The Best Of Fine
WoodWorking

Modern Woodworking
Techniques

The Best Of Fine WoodWorking

Modern Woodworking
Techniques

The Taunton Press

Cover photo by Sandor Nagyszalanczy

...by fellow enthusiasts

First printing: February 1991
International Standard Book Number: 0-942391-92-6

A FINE WOODWORKING Book

FINE WOODWORKING® is a trademark of The Taunton Press, Inc.,
registered in the U.S. Patent and Trademark Office.

The Taunton Press, Inc.
63 South Main Street
Box 5506
Newtown, Connecticut 06470-5506

Library of Congress Cataloging-in-Publication Data

The Best of Fine woodworking. Modern woodworking techniques : 31
    articles / selected by the editors of Fine Woodworking magazine.
      p. cm.
    "A Fine woodworking book"—T.p. verso.
    Includes index.
    ISBN 0-942391-92-6
    1.Woodwork   2. Furniture making.   I. Fine woodworking.
II. Title: Modern woodworking techniques.
  TT180.B43 1990
  684.1'042—dc20   90-49028
                                            CIP

Contents

Introduction

Technique without feeling and imagination is a dead proposition. At the same time, feeling and imagination without technique are often little more than wishful thinking. No matter how good we as woodworkers might be at designing furniture, we all need to know how to turn our ideas into finished construction. The wood has to be milled and cut to size, small pieces have to be joined together to make frames and carcases, doors have to be hung and countless other details handled.

This collection of 31 articles from *Fine Woodworking* magazine presents a survey of techniques suited for contemporary designs. The basics are covered in articles on doweling and mortise-and-tenon joints. Newer approaches are presented in articles on vacuum veneering, the use of plate joiners for biscuit joinery and the 32mm system for European-style cabinets. And Oriental influences are reflected in articles on shoji panels and glueless joinery.

—Dick Burrows, editor

The "Best of *Fine Woodworking*" series spans issues 46 through 80 of *Fine Woodworking* magazine, originally published between mid-1984 and the end of 1989. There is no duplication between these books and the popular *"Fine Woodworking* on..." series. A footnote with each article gives the date of first publication; product availability, suppliers' addresses and prices may have changed since then.

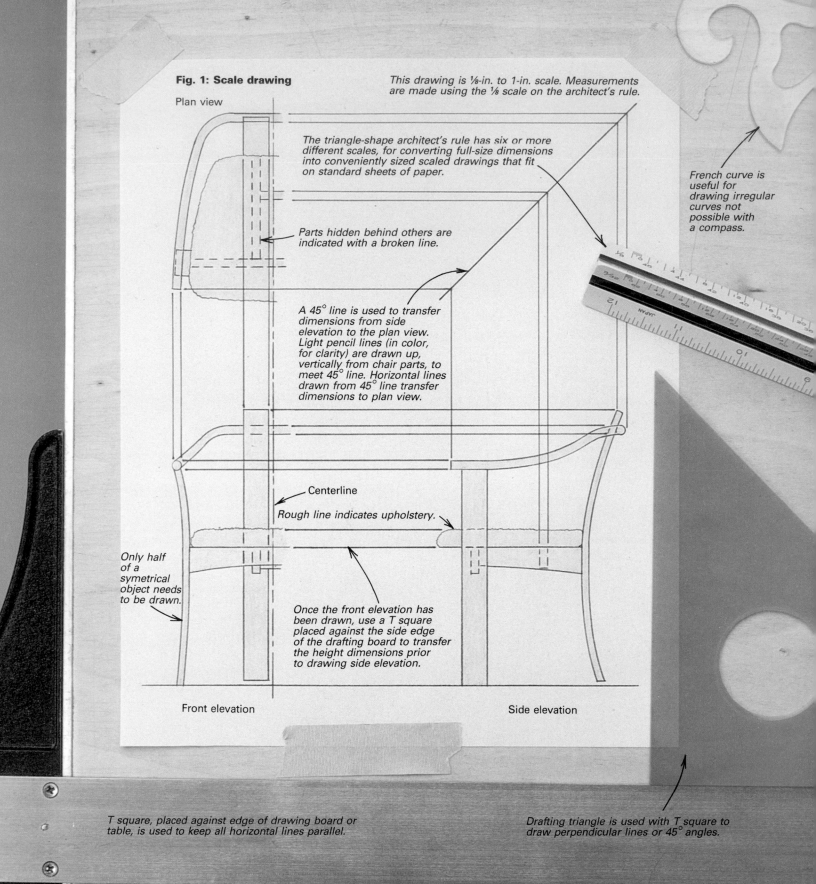

Fig. 1: Scale drawing

Plan view

This drawing is ⅛-in. to 1-in. scale. Measurements are made using the ⅛ scale on the architect's rule.

The triangle-shape architect's rule has six or more different scales, for converting full-size dimensions into conveniently sized scaled drawings that fit on standard sheets of paper.

French curve is useful for drawing irregular curves not possible with a compass.

Parts hidden behind others are indicated with a broken line.

A 45° line is used to transfer dimensions from side elevation to the plan view. Light pencil lines (in color, for clarity) are drawn up, vertically from chair parts, to meet 45° line. Horizontal lines drawn from 45° line transfer dimensions to plan view.

Centerline

Rough line indicates upholstery.

Only half of a symetrical object needs to be drawn.

Once the front elevation has been drawn, use a T square placed against the side edge of the drafting board to transfer the height dimensions prior to drawing side elevation.

Front elevation

Side elevation

T square, placed against edge of drawing board or table, is used to keep all horizontal lines parallel.

Drafting triangle is used with T square to draw perpendicular lines or 45° angles.

Drawing and the Design Process
Translating ideas into furniture

by Peter Korn

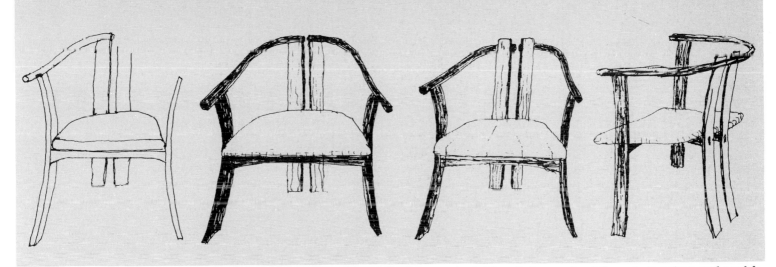

Selections from the author's sketchbook illustrate how his chair ideas begin as crude sketches that are refined through drawings and models.

At the start of my career as a self-taught furnituremaker, I focused on learning craftsmanship. I'd usually jot down some rough pictures and general measurements and go straight to the lumber pile; design was something to put up with in order to learn technique. The pieces I built incorporated the construction techniques I wanted to learn, and I worked out details as I encountered them. After a few years though, I began to take craftsmanship more for granted and found myself increasingly absorbed in the process of imagining something and then working out a successful design.

Drawing is one of the most useful tools in the design process: It helps the designer/craftsman capture that first flickering idea, then through a series of refinements, translate it into a buildable piece. Drawing doesn't create the inspiration for design, but it is a shop tool that can make the design process more fluid and efficient. There are lots of different drawing methods available for craftsmen to choose from, ranging from freehand doodling to meticulous drafting. Choosing the right kind of drawing to develop or communicate your furniture idea can be just as important as selecting the right hand or power tools to build it. In this article, I will explain how I use drawing in my design process, and I'll take you through all the stages, from rough sketches to full-scale drawings, and even throw in a few tips on making mock-ups or models and prototypes. I'll use a chair I recently designed for the contract furniture industry, pictured on p. 11, to illustrate my drawing methods and design process.

Sketching—When looking for a new chair design, the first thing I do is sit down and start doodling. I'll sketch chairs, one after the other, and let my ideas flow out onto the paper. The ideas can come from anywhere: Furniture designers can be inspired by anything from Post-Modern architecture, Mayan civilization or the work of a craftsman they admire. With maturity, the individual styles of designers/craftsmen emerge in their own design work, submerging the evidence of outside influences.

You don't have to be a formally trained artist or even know how to draw to make useful sketches. Rough sketching is for you alone, and as long as you know what your sketches mean, they serve their purpose. The first sketches I made of my contract chair, shown above, may look childishly drawn, but they were clear enough to help me conceive and nurture my ideas. I try not to be too judgemental at this stage and let the pencil do the thinking. As you sketch, remember that you're just trying out different ideas—not trying to create a visual masterpiece. If you need help improving your freehand drawing skills, I suggest reading *Drawing on the Right Side of the Brain* (see further reading on p. 11).

A bound spiral sketchbook and pen or pencil are the best imple-

ments for encouraging creativity in design. Further, because their pages don't get lost, bound sketchbooks add up to a useful record of your development as a designer. Sketches are worth saving, because even if you don't know the relevance of a particular idea now, you may come across some need for it in the future. Occasionally, perhaps once a year, I'll thumb through my old sketchbooks and rediscover some little drawing that surprises me with a useful idea.

Sketching techniques develop with practice. The basic trick to good sketching is to draw each line cleanly and continuously rather than make tentative scratches. This is often difficult at first, but it's worth the effort, because I believe we perceive through the physical motion of making the line, not just through looking at it once it is drawn. Drawing with a pen rather than a pencil encourages boldness of line, because you can't erase. I may use cross-hatching to give a form dimension or darken in parts of the sketch to get a better sense of the piece's overall form and to distinguish different materials.

I often sketch for short periods of time, leaving the sketches for an hour or a day so I can come back and view them with a fresh eye. Eventually one of my chair drawings will sing to me, and I enter a new phase of the design process—trying to capture the melody. To find out just what it is about the sketch that resonates involves more sketching: playing with proportion, fiddling with details, perhaps having the arm of a chair meet the legs in a different way.

Scale drawings—Once I've come up with a promising set of sketches, it's time to make scale drawings to turn the melody into a song. Measured scale drawings translate rough sketches into proportionally accurate views of the chair that are smaller than life-size. The trick is to keep the interesting aspects of your original idea alive while adapting it to functional proportions. Crucial considerations for my contract chair included arms low enough to slide under the apron of a table, legs with a large enough "footprint" to stabilize the chair and a curve for the continuous arm that would enclose the sitter's back comfortably. You can research chair dimensions by measuring the furniture you live with to see what's comfortable and what isn't, and you can refer to one of the design standards books listed at the end of this article.

There are three views needed in a scale drawing to fully describe a three-dimensional piece of furniture: the front elevation, side elevation and plan view, as shown in the drawings on the facing page. Front and side elevations show the piece in flat, straight-on views, without any sense of perspective. The plan view shows the furniture seen from directly above, again with no perspective. A practiced eye can look at these scale-drawing views and fairly clearly extrapolate the three-dimensional object.

Before beginning a scale drawing, you must choose an appropriate scale of conversion, where one unit of measure will represent another. For most scale drawings of furniture, I use a scale of either ⅛ in. = 1 in. or ¼ in. = 1 in. These scales allow the three views of a furniture piece to fit on a single sheet of 11-in. by 14-in. paper.

To save the trouble of mathematically converting all the dimensions of the furniture piece into scale sizes, I use an architect's rule, which has 12 different scales printed on it, including the scales I use most often. An architect designing a building employs the ¼-in. scale to mean ¼ in. = 1 ft., but it's more convenient for a furniture designer to use the same scale to mean ¼ in. = 1 in. For example, using the ¼-in. scale, a line that's 1 in. long on paper represents a true distance of 4 in.

Besides an architect's rule, there are other drafting supplies you will need to make good scale drawings. Special paper isn't required (you can use brown-paper bags if that's all you have), but it does help. Although it's more expensive than plain paper, translucent vellum paper is great for scale drawings for several reasons: It takes lead and erases well, you can trace through it and you can run it through a blueprint machine for copies. I prefer Admaster 406R, which is available at drafting supply stores. I use unlined paper, but some people prefer graph paper with a grid size that matches the scale of the drawing. Without a ruler, you can quickly count the squares to check a measurement, and the grid also helps you lay out square and parallel lines; if you use unlined paper, you'll need a T square.

Instead of using a regular wooden pencil, I find it convenient to use a lead holder with removable lead. A little hand-held sharpener keeps the lead point sharp so it will draw a line of consistent thickness. Drafting leads and pencils come in different hardnesses, with B pencils being softer and H pencils being harder. I prefer leads in the range of H to 3H, but there is no one correct hardness to use for all scale drawings. The softer the lead, the darker the line, but the lead will need sharpening more often and the drawing will smudge more easily. Besides an eraser (I like the Pink-Pearl brand), you'll want an eraser shield, a thin piece of sheet metal with various shape holes punched in it. A hole in the shield is laid over a small section of the drawing you wish to erase, protecting adjacent areas from being erased. You'll also need a drafting triangle, and depending on how curvaceous your design is, a circle template, a compass and a variety of french curves will come in handy.

Although they look more technical, scale drawings, like sketches, don't take any particular training to do. Some prefer to do the front elevation first, but I like to work out all three views simultaneously in reference to each other. If the piece is symmetrical, as in the case of my chair, you can save time and room on the paper by drawing only half of the piece and indicating the axis of symmetry with a dotted line labeled "CL" for centerline. Lay out the dimensions of the piece accurately, starting with the overall forms, then filling in the details later. At this stage of the design process, your scale drawings don't have to include every detail of joinery and construction, only the information needed to continue refining your visualization of the piece. In order to draw the irregular curves for the arm of my chair, I lightly sketched the curves freehand until they looked right, then firmed up the lines with corresponding sections of a french curve. When parts are hidden behind others, such as the seat rails in the plan view, they are indicated with a dotted line.

Measurements can be copied from one view to another by using the graph paper's grid or a T square to transfer the dimensions. Height dimensions are transferable between front and side elevations, while widths are copied from the front elevation to the plan view. You can also use the 45° method, shown in the drawing on

p. 8, to transfer depth dimensions from the side elevation to the plan view.

Occasionally it's necessary to draw a rear view or a side elevation from the opposite direction for a complex piece with details not seen in the usual three views. Cutaway views, called sections, are used when there are parts of the piece that don't show up in elevation or plan views. Sections are more likely to be useful when doing the comprehensive full-scale drawings used for construction of the furniture piece.

Full-scale drawing—If sketching encourages your creativity and scale drawings capture it, full-scale drawing is the stage where your idea becomes buildable. This form of drawing is impractical for large cabinets and unnecessary for straight-line furniture pieces that can be easily constructed using information from scale drawings. For a complex piece like a chair though, full-scale drawings are invaluable in several ways. Measurements and joinery details for a piece can be checked in actual size, minimizing the possibility of mathematical errors creating misfitting or wrong-size parts. Full-scale drawings also provide a ready source of tracing templates for curved or irregular parts, and they provide a complete record of your piece and all its details. If a full-scale blueprint drawn in America were mailed to a craftsman in Taiwan, for example, he would have all the information needed to build the piece.

Full-scale drawings are prepared in the same manner as scale drawings, only they are drawn to show more detail, including the joints, the profiles of edges and corners and the orientation of wood grain. I make the same three views as in the scale drawings described above, only I use a normal (not scale) ruler to lay out the dimensions. I like to work on Clearprint 1000H paper, which is available from drafting-supply stores. I buy the paper in 42-in.-wide rolls, more than wide enough for most chairs. I cut off a length and tape or pin it to the sheet of plywood I use for a drawing table. The drafting tools I use are the same as for scale, but a larger, 42-in. T square is helpful. After completing the three usual views, I draw separate detail drawings and cross sections where necessary to illustrate hidden parts or complex joints.

Rendered perspectives—Scale and full-size drawings that clarify proportions and construction details usually provide enough information for me to build the piece I've designed. But these mechanical drawings are often difficult for a layperson to understand. A rendered perspective is like a photograph of the piece, as it would look were it built, and is great for communicating with a prospective client or manufacturer. Though renderings can be time-consuming, they're a good sales tool and prevent misunderstandings caused by differences between what the client expects and what the craftsman builds.

There are lots of books that explain rendering and perspective drawing in detail (see further reading on the facing page), but here are the basics: In perspective drawing, the dimensions are taken directly from the scale drawings. Before you begin drawing the object, you must choose the angle and distance from which it will be seen by an imaginary viewer. The viewer's eye level becomes the horizon line on which one or two vanishing points define where horizontal lines (which would be parallel in an elevation drawing) converge. It's this convergence of parallel lines on the horizon that gives a drawing a realistic appearance, because edges of actual objects appear to come together (converge) as they recede from the viewer. Rendering is the process of shading the drawing to give it a feeling of volume and texture. You can get an idea from looking at my chair rendering (see the top, left

From *Fine Woodworking* magazine (January 1989) 74:70-73

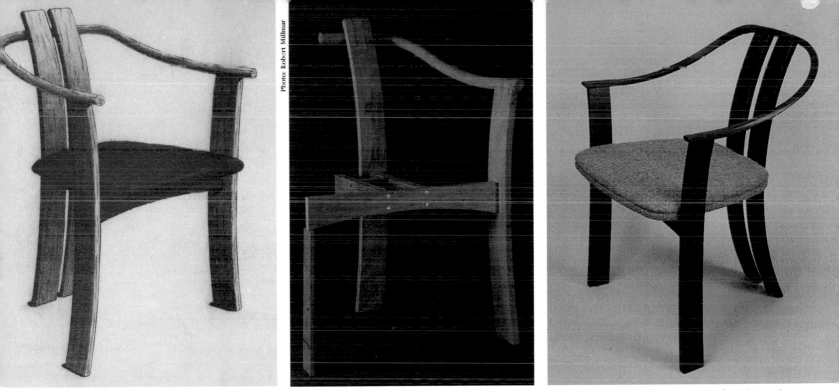

Photo: Robert Millmar

The author used shading and perspective to make the rendered drawing of his chair, above left, look like the finished chair. Also, a rendered perspective is an excellent sales tool for selling a design to a prospective client, who may not know how to 'read' a scale drawing. The full-size model, above center, helped the au- thor anticipate problems and make final changes before investing the time and materials to build the final piece. The first finished version of the author's dining chair, above right, is the culmina- tion of an idea that started as just doodles and was refined through drawings and mock-ups.

drawing above) of how the shaded cushion and sketched-in wood grain give the drawing a realistic appearance.

Mock-ups and prototypes—Once the full-scale drawing is done, I have a choice to make between building the piece or making a full-size model or mock-up first. While the drawing stages I've de- scribed are crucial to the design process, drawings of a complex piece are often insufficient for getting a clear image of how the lines will interact when the actual piece is viewed from different angles. A mock-up or model is invaluable here. Building a mock- up is much like building an actual piece of furniture, and you can measure directly from your full-scale drawings to size the parts. If the piece is symmetrical, you may build only a half model, as of my chair shown above (center). Early mock-ups can be made from cardboard and scraps that are just hot-glued or nailed together. The trick is to keep things flexible so you can experiment with changing the shape of parts or changing the way they connect to each other. Eventually, I get to a stage where I'm ready to make a better quality model—my prototype for the chair. The prototype may only be screwed-together plywood, but it's built well enough so I can sit in it to test its comfort and stability. My prototype convinced me to change the design of my chair, because the meeting of the back splat with the arm didn't look as good in life as in my drawings.

For tables and other simple forms, there's no need for mock ups, because the process can be time-consuming. But when it comes to a spatially complex piece, the work put into development of a model can help you steer clear of functional or visual problems, as the fol- lowing story illustrates. A few years ago, I began showing rendered perspectives of a chair collection (not including the chair shown in this article) to manufacturers of contract furniture. After speaking to several companies, I refined my drawings according to their feedback. In drawing each perspective of the chairs, I carefully chose the angle of view that would show off my chair in the most flattering way. One manufacturer finally signed a contract for my chair collection and made three prototypes from my full-scale drawings. Viewed from the correct angle, each chair looked as good as the original perspective drawings. But when we walked around the chair, the design lost its coherency and proportional attractiveness. I discovered that through the drawing process I had perfected one view of the chair and ignored the others. Eventually, the manufacturer decided not to produce the collection, and I am left wondering if it would have succeeded had I worked out the designs with mock-ups before submitting them. Having spent the time to extensively prototype the design of the chair in this article, I am confident it works, visually and in terms of comfort. □

Peter Korn is director of the woodworking/furniture design pro- gram at the Anderson Ranch Arts Center in Snowmass, Colo., where he teaches a workshop on basic drawing for designers. For more information, write to Anderson Ranch, Box 6194, Snowmass Village, Colo. 81615.

Further reading

Books on drawing basics:

Drawing on the Right Side of the Brain by Betty Edwards. J.P. Tarcher, 9110 Sunset Blvd., Suite 250, Los Angeles, CA 90069; 1979.

Thinking with a Pencil by Henning Nelms. Ten Speed Press, Box 7123, Berkeley, CA 94707; 1981.

Books on perspective drawing and rendering:

Color Drawing by Michael Doyle. Van Nostrand Reinhold Co., 135 W. 50th St., New York, NY 10020; 1983.

Design Graphics, 2nd edition by C. Leslie Martin. MacMillan Publish- ing Co., Inc., 866-T 3rd Ave., New York, NY 10022; 1968.

Perspective Drawing Handbook by Joseph D'Amelio. Leon Amiel, Publisher, 31 W. 46th St., New York, NY 10036; 1964.

Books on standard measurements for design:

Humanscale 1/2/3 by Niels Diffrient, Alvin Tilley and Joan Bardagjy. The MIT Press, Massachusetts Institute of Technology, Cambridge, MA 02142; 1974.

The Measure of Man: Human Factors in Design by Henry Dreyfuss. Whitney Library of Design, 18 E. 50th St., New York, NY 10022; 1967.

Form in Furniture

Six rules for creating better designs

by Seth Stem

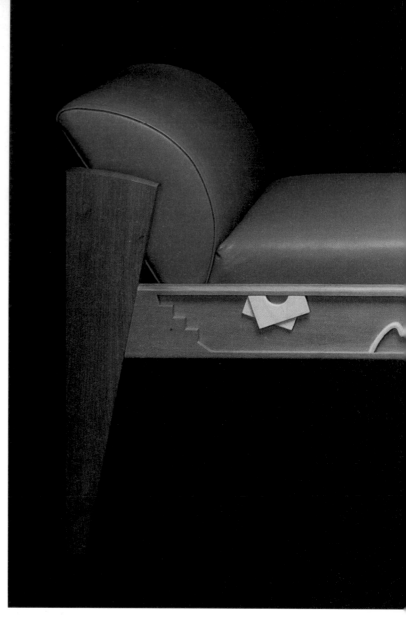

Below: The form of the Egg Desk by David Powell of East Hampton, Mass., is top-heavy and lacks depth. However, the interior's curvature and drawer-and-cubbyhole composition are pleasing. (Photo by Robert Aude.) Right: Rosanne Somerson of Westport, Mass., created an interesting interaction between this bench's armrests and legs. The curved tops of the wooden legs relate to the curved forms of the upholstered armrests. In addition, the legs overlap the upholstery so that the inside top corners of the legs fall precisely on a radius line that would bisect the central division of the curve in the armrests. (Photo by George Erml, courtesy of the American Craft Museum.)

Form is often the thing we notice first in furniture; it is the perceived geometry of the volume and mass of any object. All furniture has some sort of form, even if it appears relatively shapeless. A designer creates a piece of furniture by manipulating any combination of elements chosen from a vast menu of design possibilities. This menu is the "visual vocabulary" of design elements that gives a designer the means to express ideas clearly and eloquently in three-dimensional form.

The form of a piece of furniture should provide three levels of information. The first level lets the viewer recognize the piece as a chair, table or whatever. More subtly, form can also distinguish objects that look similar but have different functions. For instance, a viewer might be able to tell a backless bench from a coffee table only because of the slight concave form of the benchtop or the delicate form of the coffee table's understructure. Form at this level also establishes overall character—whether the piece is organic, elegant or attention grabbing.

The second level of form gives visual information on how to interact with a piece. For example, chairs have a myriad of forms, but all are for sitting; the forms of cabinets suggest storage or display. On this level, form tells the viewer where to open a cabinet door, where to grab an armrest or how to work an extension table.

The third level of form is more intimate and concerns fine detailing, such as carving, hardware, molding and inlays. This is the level of information that closely holds our interest when we

From *Fine Woodworking* magazine (September 1989) 78:64-68

interact with the piece, and it prevents boredom with the visual information presented on the first two levels.

Whether natural or man-made, forms are composed primarily of combinations of basic geometric shapes or their variations. Individually or in combination, cubes, spheres, cones, pyramids and cylinders can create a furniture form. Although a form can take shape spontaneously, uninspired designers also use conventional exercises to develop them.

Too often woodworkers rely on craftsmanship, joinery or materials to carry a design. These matters are important, of course, but no single element should dominate the others. Evaluate form in furniture under design by mentally painting it gray and asking the following questions: Does the form stand by itself? Is it suitable for its intended use? Is it interesting and visually dynamic? Does it achieve these things without material richness and structural or joinery information? If you can answer yes to these questions, the form has credibility and the design is proceeding in the right direction. By adding detail, high-quality craftsmanship, gorgeous materials, color and any other necessary elements to a successful form, a well designed piece of furniture will almost certainly result.

Designers usually deal with the piece's overall form first, and use detail either to complement it or contrast with it. This is not a hard-and-fast rule, however, and many designs are developed by concentrating on details first. But much of what's true about overall form also applies to detail form.

Six principles of form—The designer has an incredible amount of latitude in creating a furniture form, even when the piece must fulfill a narrow function. For example, a dining-room table traditionally has a flat surface atop an understructure that is arranged to accommodate diners' feet and legs. Once these requirements have been met, there are still many options. The table base may have four legs or a trestle or central pedestal. Each of these options could be executed in a way that's angular or curvilinear, massive or delicate, traditional or avant-garde. Which alternative is best? It's up to the designer.

The first principle in form development is that the form must satisfactorily express the piece's concept. A table intended to blend with a suite of traditional hardwood furniture would probably not work with an outlandish base, nor would a chair designed to appear soft and comfortable warrant a strongly rectilinear or geometric form.

Subtle variations of a form can dramatically affect its visual message. Imagine a sphere attached to a wall. If the sphere is designed with consistent curvature, it will look static, perhaps machined. If it is distorted to a slight pear shape, with most of its volume below the equator, it will look organic, as though it is responding to gravity (see the desk on the facing page). By contrast, if most of the sphere's volume is above the equator, the form will appear lightweight, as though it's on the brink of ascension. While all of these forms are fine, the choice of one over another should reflect goals specific to the concept.

The second principle of form development is that a form should have balance, either within itself or with another element. This does not mean that a form must be symmetrical, but any variations should be counterbalanced. Forms shouldn't appear top-heavy or bottom heavy without good reason. A designer must be able to "feel" when a form is balanced, rather than just engineer a physically balanced form, because the latter may be boring. Therefore, it is wise to be concerned with visual interest when exploring balance. While a balanced form often automatically yields a balanced composition, make sure the piece is interesting as well.

Third, emphasis on one or more parts is also important when considering form. When there is variation within a form, there will be dynamism; forms that are too consistent are likely to appear bland. Emphasis in form design is analogous to emphasis in a spoken sentence. Every sentence has a beginning, a middle section in which the thought is developed and ultimately an end; but at any point emphasis may be given through the choice of words or the ways the words are spoken. Similarly, emphasis can be added to any part of a form. The drawing below, left, shows one treatment of emphasis. The top table is rather indifferent because the legs have unvarying curvature and consistent thickness. Emphasizing the legs adds dynamism to the entire form. The legs of the bottom table have a well-defined beginning and end, a tighter radius toward the foot of the curve and a variation in width.

Consider the three lamps at the bottom of the drawing below, left, as another example. The base and glass reflector of the first lamp are similarly sized; without emphasis of color or texture they are about equal in importance. Enlarging the reflector and reducing the base, as in the second lamp, creates emphasis through a difference in scale. The third lamp uses the scale of the first lamp, but adds emphasis through the active shape of the reflector. As you can see, emphasis in form is closely tied to emphasis in composition. However, form emphasis deals with contour and scale relationships, while composition concentrates primarily on placement.

The fourth principle of form design is that for maximum visual interest a form should create relationships either within itself or with surrounding elements. In other words, forms should interact. Using forms sensitively creates a harmonious design, as shown in the photo of the upholstered bench, pp. 12-13, while juxtaposing dissimilar forms in a disorderly or haphazard manner gives a chaotic feeling.

Depending on their location and proximity to each other, forms can be used to create a particular mood by suggesting tension, aggression and serenity, among other qualities. For example, the point of a triangular form directed at an adjacent rectangle feels aggressive; if a side of the same triangle is adjacent to the rectangle, the feeling changes because of the compatibility of the two adjacent straight edges. Here again, the issues of form overlap those of composition.

Fifth, a piece of furniture's form must be sensitive to the materials used. Seek the most appropriate material for the form under design. If you want to use veneer, don't design a form with fragile edges or the piece will be at risk of damage. Consider, too, that the eye perceives certain weights for common materials; a form attractive in wood might look unattractive if made the same size in steel.

Last, when designing the overall form of a piece, try to consider all viewing angles. Much too often designers study only one view, usually the front view of a cabinet and the side view of a chair. In Cory Burr's chair in the photos on the left side of the facing page, it's clear that the side view was the main focus; the front view is less effective.

By contrast, the overall form of Arata Isozaki's chair in the photo on the right side of the facing page is more successful. The side of the chair has a more active form than the front, but front-view interest is generated by the long slats. Where it's not possible to strengthen an uninteresting form, the designer can use other elements of the visual vocabulary (such as texture or color) to compensate.

Details of form—When function and structure have been considered in the overall form, there is freedom in developing the details. Designs are most often successful if the detail shapes are

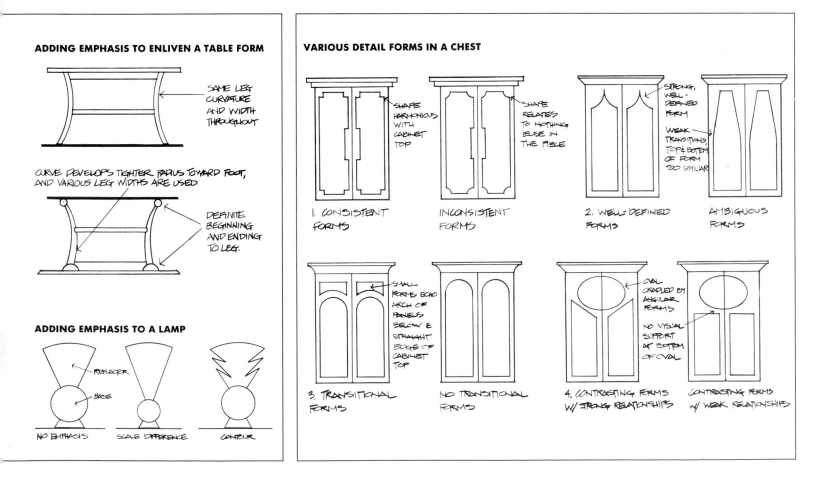

ADDING EMPHASIS TO ENLIVEN A TABLE FORM

SAME LEG CURVATURE AND WIDTH THROUGHOUT

CURVE DEVELOPS TIGHTER RADIUS TOWARD FOOT, AND VARIOUS LEG WIDTHS ARE USED

DEFINITE BEGINNING AND ENDING TO LEG.

ADDING EMPHASIS TO A LAMP

REFLECTOR

BASE

NO EMPHASIS

SCALE DIFFERENCE

CONTOUR

VARIOUS DETAIL FORMS IN A CHEST

SHAPE HARMONIOUS WITH CABINET TOP

1. CONSISTENT FORMS

SHAPE RELATES TO NOTHING ELSE IN THE PIECE

INCONSISTENT FORMS

STRONG, WELL-DEFINED FORM

WEAK TRANSITIONS, TOP & BOTTOM OF FORM TOO SIMILAR

2. WELL-DEFINED FORMS

AMBIGUOUS FORMS

SMALL FORMS ECHO ARCH OF PANELS BELOW & STRAIGHT EDGE OF CABINET TOP

3. TRANSITIONAL FORMS

NO TRANSITIONAL FORMS

OVAL CRADLED BY ANGULAR FORMS

NO VISUAL SUPPORT AT BOTTOM OF OVAL

4. CONTRASTING FORMS W/ STRONG RELATIONSHIPS

CONTRASTING FORMS W/ WEAK RELATIONSHIPS

This chair by Cory Burr of Providence, R.I., looks as though it was designed primarily from the side view. The curves introduced into the front view (above), through the edges of the seat and back, don't have the same command and character as those in the side view (below). (Photos by Seth Stem.)

The side view of the "Marilyn Chair" by Arata Isozaki of Tokyo, Japan, is more active than the front, but the backrest slats in the front view also provide the viewer with visual interest. (Photo courtesy of MIT Hayden Gallery.)

consistent throughout a piece; for example, on the legs, arm-rests, back support and seat of a chair. (Of course, the scale of the detailing has to change depending on its location in the piece.) But not all details must relate closely. Contrast and variety are needed to keep a piece visually alive. Rounded over edges on curvilinear framework create a sculptural feeling, whereas crisp edges add definition by creating shadow lines that visually separate planes and edges. The bottom, right, drawings on p. 14 illustrate how a variety of details might work in a simple rectangular chest. In the first example, a strong relationship between forms is established in the consistent detailing of the doors and cabinet top. However, rounding the door-panel corners weakens this relationship.

In the second example, the form of the panels on the left is well defined, but the panels on the right are weak. Here you can see that too much balance is a bad thing. The top of the form is too similar to the bottom, and the transition from the straight sides to the tapers is muddy and uninteresting.

The third example demonstrates how a piece can benefit from a transitional element. The smaller forms above the archs in the cabinet on the left pick up both the shape of the door panels and the horizontal line of the cabinet top, softening the contrast between the two.

The last example illustrates the importance of relationships between contrasting forms. In the cabinet on the left, the trapezoids seem to cradle the oval. This is a much stronger relationship than that of the cabinet shown on the right, in which the panels fail to interact with the oval. Here, the oval is also surrounded by too much negative space; it could use some visual support, especially on the underside.

Ideally, you should use detail form systematically. For example, the framework of a chair may be based on certain shapes, but if you think of the backrest as a complementary element framed by the chair structure, you can detail it entirely different-ly. The well-developed curvilinear profiles of the filing dividers in the writing desk, shown in the top photo at left, contrast very nicely with the straightforward lines of the rest of the piece.

While you are designing the piece of furniture, consider adding transitions between detail forms so the jump from one form to another doesn't appear awkward or abrupt, especially when there is a change in materials. Introducing a small, third detail between two existing forms is a good way to create a transition. This is evident in the table shown in the bottom photo at left, which features a small ring where the top of the cylindrical table leg ends in a ball to effect a smooth transition. The form of a transitional element need not closely relate to the forms on either side, but scale is important. The transitional element is usually a lot smaller than the forms it separates; if it becomes too large, it becomes less of a transition and more of a form in its own right.

When designing detail forms, more is not necessarily better; there really is only so much information a viewer can digest before a piece becomes visually confusing. A good rule in evaluating whether a piece is fully developed is to subtract or add information; if doing either makes the piece less attractive, confuses the visual message or clouds the concept, it's a good bet the design is complete. ☐

Above: The curved forms of the file dividers in this fall-front desk by Louis Goodman of New York, N.Y., contrast with the straightforward construction of the frame, and they become the desk's focal point. (Photo courtesy of the Gallery of Applied Arts.) Below: The blue ring acts as a transitional form between the mahogany ball and the black leg in this Roscoe-Award-winning table, which was designed by Jack Larimore of Philadelphia, Pa. (Photo by Rick Echelmeyer.)

Seth Stem teaches at the Rhode Island School of Design and designs and makes furniture in Marblehead, Mass. This article has been adapted with permission from the new Taunton Press book, Designing Furniture, *©1989, The Taunton Press, 63 S. Main St., Newtown, Conn. 06470.*

Chainsawn Seat

by Robert Erickson

Joe Felzman Studio

Methods for shaping saddled chair seats, like those of Windsor chairs and old tractors, interest me. The traditional Windsor method, with adze, scorp, travisher and handplanes, seems satisfying but slow and not well suited to the small production shop. Jeremy Singley's method of bending seats by driving wedges into sawkerfs is effective but not, I suspect, much quicker. Sam Maloof's method of bandsawing narrow boards roughly to shape, then gluing them up as a seat blank seems better suited to the small production shop. Where possible, however, I like to use one or two wide planks for the seat; ripping them first would disturb the grain continuity. I've developed a method of shaping a tractor-style seat with a chainsaw and a body grinder that solves this problem and takes only about an hour per seat.

First, I bandsaw the blank to shape, then pencil-on the outline of the saddling on the top surface and the contour on the front edge. This contour curves down each side of the center arris to a maximum depth of ⅞ in., then gently up to meet the hard line of the arris defined by the outline on top. Next, I kerf the waste wood in the saddled area with the chainsaw. I've found I can control the saw better if I hold my elbow against my side. I work to within about ⅛ in. of the finished depth at this point.

To remove the waste and begin shaping, I work with the nose of the chainsaw at right angles to the saw kerfs, the bar at an acute angle to the surface, angled toward the seat center, as shown at right. Start at the seat back, about ¾ in. from the pencil line, and slowly sweep the saw back and forth. After removing the waste, fine-tune the shape, working carefully back toward the outline and in to the center arris, letting the radius of the bar's nose define the curve of the saddle up to the hard lines of the arrises. The depth of cut is shallow, so there shouldn't be kick-

With a chainsaw and body grinder, Erickson can sculpt the tractor-seat saddle of his chairs in about an hour. After penciling the saddle outline on the top surface and the contour on the front edge, kerf the seat with a series of chainsaw cuts to approximate depth (left). Shape the seat by sweeping the nose of the chainsaw slowly from the arrises into the depressions. A body grinder refines the saddling and cleans up chainsaw marks (right). The chair shown at top is made of California madrone.

back problems. As with any chainsaw operation, however, be very careful.

To complete the shaping and clean up the chainsaw marks, I use a Bosch Model 0601 body grinder and 50-grit sandpaper mounted on a 4-in.-diameter flexible backing pad. My backing pad is a Rockwell #55746, and its ¼-in.-thick rubber is fairly stiff. I've tried grinding with a 6-in. disc and found it more difficult to control.

Sweep the grinder from the arrises into the seat's depressions. For better control, I choke up on the grinder's grip and press an elbow against my body while grinding. I finish-sand with a Makita pad sander with a 6-in.-diameter circular base, working from 60 grit up to 400 grit. ☐

Bob Erickson makes chairs and furniture in Nevada City, Calif.

From *Fine Woodworking* magazine (May 1986) 58:65

Inspired by James Krenov's understated aesthetic, the author built this showcase cabinet from European maple. The carcase is joined by dowels, allowing delicate shaping of the cabinet top and bottom that wouldn't be practical with other corner joints.

Carcase Doweling
Accuracy and patience ensure success

by Monroe Robinson

I learned about cabinet doweling from James Krenov at the College of the Redwoods. Krenov is well-known for his graciously proportioned wall and showcase cabinets, delicate carcases that are ideally suited for doweled corner joints. But the technique is just as appropriate for larger cabinets and, if done accurately, dowels are as strong as any other corner joint and can be made fairly quickly with few tools. More important, doweling is versatile, offering design options not available with other joints.

For the European maple showcase cabinet I built to illustrate this article, doweling was really my only choice. Because I wanted to plane a decorative profile on the edges of the cabinet's solid-wood top and bottom, I extended them slightly past the carcase sides. Dovetails here would have been difficult to lay out and cut on the curved carcase sides and would have prevent-

ed me from shaping the overhanging top and bottom.

Doweling has one advantage over almost any other joint (except perhaps plate joinery in some applications)—it's equally effective in solid-wood or veneered panels or in combinations of the two. In the rosewood china hutch on p. 20, for example, I wanted the appearance of frame-and-panel construction but the rigidity of veneered panels. To achieve this, I glued rails and stiles to panels made of lumbercore plywood veneered with $3/32$-in. rosewood. Even the rails and stiles are veneered plywood, and the entire lower case is doweled into the base, forming a rigid structure.

Tools for doweling—Since boring accurate holes is what doweling is all about, you need brad-point drill bits and, ideally, a mortising machine or horizontal borer, both to make a doweling

From *Fine Woodworking* magazine (May 1988) 70:69-73

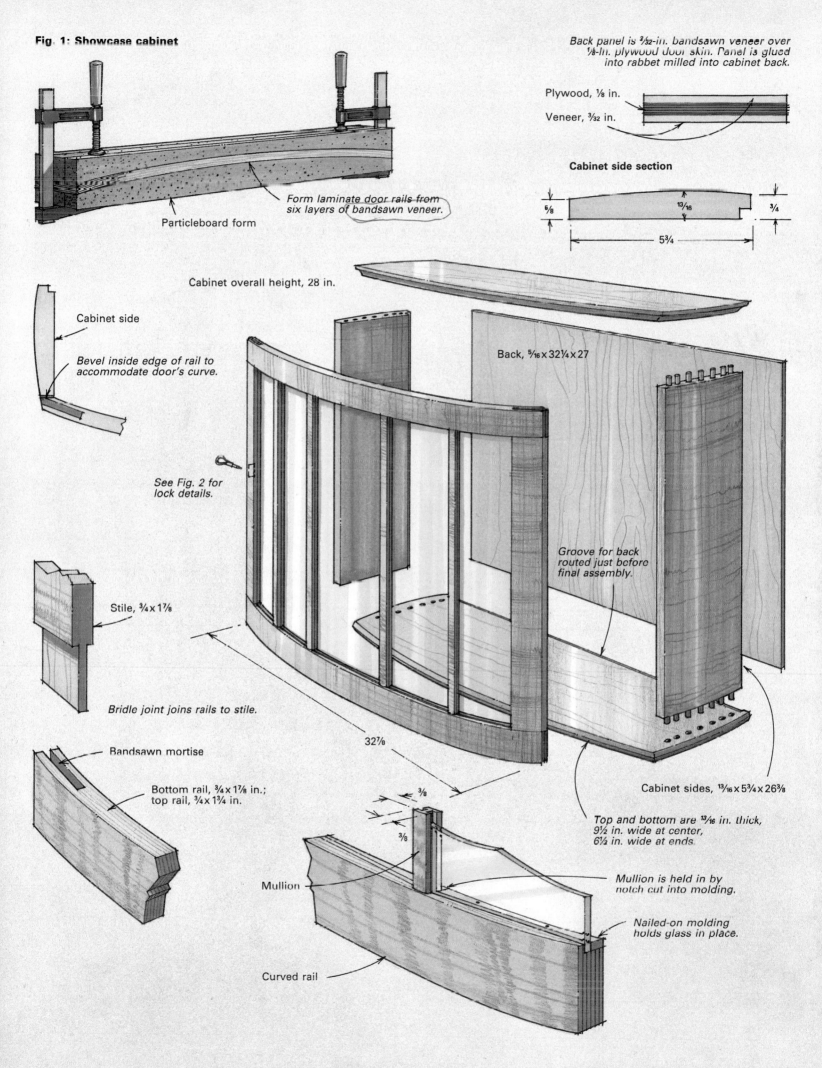

Fig. 1: Showcase cabinet

Back panel is ³/₃₂-in. bandsawn veneer over ¹/₈-in. plywood door skin. Panel is glued into rabbet milled into cabinet back.

Plywood, ⅛ in.

Veneer, ³/₃₂ in.

Cabinet side section

⅝

¹³/₁₆

¾

5¾

Form laminate door rails from six layers of bandsawn veneer.

Particleboard form

Cabinet overall height, 28 in.

Cabinet side

Bevel inside edge of rail to accommodate door's curve.

See Fig. 2 for lock details.

Back, ⁵/₁₆ x 32¼ x 27

Groove for back routed just before final assembly.

Stile, ¾ x 1⅞

Bridle joint joins rails to stile.

32⅞

Bandsawn mortise

Bottom rail, ¾ x 1⅞ in.; top rail, ¾ x 1¾ in.

Cabinet sides, ¹³/₁₆ x 5¾ x 26⅜

Top and bottom are ¹³/₁₆ in. thick, 9½ in. wide at center, 6½ in. wide at ends.

⅜

⅜

Mullion is held in by notch cut into molding.

Mullion

Nailed-on molding holds glass in place.

Curved rail

Robinson's rosewood china hutch, above, is also doweled. The lower carcase consists of a mock frame-and-panel structure doweled into a base and a solid-wood top, while the upper carcase is made of frames into which glass panes have been set. He stiffened the structure by gluing veneered panels into the solid-wood frames that form the backs of both upper and lower carcases. Normally, panels would float freely in the frames.

To accurately align dowels in parts being joined, the author makes a scrapwood doweling jig to serve as a boring guide. In the photo above, he has nailed the jig to the cabinet side for endgrain boring. Below, it's reversed and nailed to the cabinet bottom to bore matching holes. The doweling jig is bandsawn to the profile of the carcase side, and a heel is glued and nailed to one end to aid in alignment.

jig for the specific carcase you'll be building and to bore holes in the endgrain pieces. If a mortiser or horizontal-boring machine is beyond your budget, you might consider building one, but the truth is, you can get by with just a drill press and/or a portable electric drill. These two tools can drill holes accurately enough for doweling, but they will of course require careful setup to achieve good results.

A brad point will bore a much cleaner hole in wood than a regular twist drill. Typically, a selection of ¼-in., 5/16-in., 3/8-in. and ½-in. brad points will be sufficient for matching the dowel sizes you'll be using. If the available brad points won't match an undersize or oversize dowel, standard metal drills—available in a far greater range of sizes—can be ground to make a brad point of the exact size. To regrind a bit, I use a regular bench grinder with an aluminum-oxide wheel. The corner of the wheel has been rounded off slightly, which makes reshaping the bit much easier. For a larger-diameter bit, you need to shape a larger radius on the edge of the wheel. I use a diamond-tipped dressing rod to true the face of the grinding wheel and shape the radius edges. In grinding a point on a metal bit, the exact angles aren't critical but the point must be perfectly centered, so don't rotate or move the bit from side to side while you're grinding. Be careful not to overheat the bit by grinding too aggressively.

Dowels are available in two types: fluted and spiral groove. The flutes and spirals help spread the glue, making a better bond between the dowel and hole. Either type of dowel is fine, although I prefer the fluted ones, because they are machined more precisely and thus fit into the hole more easily. Also, fluted dowels allow excess glue to escape, preventing the dowel from being forced out of the hole by hydraulic pressure. Some people make their own dowels out of standard, hardware-store dowels. If you do this, make sure the dowels match the diameter of the bits you have and chamfer the ends of each dowel so they'll slide easily into the holes. In any case, the diameter of the dowel should be slightly greater than one-third the thickness of the stock you are using. I have no rules on dowel length, but generally I bore side-grain holes to within about ⅛ in. of breaking through the opposite side; the endgrain holes are bored to an equivalent depth.

The trick to strong carcase doweling is accuracy, and this is achieved with a doweling jig made specifically for each carcase. The jig I learned about from Krenov is shown in the photos at left. It's nothing more than a block of wood with holes matching the dowel spacing bored through it. The jig is nailed and/or clamped to the carcase parts and aligns the drill bit for boring. I make the jig from a scrap of dense hardwood to minimize wear during boring. Make sure the stock for your jig is perfectly square in section, otherwise your dowel holes will be at an angle, spoiling accuracy. This is especially true if you're boring with a portable drill.

Hole spacing is a matter of personal preference. On my showcase, I spaced the ½-in. dowels about 1 in. apart (center to center), but near the edges of the joint, I spaced them closer to help the joint resist cupping. With the holes marked out on the jig, I bore them on the mortising machine or drill press. I like to bandsaw the jig precisely to the carcase side's cross section—this helps me see if I'm using the jig in the correct relationship to the cabinet during all steps of construction. Finally, I glue and nail a small wood heel on the squared end of the jig to help locate it exactly within the board's width.

Order of events—Because doweling lends itself to so many construction styles, the actual joinery of a piece can happen at any of various stages. If the parts are all square in section and no subsequent shaping is desired, you can simply cut your cabinet

Photos: Sean Sprague; Drawings: Joel Katzowitz

Allowing for springback of the door's form-laminated rails was hopeless guesswork, so Robinson built the curved door first, then made the carcase to match. He dry-assembled the cabinet sides, above, to an oversized top and bottom, then traced the outline of the sides, right, using a compass to allow extra material for shaping. After doweling, the top and bottom were shaped with hand tools.

A carver's burr chucked in a hand drill, left, cleans up the dowel holes and forms a slightly enlarged opening to ease entry of the dowels. To set dowels to the proper depth, above, a scrap makes a handy depth gauge. Spacing of dowels isn't critical, but to prevent cupping from opening the joint, the two outermost dowels should be spaced more closely than the rest. In the photo below, the cabinet is being test assembled. Before final glue-up, Robinson chopped mortises for the door's knife hinges.

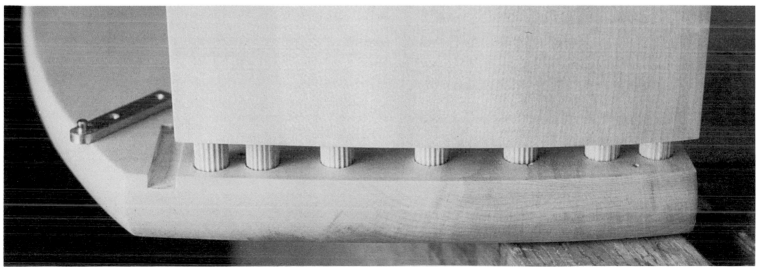

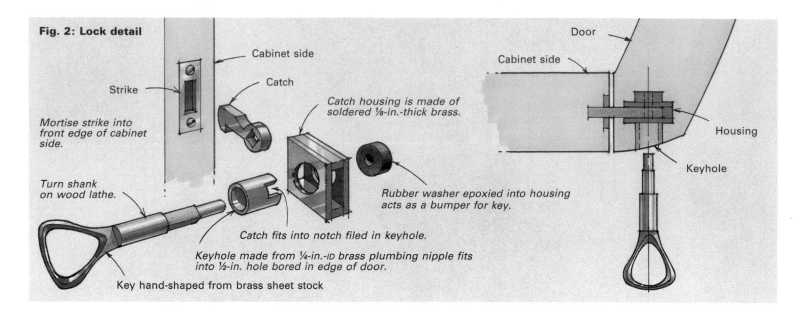

Fig. 2: Lock detail

Cabinet side

Strike

Mortise strike into front edge of cabinet side.

Catch

Catch housing is made of soldered ⅛-in.-thick brass.

Turn shank on wood lathe.

Rubber washer epoxied into housing acts as a bumper for key.

Catch fits into notch filed in keyhole.

Keyhole made from ¼-in.-ID brass plumbing nipple fits into ½-in. hole bored in edge of door.

Key hand-shaped from brass sheet stock

Door

Cabinet side

Housing

Keyhole

parts to size and dowel them together. Because the curved rails of the cabinet door shown here were form laminated, however, and thus subject to springback, there was no way to predict just how the curve would come out. Thus, I made the door first, reasoning that it's far easier to shape the cabinet parts to match the door's curve than vice versa. (The amount of springback can, however, be reduced by increasing the number of laminates in the curve.)

When I had finished the door, I cut the carcase sides to the exact length and shaped their convex profile with handplanes. Next, I surface-planed the lumber for the carcase top and bottom and finish-planed their inside surfaces. But at this point, the top and bottom were left longer and wider than their finished dimensions. To locate the dowel holes in the top and bottom, I set the carcase sides up with the top and bottom and with the door in place, and then checked everything for a good fit. Next, I traced the outline of the sides onto the oversize top and bottom, marked all the parts so I could reassemble them correctly and took down my mock-up to bore the dowel holes.

It doesn't matter whether you bore the endgrain or side-grain holes first, but in either case, align the doweling jig so its profile matches the appropriate surface and the glued-on heel is firmly butted to the correct edge. Don't attempt to hold the jig in place by hand. It will surely slip and mislocate the holes. Instead, nail it in place. I use 1⅝-in. hardened paneling nails that push snugly through pre-drilled holes in the jig. The nails are tapped only part way in for easy removal. For boring the endgrain holes in the carcase sides, I use my mortising machine, set at the same boring height I used to make the doweling jig. If you're going to use a portable drill instead, I suggest clamping the doweling jig with a bar clamp to make absolutely certain it won't move. Use a scrap block to keep the clamp from marring the opposite end of the work. Set a stop collar or masking-tape marker on the drill bit so the hole depth is just slightly deeper than the length of the dowel. This will keep the dowel from bottoming, preventing the joint from closing.

To bore the holes in the corresponding piece, in this case the cabinet top or bottom, the jig is reversed and the nails are pulled and put in from the opposite side. Align the jig and tap the nails in. I use a drill press to bore holes in the top and bottom but again, a portable drill is fine, as long as you clamp both the board and the jig firmly to your bench. Once all the holes are bored, I use an eggbeater drill with a countersink or carver's burr to enlarge the lip of the hole a bit so the dowel enters more easily.

Assembly—The beauty of doweling is in allowing an almost unlimited freedom of expression at the points where two boards join at a right angle. After all the dowel holes are bored, I mark out the carcase top and bottom and cut them to the final size to ready them for final detailing. The edge of the carcase bottom was then detailed with a gently sloping bevel, which I formed with a handplane and chisels. I routed a cove along the top edge and then used carving tools to texture the machined surfaces.

The final fitting and a test assembly follow the detailing. For test fitting, glue the dowels into the cabinet side only, using a short scrap of undersized dowel to spread glue evenly in the hole. Dab just a little glue on the dowel itself, not too much or you'll have a mess to clean up. Tap the dowels into their holes, using a scrap block of the appropriate thickness as a depth gauge. Now, do a complete dry clamp-up of the cabinet, making sure the dowels seat completely and the carcase is perfectly square. Check for square by measuring diagonally from corner to corner either with a tape measure or with a pair of sticks or pinch rods. The dry assembly is a good time to iron out any problems in clamping strategy. Now's the time to find out if you don't have enough clamps and/or pads to do the real thing.

If everything checks out, I knock apart the test assembly using padded blocks and finish any pre-assembly details. This cabinet involved routing the rabbet for the back panel and chopping mortises for the door's knife hinges before proceeding to the final glue-up. I finished the cabinet with several coats of very thin shellac, sanded between coats with 400-grit sandpaper and finished up with a coat of Goddard's furniture wax.

One final note about hardware: The knife hinges for the cabinet door are available from many local hardware stores and various mail-order supply houses, but the lock and key are custom-made. Although this might seem difficult to do, cutting and shaping brass is quite easy. The drawing above shows how the lock was made, using a hacksaw, files and soldering iron. The parts were made from brass sheet stock, except for the keyhole, which is a standard ¼-in.-ID plumbing nipple. The key's shank was turned round on a wood lathe. ☐

Monroe Robinson is a graduate of the College of the Redwoods in Fort Bragg, Calif., and a professional furnituremaker in Little River, Calif. Goddard's wax is available from Woodcraft Supply Corp., P.O. Box 4000, Woburn, Mass. 01888, and in Canada from Lee Valley Tools Ltd., P.O. Box 6295, Station J, Ottawa, Ont. K2A 1T4.

Mortise and Tenon

Chop the mortise by hand,
but a machine's best for the tenon

by Michael Podmaniczky

Easily cut by a combination of hand and machine methods, the mortise and tenon is among the most versatile of all furniture joints.

I've always considered the basic mortise and tenon the work-horse of joinery and the primary joint to master for most furniture work. Like the dovetail, the mortise and tenon allows wood to "turn the corner." It's also the basic joint we use for frame joinery to join rails and stiles to make doors, join aprons to legs to make tables and join rails to posts for chairs. Marked out and cut in multiples, it's a perfectly acceptable—albeit more time-consuming—alternative to sliding dovetails, miters or lap joints for carcase work, but I'll limit my discussion here to frame joints.

When I grit my teeth and do the very best I can to remain objective, neither falling into the argument that the old ways work best nor advising that nothing really works well in the 20th century unless it does so at deafening decibels, I have to admit that I usually cut my mortises by hand and my tenons by machine. I've arrived at this method after years of working in shops with no proper mortising equipment. Certainly, the router will do a decent job on a shallow mortise, but most furniture work will require a mortise at least 1 in. deep and probably deeper. If you have a slot mortiser or a hollow-chisel setup, you're lucky. Most of us don't have these tools, so it makes sense to learn to mortise by hand. Tenoning is another matter. For just a few rails, sawing tenons by hand is quite reasonable and not all that hard to learn. But one tool that almost all shops have—the tablesaw—is easy and safe to set up for tenoning.

Chopping a mortise by hand doesn't require mind-numbing attention to accuracy. Unlike an edge-glued joint, which is jointed straight and then clamped tight, the mortise and tenon needs to be really "tight" only where the tenon shoulder meets the mortise face. It's possible, of course, to achieve a piston-like fit on the tenon, but there's no practical need to do so since modern glues

are more than able to fill minor gaps. In fact, if the fit of the joint was as tight as a clamped edge joint, you'd probably split the mortise apart during assembly. Still, it's a good idea to cut the joint precisely, and I'll describe my procedures for doing so.

But, first, the mortise. You'll need these tools: a combination square, a mortise-marking gauge, a layout knife, a hefty mallet and, of course, a mortise chisel. An accurate square (I like my Starrett combination) is a must for marking both the mortise and the tenon. For marking lines that must be carried completely around the stock, nothing is more annoying than an untrustworthy square that multiplies its error at every turn. For marking out the mortise (and later the tenon), you'll need a mortise-marking gauge—essentially a regular marking gauge, except that it has two spurs instead of one. One spur is fixed to the gauge's beam; the other is adjustable, and both can be moved in relationship to the gauge fence. This allows mortises and tenons of various thicknesses to be marked out and positioned anywhere in the stock thickness.

I realize that some tool catalogs sell what they refer to as "mortise chisels," and there are plenty to pick from. Essentially, a mortise chisel differs from bench and paring chisels in that it has a rectangular section that's deeper than it is wide, with sides that should be parallel to each other (and, with careful sharpening, perpendicular to the cutting edge). I consider the proper mortiser one that can be driven into the side of a utility pole and jumped on by John Madden without breaking or bending. I haven't found a commercial tool that completely fills the bill, so I've taken to making my own by a process described on p. 27.

You can try to sneak by with a paring chisel—I suppose small, shallow joints can be cut this way. But as soon as you start getting into deep mortising, your little paring chisel will twist and there's just no way that the mortise cheeks are going to stay par-

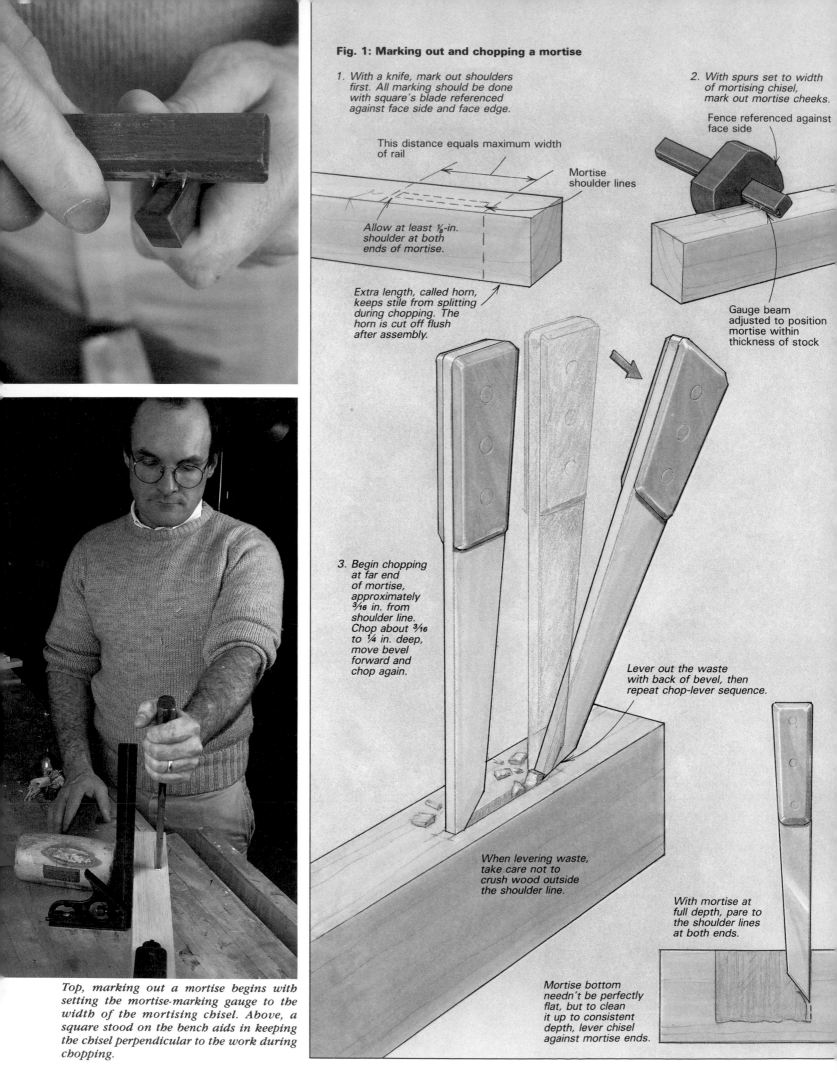

Fig. 1: Marking out and chopping a mortise

1. With a knife, mark out shoulders first. All marking should be done with square's blade referenced against face side and face edge.

2. With spurs set to width of mortising chisel, mark out mortise cheeks.

Fence referenced against face side

This distance equals maximum width of rail

Mortise shoulder lines

Allow at least ⅛-in. shoulder at both ends of mortise.

Extra length, called horn, keeps stile from splitting during chopping. The horn is cut off flush after assembly.

Gauge beam adjusted to position mortise within thickness of stock

3. Begin chopping at far end of mortise, approximately ³⁄₁₆ in. from shoulder line. Chop about ³⁄₁₆ to ¼ in. deep, move bevel forward and chop again.

Lever out the waste with back of bevel, then repeat chop-lever sequence.

When levering waste, take care not to crush wood outside the shoulder line.

With mortise at full depth, pare to the shoulder lines at both ends.

Mortise bottom needn't be perfectly flat, but to clean it up to consistent depth, lever chisel against mortise ends.

Top, marking out a mortise begins with setting the mortise-marking gauge to the width of the mortising chisel. Above, a square stood on the bench aids in keeping the chisel perpendicular to the work during chopping.

allel. So the loose joint is loaded up with gap-filling glue, and the door (chair, table, whatever) lives happily ever after. Best to do it right and buy (or make) a set of mortising chisels.

Mortising chisels are most commonly sold in four widths: ¼ in., 5/16 in., 3/8 in. and ½ in. If you aren't going to buy a set, choose a size or two most likely to fit your needs. This leads us to the question of sizing the mortise in width, length and depth. To determine mortise width, some woodworkers simply divide the stock thickness by three. Thus, ¾ in. stock would require a mortise ¼ in. wide with a tenon of matching thickness, less a bit of clearance. Most furniture is, however, frightfully overbuilt and anything reasonably close to this rule is plenty strong.

To begin, cut out your stock to the desired dimensions and make sure you've gotten the faces square to the edges—otherwise your mark-out lines won't align as you carry them around each piece. Allow extra length on the part being mortised (which I'll call the stile), and plan to position the mortise to leave at least 1 in. of additional material between the end of the piece and the edge of the finished joint. This extra length (called the "horn") will keep the stile from splitting out as you chop the mortise. Later, the horn will be cut off flush.

Mark the length of the mortise (allowing for shoulders of at least ⅛ in. on both ends) and the horn on the end of the stile. Then, scribe the lines for the mortise with the double spurs on your marking gauge set to the width of your mortising chisel (see top photo, left), and the gauge fence set to roughly center the mortise in the thickness of the stock (unless you want it closer to one edge, as in an apron-to-leg joint for a table). Once I've marked the mortise, I cut the lines a little deeper with my knife. This makes them read well and also allows the first cuts with the chisel to pop waste out without tearing up the edges.

To chop the mortise, clamp the stock to your bench with the joint positioned over a leg so that the shock of your mallet is directly transferred to the floor. You'll be doing some pounding, and even though vises are tough, they really aren't designed for this kind of punishment. The position of your body is critical to hand mortising, so don't try to cheat. With the chisel in your hand, positioned in the marked-out joint, stand in such a way that you can sight down the piece and—with your back straight and arms extended—get the feel of the tool's relationship to the work. This exercise will enable you to develop the skill of perpendicular chopping. To gain confidence, try standing a square on the bench near your work to give yourself a reference to eyeball to keep the chisel perpendicular to the benchtop (see bottom photo, left).

Begin chopping at the far end of the mortise. Start the chisel about 3/16 in. in from the line marking the finished edge of the joint (see figure 1) with the bevel toward you. Hold the tool as plumb as you can, and give it a good whack with your mallet. Move the bevel about a ¼ in. closer to you and have at it again. After this shot, lever the chip out of the slot, being very careful to keep the arc of the levering in the same plane as the mortise. Repeat this process until the levering almost crushes your mark-out line at the near end of the mortise. Now, turn the chisel around and march back in the other direction, repeating the process in reverse.

You'll quickly notice how nicely the thick blade of the mortise chisel is jigged along the waste-leveling arc in a single plane by the slot you've already cut. The parallel sides keep the blade from twisting and digging in, so that if you're careful at the start, the blade will virtually follow a straight line, right to the bottom. The deeper you go, the more muscle you'll need to put into levering out the waste, and the more you'll appreciate the extra meat you left on at both ends of the mortise: This provides a

fulcrum so that the crush doesn't encroach on visible wood outside of the joint.

The force you can apply in this process is considerable, and you'll be thankful for the extra length of the horn. Were it not there, you'd probably rip the endgrain right out of the wood with a deep, waste-clearing pry. Check the depth of the mortise from time to time, measuring with a metal rule or a combination square. How deep is deep enough? That depends on the application. A good rule of thumb is to make the mortise as deep as possible, chopping to within ¼ in. to 3/8 in. of the backside of the wood. Obviously, if you're mortising into very wide stock—say a 6-in.-wide door stile—you needn't go as deep. The mortise should be slightly deeper than the length of the tenon, and the depth can be checked with the blade of your combo-square set ⅛ in. longer than the length of the tenon; after all, you don't want the tenon bottoming out before the shoulder is tight against the mortise face.

Once you're as deep as you want to be, scrape the bottom reasonably flat with levering strokes. Finish up by paring away the material left shy of the line at the ends of the mortise. You can trim up to the final line with shallow paring cuts or with careful, mallet-driven chops, with the chisel's bevel facing into the mortise. Check again that the depth is consistently correct, and the mortise is done.

If you aren't really inclined to doing handwork or if you've got dozens of mortises to chop, there's one method that speeds things along. I have, on occasion, set up a right-angle fence on the drill-press bed, bored out most of the waste and pared to the final line. If the diameter of the drill bit used is the same as the width of the mortise, paring merely involves cleaning off the ridges between overlapping drill holes with a wide paring chisel worked parallel to the mortise length. A reasonably accurate mortise results. I say "reasonably accurate" because any paring of mortise cheeks runs a very high risk of taking them out of parallel.

I usually cut tenons by machine, but there are times that hand cutting makes more sense, is faster and more enjoyable. I'm about to build a reproduction of an 18th-century spice chest, the top case of which is closed with a pair of raised-panel doors. Since everything else is dovetailed together, I'll only have to produce eight mortise-and-tenon joints—hardly a backbreaker. In fact, it's hardly worth the time to set up the jigs and robots to do the job. When I finally succumb to the familial pressure for new kitchen cabinets, however, I plan to defeat that endless army of tenons with the tablesaw. The set-up time will be insignificant relative to the total job, and I can expend my energy on more creative concerns.

Gaining time by machine-jigging exacts a price: There must be absolute uniformity of materials. You don't have to mark out every tenon, nor do you have to concentrate on each jigged cut. But because both edges and/or faces of a rail are used alternately to reference against your jigs, all of the stock must be exactly the same thickness and length, and must also be dead square. Otherwise, the tenons aren't going to be uniform—they just won't fit right.

Hand-cutting the tenon is demanding in a different sort of way. Each piece must be individually marked, usually from only one reference surface or edge, and cutting is done freehand to the lines, requiring skill with the saw and absolute concentration. A tweak here with a shoulder plane, a trim there with a chisel and the piece goes together the way you want it to.

So, on to hand-cut tenons, beginning with stock preparation. In determining the length of a part to be tenoned, some woodworkers add the length of tenons to the distance between tenon shoulders. They then set a marking gauge to the length of the tenon and, working off the end of the board, mark back to the shoulder. Not only is this a bit like driving from New York to Cleveland, it doubles the effort required for accurate shoulders by requiring that the end of the tenon be made perfectly square, which—as far as joint fitting and strength is concerned—it doesn't have to be.

To me, the more sensible approach is to roughly cut the rail to overall length, mark where the shoulders will be (leaving equal lengths of tenon on both ends of the board) and then scribe a crisp line around the stock with your combination square and layout knife. Since there are always at least two rails of the same length in any job, gather them together on the bench after marking shoulder positions on one and knife one edge of each shoulder on all of the pieces simultaneously. The remaining three sides of each tenon can be marked off these initial lines.

The tenon cheeks can now be marked with the gauge set to the same dimension you used to lay out the width of the mortises. If the rails and stiles are to be flush on the face—as on a cabinet door—the gauge setting doesn't have to be touched. If the stile is to be proud of the rail (as some table legs are proud of the apron face) the depth of the gauge must be reset to reflect this. Strike lines across the ends and edges of each tenon, being careful to always work off the same outside face of each piece.

Figure 2 illustrates how to saw the tenon. A good backsaw will do the job nicely. The cheeks needn't be perfectly smooth and crisp, but the shoulder wants to have a nice, clean edge. So, I knife a second line at a slight angle to the first on the waste side of the line, creating a deeper notch to help guide the saw for the first few strokes. If the shoulders aren't right to the line or if they aren't smooth, true them up with a paring chisel if the tenon is narrow, or

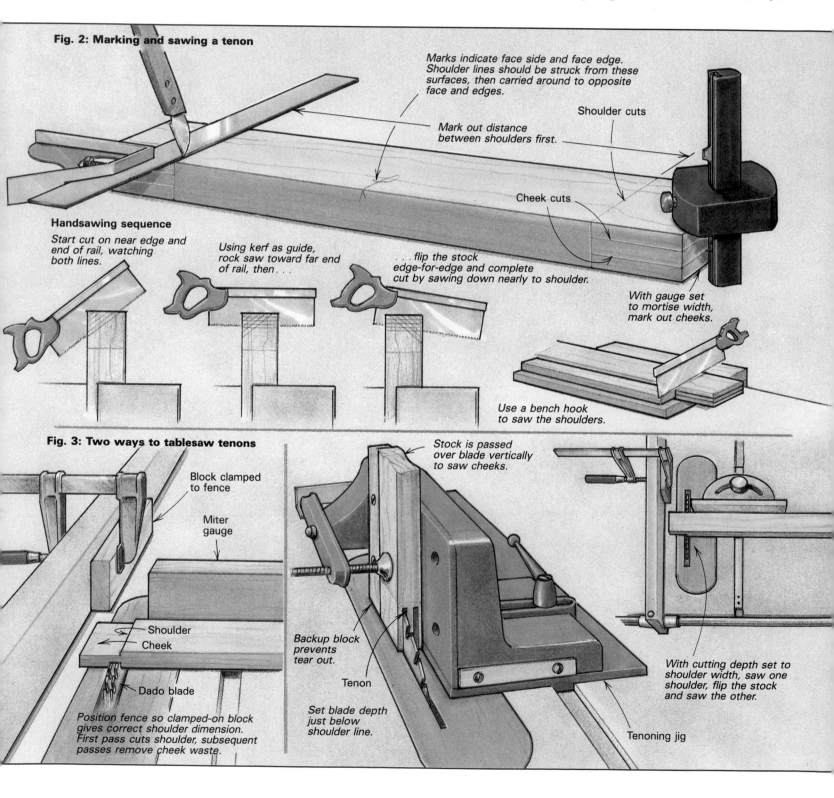

Fig. 2: Marking and sawing a tenon

Marks indicate face side and face edge. Shoulder lines should be struck from these surfaces, then carried around to opposite face and edges.

Shoulder cuts

Mark out distance between shoulders first.

Cheek cuts

Handsawing sequence

Start cut on near edge and end of rail, watching both lines.

Using kerf as guide, rock saw toward far end of rail, then . . .

. . . flip the stock edge-for-edge and complete cut by sawing down nearly to shoulder.

With gauge set to mortise width, mark out cheeks.

Use a bench hook to saw the shoulders.

Fig. 3: Two ways to tablesaw tenons

Block clamped to fence

Miter gauge

Shoulder

Cheek

Dado blade

Position fence so clamped-on block gives correct shoulder dimension. First pass cuts shoulder, subsequent passes remove cheek waste.

Stock is passed over blade vertically to saw cheeks.

Backup block prevents tear out.

Tenon

Set blade depth just below shoulder line.

With cutting depth set to shoulder width, saw one shoulder, flip the stock and saw the other.

Tenoning jig

Making a mortising chisel

I've never been able to find commercially made mortising chisels capable of withstanding the considerable pounding of heavy work, so I designed my own set a few years ago. I know very little about blacksmithing, but I took drawings of what I wanted to a machine shop and asked them to make up a set of three chisel blades, each a different width. The shop used ordinary oil-hardening tool steel, hardening it in an oven after the blades were shaped and then tempering them.

If you don't have a suitably equipped machine shop nearby, you can make the chisels yourself just as well. A good general-purpose oil-hardening tool steel is O-1 (Source: Cardinal Engineering, Route 1, Box 163, Cameron, Ill. 61423). It's available in the annealed (or soft) state, and can be shaped by grinding or with a hacksaw and file. Don't grind too aggressively, however, or else you risk heating the steel and hardening it prematurely. Drill the holes for the scales before heat treating.

To harden O-1, heat it cherry red with a pair of propane torches, then quench it in a bath of clean motor oil. Since there's a lot of

Author Podmaniczky designed his own mortising chisels and had them made. The chisels are fashioned from oil hardened tool steel with bronze handles.

steel in these chisels, small torches may be capable of heating only the lower third or lower half of the blank. As long as the cutting edge is hardened, this will work fine. Then reheat the hardened steel to about 500° F (a process known as tempering) to reduce brittleness and give a good, tough tool edge. Tempering can be done in a kitchen oven or with the propane torches.

At the time I made these chisels, I planned to produce them in quantity, so I shaped patterns for scales out of wood and had them cast in bronze. If you want to make just one set, you can easily shape quarter-hard brass with files and/or a belt sander. I lightly countersunk the holes in the scales, then riveted them on with 1/4-in. brass rod stock (see photo, left).

To ensure that the leading edges of the blade's back were straight and sharply squared, I hollow-ground the blade's length to within 1/4 in. of the cutting edge (similar to a Japanese chisel) and stoned it. I then ground the bevel flat and a bit more obtuse than a bench chisel. Finally, I stoned the bevel flat on a fine India.   —M.P.

---

with a shoulder plane if it's wide. To trim a tenon that's too thick for its mortise, pare the cheeks evenly, either with a wide chisel or a rabbeting plane.

There are two ways to saw tenons on the tablesaw (see figure 3). The method I prefer is to cut cheeks and shoulders at the same time by multiple passes over a dado blade. The other method is to saw the cheeks in one pass using a rip blade with the part standing vertically, held by a jig or running against the fence. The shoulders are then cut with a cross-cut or planer blade with the rail lying flat and the end of the tenon jigged against the fence. It's important to clamp a block on the fence. Otherwise, the off-cut cheek can jam and shoot back at you like a cannonball.

If you're really confident at machine setup, you don't have to mark even one tenon, but I always feel better when I have a line to work to. One of the secrets of machine tenoning is to have plenty of waste stock so you can run test pieces for each new setup, making practice tenons than can be tested in the mortise they're intended for before committing actual stock. Knife-in one shoulder on a scrap piece and strike one set of cheeks with the marking gauge you used for the mortises earlier.

You're going to remove cheek material with a cross-cut motion over the blade, so for maximum stock removal per pass, it's expedient to install all of the dado chippers. Set the depth of cut to just less than the depth of the tenon shoulder and, using your miter gauge, make a test cut. If your tenon is centered in the rail, the other cheek can be cut by flipping the stock over and repeating the same procedure. Test the tenon fit and adjust the depth of cut so that the tenon enters the mortise with just the slightest resistance. Better a little loose than too tight. If the tenon isn't centered, every tenon will have the same cheek cut before flipping it over. Then, the depth of cut must be reset to give the correct tenon thickness.

The stand-up method of tenoning requires a shop-built vertical jig or one of the commercial jigs sold for the purpose. Woodcraft Supply sells a lightweight aluminum jig (catalog number 17L21, $69.50). Delta makes a nice, heavy, cast-iron tenoner that attaches to tablesaws and shapers (catalog number 34-172). All of the jigs do the same thing: They clamp the stock firmly to a fence so it can be passed safely through a rip blade on the tablesaw. The jig travels in the miter gauge slot (see figure 3 on the facing page). As with the dado method, set up the tenoning jig using a piece of scrap marked out with shoulder and cheek lines. I cut the cheeks first by setting the saw's depth of cut so the top of the kerf will be just shy of the shoulder line. Saw one cheek on each of the pieces, flip the stock edge-for-edge, readjust the jig (for off-center tenons only) so the tenon thickness is correct, then saw the other cheeks.

Before committing all of your tenons to that second cheek cut, however, it's a good idea to make the second cut on your scrap piece and then saw the shoulder lines so you can test the tenon's fit. Instead of messing around resetting the tablesaw's depth of cut, you can roughly handsaw or bandsaw the cheeks on your scrap to try the fit. If it's satisfactory, complete the second cheek cuts, then set up your miter gauge for the shoulder cuts (see figure 3).

In assembling mortise-and-tenoned parts, clamp just firmly enough to ensure that the shoulder is solidly positioned against the mortise face—don't crush anything with overclamping. Correct for square and true, if necessary, by canting the clamp slightly. When the glue has set up, saw off the horn and you're in business. □

Michael Podmaniczky is a contributing editor to Fine Woodworking *and a furniture conservator at The Winterthur Museum in Winterthur, Del.*

Making Shoji by Machine
Traditional joinery with drill press and tablesaw

by Ben Erickson

Traditional Japanese shoji panels adapt beautifully to Western architecture and interior decors ranging from ultramodern to traditional, as in my home, shown in the photo below. I installed shoji in front of the windows, and they take the place of curtains or blinds. In the day, they produce a stunning effect as the light filtered through the translucent shoji paper bathes the room in a stunning warm glow; at night, they provide the same privacy as curtains. Shoji also help keep the house cooler in the summer by reflecting sunlight, and warmer in the winter by reducing heat loss through windows.

Despite their intricate look, shoji aren't difficult to build. In this article, I'll tell you how I build shoji in my workshop in Eutaw, Ala., including how to glue on the paper, make the track and install a set of sliding panels. While shoji screens are traditionally made with only hand tools, they are well suited to the machine setups I use, due to the number of repetitive operations involved—such as cutting mortises, tenons and dadoes—that must be performed without deviation. Indeed, Japanese apprentices being trained to-day use tablesaws and thickness planers for preparing shoji panels.

Shoji anatomy—A shoji panel consists of a through mortise-and-tenon frame that holds a lattice of lap-jointed muntins or "kumiko," as shown in the drawing on the facing page. These muntins are woven together for strength and to prevent the individual kumiko from bowing. Both the vertical (long) and horizontal (short) kumiko have stub tenons on their ends that fit into square mortises chopped in the inside edges of the frame. The kumiko and frame are flush on the side facing away from the room. Shoji paper (a modern synthetic-paper blend that doesn't yellow as traditional shoji rice paper does) is glued to this side.

While a shoji panel can be 4 ft. or more wide, and the dimensions of the individual components can deviate from the ones given in the article, the spacing of the short kumiko should be 5⅜ in. center to center, to accommodate the width of the shoji paper covering, which comes in a 28-cm-wide roll (about 11¹⁄₁₆ in.). One piece of glued-on paper spans two short kumiko, overlapping at the seams by the thickness of one kumiko (⅜ in.). The paper also overlaps the inside edges of the frame by the same amount. While height requirements will dictate how many short kumiko are used in a panel, a typical 3-ft.-wide shoji traditionally has three long kumiko. However, I use two in my shoji, as I prefer the look of the longer horizontal rectangles that result.

For use in front of a window (or door), two, three or four shoji may be held in a two-lane track attached to the casing around the opening. The grooved track holds the shoji at top and bottom and allows them to slide past one another.

Building the frames—To ensure frame parts will fit together properly, the shoji stock must be uniform in thickness, with square and straight edges. To guarantee this, I first cut the rough frame stock oversize, and then lean it against a wall for a couple of days until it adjusts to the shop's humidity. Frames are traditionally made from lightweight softwoods, but I use Honduras mahogany; any easily worked stock will do. I plane the stock until its thickness is 1¼ in., taking the final pass on all the frame stock with the thickness planer at one setting, pushing the pieces over the same part of the bed, in case the planer knives aren't exactly parallel. Next, I joint the edges of the frame members to dress them to final width: 1¼ in. for stiles, 3½ in. for rails. Rail width may be varied to fine-tune overall height of shoji.

The stiles are crosscut 2 in. to 4 in. longer than their final length to allow for horns on the ends. The horns keep the stiles from splitting while the tenons are driven and can be trimmed off afterwards. Cut the rails so their length equals the final width of the shoji plus ¹⁄₁₆ in. to ⅛ in. for trimming the ends of the through tenons.

Next, chop the through mortises in the stiles with a ⅜-in., hollow-chisel mortiser in the drill press. Their shoulders stop ¾ in. short of the final length of the stile. An extra-long fence and table are attached to the drill press to support the long stock. The mor-

Japanese shoji screens can blend harmoniously with practically any interior, like this three-shoji arrangement in the author's antebellum home. Installed in front of an existing window, the translucent shoji-paper screens provide the privacy of curtains, yet allow a warm light to come through during the day.

From *Fine Woodworking* magazine (September 1989) 78:82-85

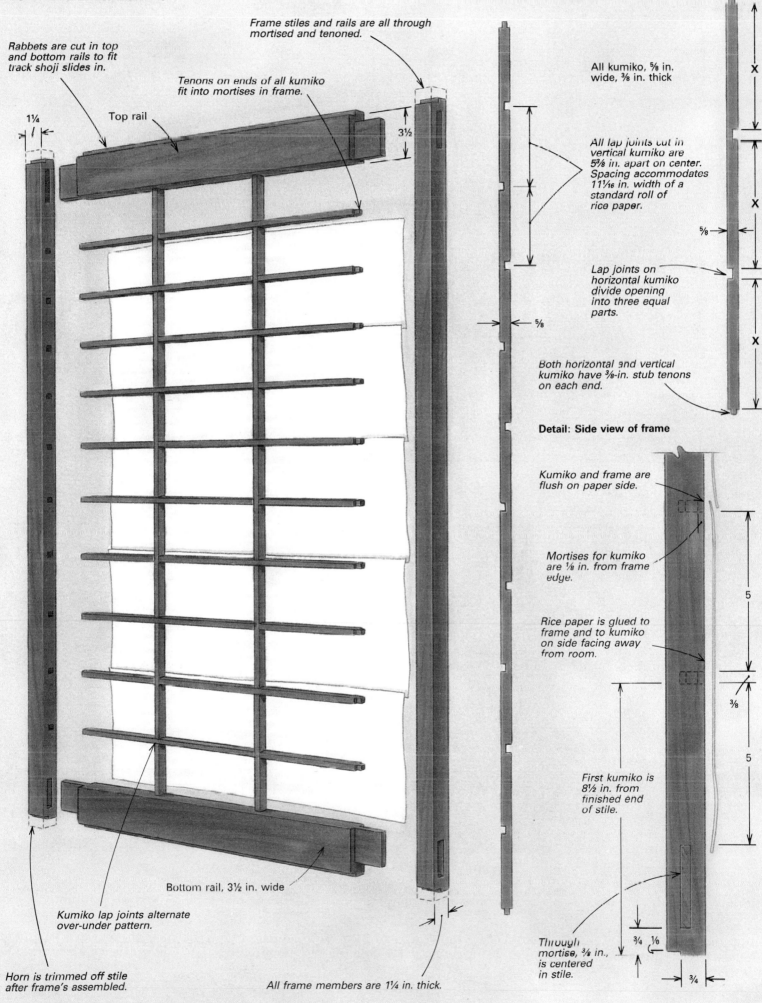

The author uses a hollow-chisel mortiser on the drill press to chop mortises in the shoji frame for the kumiko. By referencing the end of the frame against a line of blocks laid end to end (the block on the far end clamped to the fence), mortises can be accurately spaced, removing one block after each mortise.

Erickson weaves the horizontal and vertical kumiko together, alternating the direction of the lap joints of each horizontal layer. A squeeze bottle is used to apply glue to each lap before it's assembled and pounded home with a hammer.

The shoji-paper covering is glued to the flush surface of the shoji frame and kumiko on the side that will face away from the room. A pair of clamping blocks helps the author keep the paper taut as it's lowered onto the shoji members that have been precoated with wallpaper glue.

tises are centered in the thickness of the stiles, so mortising can be done on both ends without having to change the fence setting. To prevent tearout, start by mortising a little over halfway through the stile. Make the two end cuts first, remove the waste in between, then flip the stile and complete the through mortise. Next, cut the 3/8-in.-wide tenons on the frame rails by whichever method you prefer; I use a tenoning attachment on the tablesaw.

The mortises for the kumiko are done next. These square mortises are the same size as the kumiko's thickness (3/8 in.) and are located so the assembled lattice will be flush on one side. Set the drill-press fence so the mortises are 1/8 in. (the width of a kumiko shoulder) from the outside-facing edge of the frame. Chop the two kumiko mortises in each rail first, dividing the distance between tenon shoulders evenly in thirds to locate the mortises. To cut the kumiko mortises on the stiles accurately, you'll need to make the same number of spacer blocks as short kumiko from 2x2 scraps. Using a stop block on the radial-arm saw, cut each spacer block 5 3/8 in. long—the spacing of the short kumiko. Keeping the same fence setting as for the frame mortises, locate the first mortise 8 1/2 in. from the finish end of the stile (see the detail in figure 1 on the previous page). Lay the spacer blocks along the fence end to end, with the first block against the stile and the last one clamped to the fence, as shown in the top photo at left. Remove a block after making each mortise until they're all done.

Making the kumiko—I thickness-plane the kumiko stock to 5/8 in., and then rough-cut it and allow it to adjust to the shop's humidity. Instead of cutting the lap joints, where the long and short kumiko intersect, on all the thin kumiko separately, I cut one wide board for all the long kumiko and one or two for all the short kumiko. By adding enough extra width for sawkerfs and trimming, I can slice off individual kumiko after cutting the laps. This ensures identical joints, prevents tearout and saves time. First, trial-assemble the shoji frame to determine exact kumiko length, which equals the inside frame measurements plus 3/4 in., for stub tenons on each end. After trimming the boards to length, I cut the lap joints on the radial-arm saw, using a 3/8-in.-wide dado blade set for a 3/8-in.-deep cut. Make trial cuts first, to check the fit and squareness of cut, then use the set of spacer blocks to locate the joints on the long kumiko just as you used them for making the mortises earlier. Flip the kumiko stock over after each cut, so the laps alternate sides. The lap joints for the short kumiko are cut using a regular stop block.

The radial-arm saw also cuts the stub tenons on the ends of the kumiko boards. By taking passes from both sides of the stock, the 3/8-in.-thick tenons are automatically centered. Set a stop block so the blade cuts 3/8 in. into the end of each board—the correct length of the tenons. After these cuts are taken on each board, the individual kumiko are bandsawn apart. Set the bandsaw's rip fence for a little over 3/8 in., and rip the kumiko off one at a time. Joint the edge of the stock before bandsawing and after each cut, and thickness-plane the kumiko so the lap joints fit tight.

Assembly—I assemble the kumiko lattice first, then the frame around it. I start by laying the two long kumiko parallel on the bench. After applying a drop of yellow glue to the lap joints on a short kumiko, I fit it onto the long kumiko, tapping the joints home with a hammer protected by a block of softwood. This process is repeated, weaving the kumiko together (shown in the middle photo at left), until the lattice is complete. Friction holds most joints tight, but I secure any loose ones with a small clamp until the glue dries. Using a 1/16-in.-radius roundover bit in the router, I round the edges on the non-paper side of the lattice, as well as the inside edges of the frame on the non-paper side, stopping short of the corner joints.

For final assembly, I insert the long kumiko tenons into the top and bottom rails, driving the joints home with a rubber mallet. Next, I coat all the frame mortises and tenons with yellow glue and also dab a drop on the inside of each kumiko mortise. I fit one stile on the rails, starting the short kumiko stub tenons into their mortises as I work from one end to the other. When the tenons are all partially inserted, I drive the stile on with the rubber mallet, stopping when the rail-to-stile joints are home. Working quickly before the glue dries, I repeat this process with the other stile, and then apply pipe clamps and pull the frame joints home. Finally, I check the frame's diagonals for squareness.

After the glue dries overnight, I plane down any irregularities in the frame and trim the through tenons flush. I cut off the horns on the ends of the stiles and round the outside edges of the stiles with a ⅛-in. roundover bit in the router. If the shoji will be used in a track, a tongue needs to be rabbeted in the top and bottom frame edges, to fit the track grooves. Using either a router or a shoulder plane, cut a ⅛-in.-deep rabbet on the bottom rail and a ⅝-in.-deep rabbet on the top.

Although Japanese customarily leave the shoji unfinished, I prefer to finish with three coats of tung oil, sanding lightly between coats. Do not apply finish to the paper side of any kumiko or within ⅜ in. of the frame's inside face, as the glue used to attach the shoji paper sticks better to unfinished wood.

Making the track—The track the shoji panels slide in can be made before or after the shoji themselves. I usually make the track first and size the shoji to fit. The shoji track consists of upper and lower grooved rails that are joined on the ends into a four-sided frame with the corners rabbeted and screwed together. The frame is made from stock that's 1¼ in. thick and 3½ in. wide. You may need to make it wider, to clear door or window casings. The height of the opening in the assembled track frame should be ⁹⁄₁₆ in. less than the overall height of the shoji. Track length equals the total width of all shoji plus 2½ in. (the thickness of the track's side frames) minus one shoji stile width wherever shoji will overlap in the track. The tongues on the shoji panels ride in grooves in the tracks: The lower track has two shallow grooves and the upper has two deeper grooves that allow the shoji to be lifted in or out. These are all cut on the tablesaw with a dado blade. The track dimensions, shown in figure 2 at right, provide a ⅛-in. gap for clearance between shoji as they slide past each other.

After the track frame is assembled at the work site, it may be screwed to the wall studs or casings. The track frame should completely cover the door or window casing and should screw into the edge of this casing, if it protrudes enough from the wall's surface; if not, a 1-in. by 2-in. strip can be screwed to the tracks as a fastening strip. Check the frame's diagonals for squareness as you attach them.

Applying the paper—Shoji paper is best applied on humid days, because the paper expands and contracts with changes in moisture. If I have to put the paper on in dry weather, I create my own humidity by running a vaporizer for several hours before applying the paper. Working on a clean surface, I first cut the paper pieces to the width of the shoji plus a couple of inches, using a square and sharp utility knife. Special shoji glue comes with the paper. (Shoji paper is available from Highland Hardware, 1045 N. Highland Ave. N.E., Atlanta, Ga. 30306; 404-872-4466. For orders, call 800-241-6748.) While you can substitute a clear cellulose wallpaper adhesive, such as "Shur-Stik" (available from a wallpaper and paint store), I find the

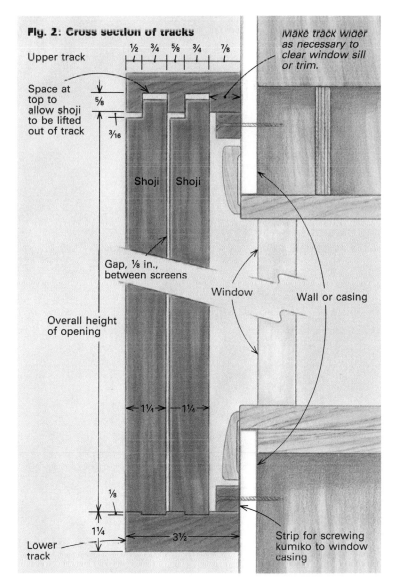

Fig. 2: Cross section of tracks

Upper track

Make track wider as necessary to clear window sill or trim.

½ ¾ ⅝ ¾ ⅞

Space at top to allow shoji to be lifted out of track — ⅝ — ³⁄₁₆

Shoji Shoji

Gap, ⅛ in., between screens

Window Wall or casing

Overall height of opening

← 1¼ → ← 1¼ →

⅛

1¼

Lower track

3½

Strip for screwing kumiko to window casing

shoji glue has a smoother consistency that brushes out better. The directions for the special glue, in case you don't read Japanese, are as follows: Slowly add the packet of glue to 400cc (1⅝ cup) of water, stir well and let it sit for 10 minutes before using.

With the shoji panel lying flush side up on the bench, I start the papering at the bottom of the frame and work my way up. The glue is applied to the short and long kumiko and within ⅜ in. around the inside edge of the frame using a small plastic squeeze bottle. To hold the paper evenly for application, I made two paper holders by hinging together two pieces of 12-in.-long scrap with duct tape. It helps if the halves of each holder bow slightly away from each other in the center, so finger pressure in the center firmly grips both edges of the paper. Grip each end of the paper in a holder and pass the paper once or twice over the vaporizer. Carefully align it with the kumiko and set it into the glue, as shown in the bottom photo on the facing page. Run your fingertip down the kumiko and the edge of the frame to press the paper into the glue and to carefully pull out any wrinkles. Then repeat the process, lapping the next paper over the previous one by the width of a kumiko. If the paper is still not tight enough after the glue is dry, it may be lightly wetted with a spray bottle to further shrink the paper. Damaged or misaligned paper may be removed by dampening the glued areas and peeling it off. □

Ben Erickson is a woodworker in Eutaw, Ala.

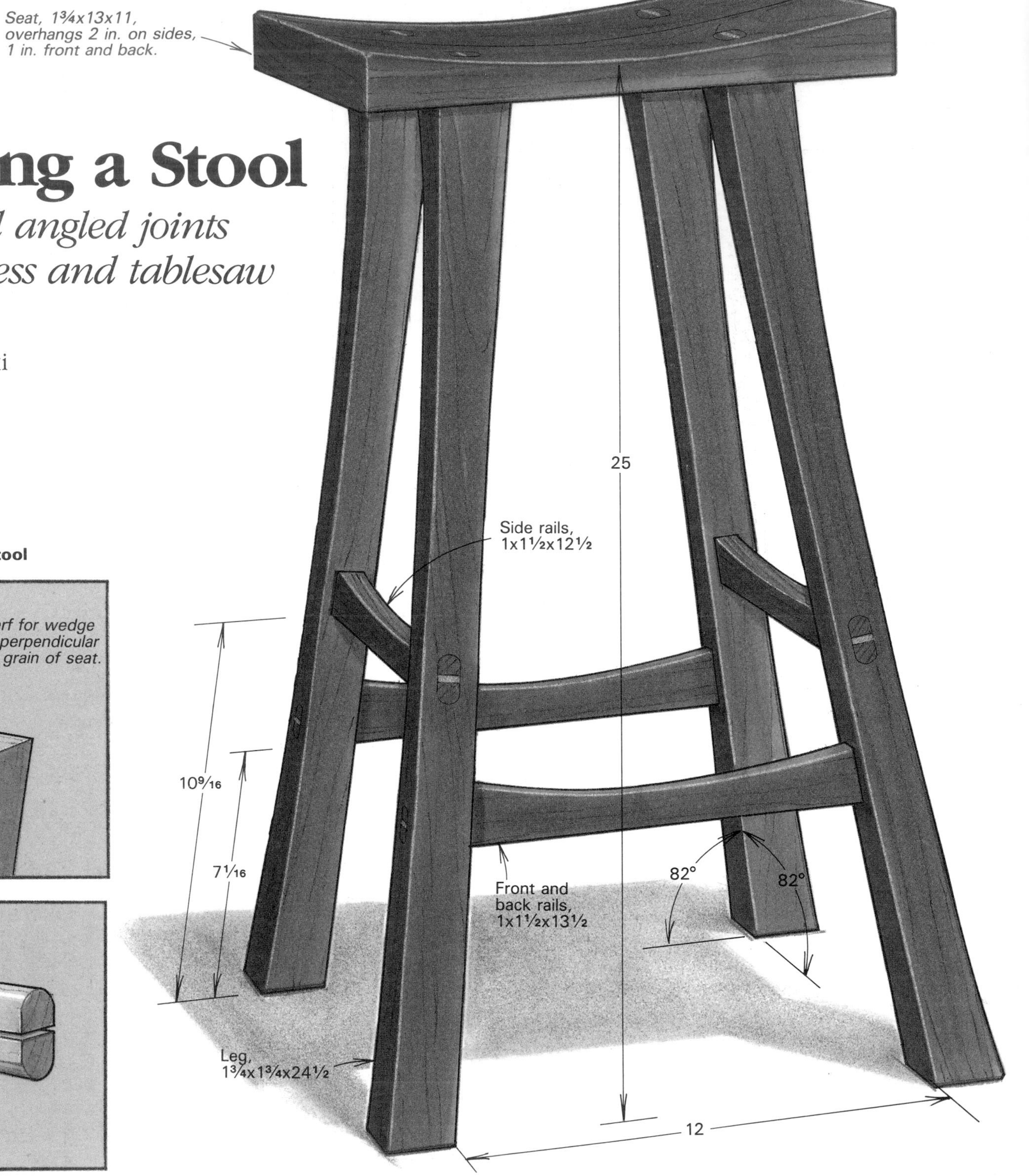

Seat, 1¾x13x11,
overhangs 2 in. on sides,
1 in. front and back.

Building a Stool
Compound angled joints on drill press and tablesaw

by Gary Rogowski

Fig. 1: Rogowski's stool

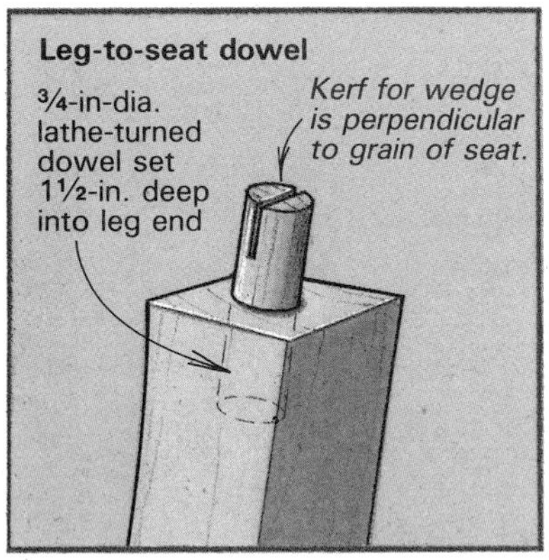

Leg-to-seat dowel

¾-in.-dia.
lathe-turned
dowel set
1½-in. deep
into leg end

Kerf for wedge
is perpendicular
to grain of seat.

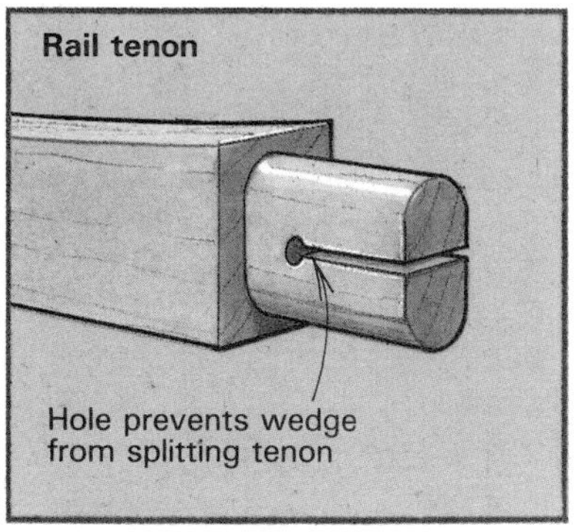

Rail tenon

Hole prevents wedge
from splitting tenon

Side rails,
1x1½x12½

25

10⁹⁄₁₆

7¹⁄₁₆

Front and
back rails,
1x1½x13½

82°   82°

Leg,
1¾x1¾x24½

12

I t was not in the sometimes-a-great-notion category that I decided to build a stool a few years ago. I needed something
sturdy to sit on. "How hard could it be to knock out a stool?"
I asked myself. My first attempt ended in a three-legged triumph
of material over maker. It was astonishingly ugly and so precar-
ious that you could sit on it only with great caution. It did hold a
plant very nicely though.

In the process of building my first stool, I learned a basic
lesson. Effort, not luck, and planning, not good intentions, are
required to successfully build a piece of furniture. This involves

a thoughtful approach to design, accurate drawings and careful
construction. Gone is the innocent notion that one relaxing
weekend of humming and puttering is enough to concoct a
piece with style, grace and strength. So, I started over.

Designing a chair or stool is a deceptive task, like setting up a
model train. Kind thoughts blessed with the vision of an innocent
invariably produce some degree of frustration. It only looks simple.
You soon find the job involves more work than you expected.
The process is a lot like designing other types of furniture in that
it involves solving a series of problems, both aesthetically and

From *Fine Woodworking* magazine (March 1988) 69:40-44

structurally. Stools do present unique design difficulties, however. A stool's parts must strike a delicate balance between looks and weight. Stools look jaunty compared to chairs, are comparatively lighter and easier to move. Yet, looks can't come at the expense of strength. Thus, a stool is built with the strength of a timber-frame house even though its airiness gives the impression it is built of matchsticks.

As if this didn't present enough of a challenge, recall that, by design, stools are meant to put you high off the floor or close to it. Generally, the former design is more popular because there are more reasons in this world for sitting at workbenches, counters and bars than there are for sitting a few inches off the ground. Thus, stools are generally higher than chairs and narrower in front and side profile. This makes for a weight distribution problem. Chairs are comparatively wider and more stable, so their legs can be perpendicular to or angled from the seat. Stools need all the stability they can get, are more stable and look best if their legs are splayed (i.e. they slope at a compound angle). A stool with splayed legs distributes a person's weight over a greater area than one with legs perpendicular to the seat. Thus, a person sitting on a stool with splayed legs must tip through a greater arc before falling over.

Splayed legs help, but don't entirely solve the stability problem. A stool's stability and attractiveness rely heavily on its proportions. In my case, these were quickly arrived at through an empirical method. I wanted to sit comfortably at my workbench and knew that chair height, about 17 in. or 18 in., would be too low. I put a chair on top of bricks, placed phone books on its seat and finally, sat myself on top of the phone books. I discovered the correct seat height was about 25 in. With the stool's height established, I went to the drawing board and made a series of drawings at ¼ in. scale, experimenting with various leg angles and spacing arrangements. I finally decided to locate the legs so they were 12 in. apart at the base and sloping 82°. Given the stool's height, the slope of the legs looked just right. I used a sliding protractor to copy the angle of the legs off the drawing.

Angled joinery—It soon occurred to me that although the sloping legs add to a stool's attractiveness and stability, they presented quite a challenge in joining together its parts—both in terms of rung-to-leg and leg-to-seat joinery. This was particularly troublesome in my case because, being influenced by James Krenov's work, I wanted to use exposed mortise-and-tenon joinery throughout. This meant the eight rung mortises would have to be cut to compensate for the slope of the legs, and the tenons on the ends of the rungs would need sloping shoulders. Furthermore, the compound angle does funny things to the geometry of the legs. The footprint seen in figure 3 shows an exaggerated view of what happens. Fortunately, the gentle curve I added to the legs had no effect on the joinery, because the legs curve only on their outside surfaces and were shaped after the joints were cut.

Joining the seat to the legs seemed similarly tricky, but after some head scratching, this problem was easily solved by letting a lathe-turned dowel into the top of each leg (I explain how to do this below). A dowel joint eliminated the need to cut a tenon with compound-angled shoulders on the end of the leg.

I started work on the stool by milling up my stock for the legs, rungs and seat. Cutting the compound angles on the ends of the legs seemed the trickiest job, so I started with them. I cut an accurate 8° compound angle on the ends of each leg on the table-saw. With an extra-long fence on the miter gauge, I tilted the

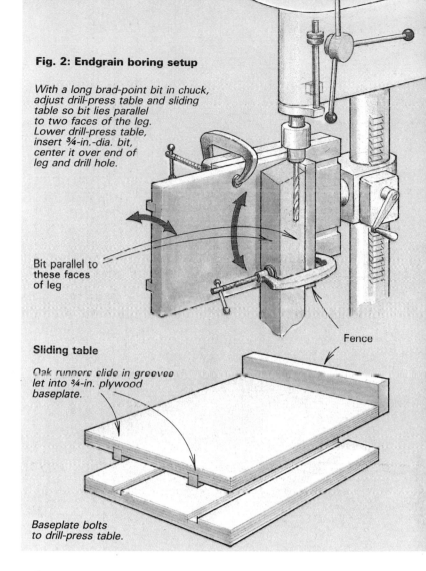

Fig. 2: Endgrain boring setup

With a long brad-point bit in chuck, adjust drill-press table and sliding table so bit lies parallel to two faces of the leg. Lower drill-press table, insert ¾-in.-dia. bit, center it over end of leg and drill hole.

Bit parallel to these faces of leg

Fence

Sliding table

Oak runners slide in grooves let into ¾-in. plywood baseplate.

Baseplate bolts to drill-press table.

blade over 8°, made a test cut and then checked it with the protractor. I repeated and tested the cuts until the saw cut a perfect 8° slope. To complete the compound angle, I set the miter gauge to 8°, make another test cut and check as before. When I can produce a perfect compound miter, I clamp a stop to the miter-gauge fence. Then, I cut one end, tip the miter gauge to 8° in the other direction, flip the leg over and cut the leg to finished length. Be sure to check that the top and bottom of the leg are parallel after it is cut to length.

To bore the dowel hole in the end of each leg, I clamp the leg to a vertical sliding table bolted to the drill-press table. The sliding table moves toward or away from the drill-press column (see figure 2, above). To ensure the leg is plumb to the bit, I swivel the drill-press table around until the leg butts up to a long brad-point bit chucked into the press, adjusting the drill-press table so the leg lies along the bit's length. I then reposition the sliding table so a second face on the leg lies along the bit's length (referencing off a face perpendicular to the first face). Once I'm sure the leg is plumb to the drill bit, I switch to a ¾-in.-dia. bit, center the leg's end under it and bore a 1½-in.-deep hole.

Next, I crosscut the rungs on the tablesaw with a plywood crosscutting jig with an 82° wedge tacked to its fence. With the wedge to the right of the blade and its narrow end pointed toward the left, I cut one end of each rung. Then I positioned the stop block, flipped each rung over and cut it to length. Next, I lowered the blade and repositioned the stop block to cut the tenon shoulders. On each rung, I cut one shoulder, flipped the rung end for end and cut the shoulder on the opposite face. I then switched the wedge and stop block to the other side of

Tenons are cut square and then rounded with a file to fit the mortise, above. Their shape is checked with a template with a slot cut by the same end mill that bored the mortises. With addition of a shopmade sliding table, right, the author's drill press does double duty as a slot mortiser. Clamps under the table hold stop blocks to set length of mortises, which are first bored with a brad-point bit, then finished with an end mill. The sliding table is sloped to the left or right to angle the mortises, accounting for the legs' slope. A test leg to establish table angle and locate stops is shown in place.

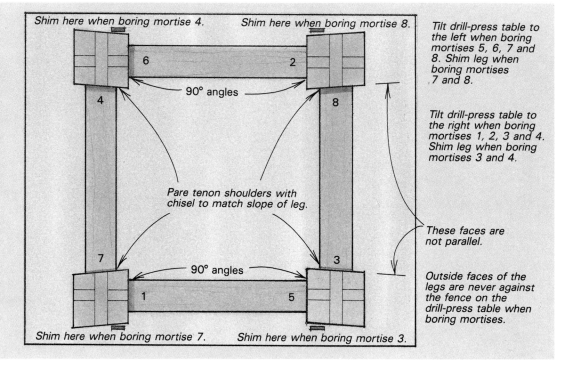

Fig. 3: Boring mortises

This diagram of the legs and rungs, viewed from above, shows the geometric relationship between them. Since the legs lean in at a compound angle, they're diamond shaped in cross section. The rails are parallel to the seat and floor. The tenons on the rails and mortises in the legs must accommodate the diamond-shaped section of the legs. Rogowski put shims under the legs when boring four of the mortises and shaved the shoulders on the matching tenons.

Shim here when boring mortise 4.
Shim here when boring mortise 8.

Tilt drill-press table to the left when boring mortises 5, 6, 7 and 8. Shim leg when boring mortises 7 and 8.

6   2

90° angles

4   8

Tilt drill-press table to the right when boring mortises 1, 2, 3 and 4. Shim leg when boring mortises 3 and 4.

Pare tenon shoulders with chisel to match slope of leg.

90° angles

These faces are not parallel.

7   3

1   5

Outside faces of the legs are never against the fence on the drill-press table when boring mortises.

Shim here when boring mortise 7.
Shim here when boring mortise 3.

the blade and repeated the procedure to cut the remaining two shoulders.

Next, I roughed out each tenon cheek on the bandsaw to prevent the offcut from flying back at me and finished sawing the tenon with a tenon jig on the tablesaw. Back at the bandsaw, each tenon was trimmed on its top and bottom edge to give it a shoulder on all four sides. Shoulders of two rungs must be pared, as described in figure 3, to compensate for the slight diamond shape of the legs. The tenons were rounded with a file to match the curve of the mortise and each was slotted on the bandsaw to receive a wedge. A ³⁄₁₆-in. hole was bored at the bottom of the slot to prevent the wedge from splitting the tenon.

Drill-press mortising—I moved on to cutting the leg mortises. I don't own a slot mortiser, but have the next best thing—a horizontal sliding table for my drill press (see photo above, right). I set the table's angle for the sloping mortises using the angle on a rung end as a guide. I chucked a long drill bit into the drill press to serve as a positioning guide, stood the rung up on the table,

tipping the table until the rung laid flat against the drill bit.

Without changing the drill-press alignment, I removed the drill bit and chucked a four-flute end mill into the drill press. The end mill badly mauled a test leg at every speed I tried. The remedy was to bore out the bulk of the mortises with a brad-point bit. The mortises were cleaned up taking shallow passes with the end mill, running the drill press at 1,600 RPM. In boring with both the brad-point bit and the end mill, I prefer to stop ¹⁄₁₆ in. or so shy of boring out the other side of the mortise. The leg's outside is shaped after the mortises are cut, so the remaining wood is cut away, leaving a clean opening. If you bore through the other side, you will have to put a piece of scrap under the leg to keep from cutting into your sliding table; you also risk tearing out the exit hole. The final shaping may not be able to remove the tearout if it's too severe. Mortises 1, 2, 3 and 4 are cut with the table sloping to the right; mortises 5, 6, 7 and 8 are cut with the table sloping to the left, as shown above. Remember to mark the table for two different sets of stops for boring the upper and lower rung mortises. When boring for mortises 3, 4, 7 and 8, I had to

Fitting rungs

by Jeremy Singley

I wish I had an extra 10 minutes for every time my mother told me not to tip back in my chair. I could retire. Mothers know a chair or stool's rungs are its weakest link; to the woodworker, rungs are a pain in the neck.

Not only do rungs have to fit tightly to the leg, in some cases they have to fit tightly to each other—double jeopardy. This requires rung holes be bored in the leg at the correct angles and cut to an accurate length. If these requirements aren't met, the assembled stool or chair will have legs sloping at different angles.

Fortunately, I've developed a bunch of techniques and jigs to make the job of fitting rungs to legs easier. For example, when I have just one or two stools to build, I bore the leg holes in the seat with a hand drill sighting along a sliding bevel gauge set to a leg axis line as a guide. I dry assemble the legs to the seat, then eyeball the alignment of the rung holes. The rungs are bored from inside the legs with an electric drill. If the room between the legs isn't enough to accommodate the drill and a full-length bit, I use a ground-off Powerbore, spade or twist bit.

The tricky part here is getting the rung holes centered. I solve this problem with a marking tool or a try square and straight-edge, shown in figure 7. I bore on the marks and measure for rung length. I check that the legs are the correct distance between their ends, use an extension rule with a sliding tongue to measure the distance from the shoulder of one hole to the bottom of another, then add the depth of the second hole. If you find reading the ruler in this situation awkward, you can simply measure the depth of each hole and then measure the span between them. The rung stock is cut to this length, and its ends are shrunk to a snug fit with a heat lamp just prior to turning and reshrunk just before the stool is assembled. The tenons swell from the moisture in the glue, locking them firmly in their holes.

The eyeball rung-boring method works if you have only a few stools to build; if you have a large batch, it pays to set up a jig.

It's crucial to keep the legs organized as you bore. A box of 50 unmarked legs with two rung holes in each makes a fine solution to the leisure-time problem—you can spend your day off sorting legs. To avoid this, before each leg leaves the jig, I mark its end with a number from one to four, corresponding to the four clockwise des-

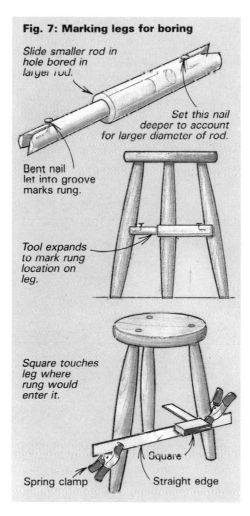

Fig. 7: Marking legs for boring

Slide smaller rod in hole bored in larger rod.

Set this nail deeper to account for larger diameter of rod.

Bent nail let into groove marks rung.

Tool expands to mark rung location on leg.

Square touches leg where rung would enter it.

Spring clamp

Square

Straight edge

ignations of leg positions: 1—front left; 2—front right; 3—rear left; and 4—rear right. This system assumes the stool is flipped over (the position it will be assembled in) so its left, front leg becomes the leg sticking up at the left rear. I use a color code to keep track of rungs. I crosscut boards and paint their ends a color to match rung length. No further coding is necessary, because turned rungs are not handed—a top rung that fits on the right side of the stool would also fit the left side. Then I rip the boards into rung blanks.

A final question: What do you do if you botch a rung hole? First, act innocent. Why bother the world with more bad news than it has already? Usually, turning a new leg is more work than the following alternatives. If the hole location is wrong and you plan to paint the stool, simply fill the hole with a plug and sand it flush. If the angle is wrong, turn a rung and then whittle the oversized tenon at an angle by eye to fit the hole (see figure 8, below). You can also glue a lathe-turned dowel into the hole and rebore. Since you have to bore the new hole exactly on the center of the dowel, position the plug with the tail center mark facing up and bore into the center mark with a brad point bit. □

Jeremy Singley makes chairs and stools in East Middlebury, Vt.

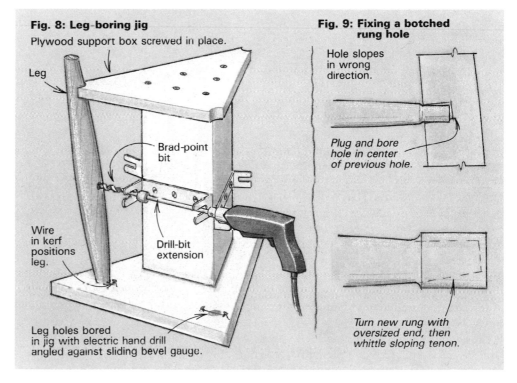

Fig. 8: Leg-boring jig

Plywood support box screwed in place.

Leg

Brad-point bit

Wire in kerf positions leg.

Drill-bit extension

Leg holes bored in jig with electric hand drill angled against sliding bevel gauge.

Fig. 9: Fixing a botched rung hole

Hole slopes in wrong direction.

Plug and bore hole in center of previous hole.

Turn new rung with oversized end, then whittle sloping tenon.

The curves on the outside of the legs are roughed out on the bandsaw and then cleaned up with a straight bit and template on the router table. Note that the template curves in two planes to accommodate the curve routed during the first pass. Always test such a setup before trying an actual leg.

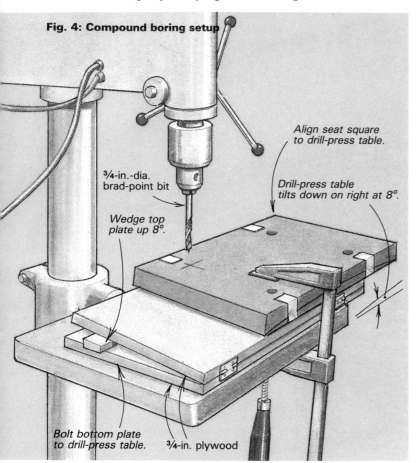

Fig. 4: Compound boring setup

Align seat square to drill-press table.

¾-in.-dia. brad-point bit

Drill-press table tilts down on right at 8°.

Wedge top plate up 8°.

Bolt bottom plate to drill-press table.

¾-in. plywood

shim the legs with a slip of paper under the rear, back edge to compensate for the compound slope of the legs.

With the setup fine-tuned, I cut the mortises and moved on to shaping the legs. Working from a full-size drawing of the stool, I made Masonite templates shaped to the curve of the legs and seat. I transferred the marks from the Masonite leg template to one made of alder, which I curved in depth and plan view (see photo, above) to match the curve of the legs. I marked the legs out, rough sawed them on the bandsaw, then taped the template on top of one leg and finish shaped it on the router table with a straight bit and ball-bearing pilot bearing against the template. I then flipped the leg over 90° and used the alder template to guide the straight bit while cutting the second curve. As can be seen in the photo, the curve in the template's depth accommodates the first curve cut in the leg.

I sand the legs and rungs before assembly because it's impossible to do a quick and neat job after the legs are assembled. There is no way of simultaneously assembling all four legs and rungs on a stool single-handedly. Because I work by myself, I

had to glue and clamp the stool in subassemblies. I glued up the front and back pairs of legs and rungs (the legs perpendicular to the long axis of the seat) and hammered the wedges into the tenons. When the glue was dry, I inserted the remaining two rungs and then glued and clamped the two pairs together.

Seat shaping—I was moving into the homestretch and started work on the seat. To save time shaping, I wanted to saw out the curve in the seat, but my bandsaw wasn't large enough to accept the seat blank turned up on edge. I solved this by making the seat from two narrower halves; I sawed the curve in each half then glued them together. I don't cut to the curved line, but leave a slight amount of wood to allow for tearout when boring the leg holes. Save the curved offcuts, you'll need them later to back up the seat when you bore the holes through it.

To mark for boring, I set dowel centers into the top of each leg, placed the seat top down on the bench and set the legs with dowel centers against the seat's bottom. After checking that the seat was positioned correctly relative to the leg, I tapped on top of each leg to mark the seat bottom and then returned to the drill press.

I use a hinged jig that bolts to the drill-press table to bore the leg holes (see figure 4). This is simply two pieces of plywood connected by a piano or butt hinges. The jig is placed with the hinge knuckle opposite the drill-press column and the jig's edge parallel to the drill-press table. The top plate is wedged up from underneath until it's at an 8° slope, then clamped in place so the wedges can't move. Next, I tilt the table 8° to the left or right, using a rung, as before, to align the table relative to the bit. I rest the seat top down on the table with the offcuts taped together underneath the seat. The brad-point bit enters the offcuts as it exits the seat, reducing tearout on the top of the seat. The seat is parallel to the edge of the jig.

Assembly is relatively easy compared to the rest of the project, but it takes considerable clamping force to bring the stool parts together. I set concrete blocks on the shop floor and then put a piece of plywood that is slightly larger than the area covered by the stool's base on top of the blocks. I set the legs on top of the plywood and the seat on top of the legs, then rest cauls on the seat's long axis (the cauls are notched to allow the leg dowels to project through the seat). I bring the seat and legs together with bar clamps running from the plywood to the cauls. I have to flex the legs a few degrees to get them into the holes; this requires a fair amount of force. Once the legs fit in the holes, a generous amount of clamping pressure is required to bring the legs and seat together. Once the legs butt up to the seat, I take the clamps off, spread some glue on the wedges and bang them in place.

After the glue has dried, I file down the seat dowels and spokeshave and sand the seat to its final curve. I file down any remaining projecting tenons. I lightly sand any areas that require it and then finish the stool with Watco or a similar oil. I prefer oil finishes because stools are prone to being roughly handled, and oil finishes are easy to retouch.

Through the years, I have made a number of variations of these stools to suit the customer's needs. Their heights have ranged from 24 in. to 27 in. and with different rung heights, but I haven't changed the basic design; neither have I changed my attitude toward building them—another relaxing, uncomplicated weekend project. I'll get started after brunch. □

Gary Rogowski builds stools and other intriguing projects in his Portland, Ore. shop.

Laying Out Compound Joints
Getting an angle on splayed sides

by Graham Blackburn

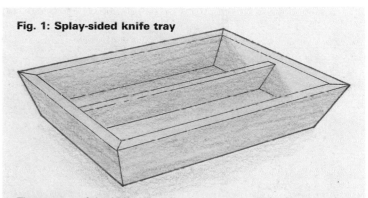

Fig. 1: Splay-sided knife tray

The corners of the knife tray, above, are compound miters. By drawing, you can determine the cutting angles for the miter. The first step is to draw the top, end and side views.

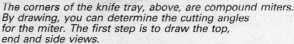

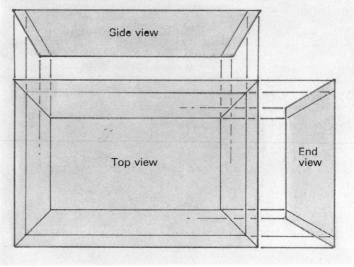

Side view

Top view

End view

Projects involving angled joinery are not difficult: The main challenge is determining the compound-angle cuts needed to join splayed sides. The true shapes and complex angles of even the simplest projects aren't easy to visualize and can't be measured directly from the usual plan drawings showing top, front and side views. You can always look up angles in a reference book, but learning how to work them out will give you the confidence to attack sophisticated projects you never thought possible.

There are many occasions when splayed joinery is desirable and some cases where it's unavoidable. Thin crown molding for cornices, for example, is designed to fasten at an angle and requires splayed joinery in corners or wherever the molding changes direction. Elegant "poche-vides," the unenclosed drawers hung beneath small worktables, are invariably made with splayed sides. And the design of knife trays, hoppers, troughs, flower boxes, planters and innumerable other articles can be enhanced with sloped sides.

Here I'll explain the graphical procedure I use to lay out simple or housed butt joints and splayed (or compound) miter joints. The method works equally well for splayed dovetail joints. It applies to special cases where, for example, different thickness wood is used for the sides and ends, or where the splay angle of the sides and ends are different—cases where references are annoyingly incomplete or not applicable. You will need to refresh your skills in representing three-dimensional objects in two dimensions, but no special tools, apart from a compass, protractor and straightedges, are required. An electronic calculator with the geometric functions might be helpful in some cases, but it's not essential.

One word of caution: It's important to make your drawings accurate, because the accumulation of small measurement errors will lead to sloppy joints. This is particularly true for angle measurements, where errors are magnified: A small error in the 45° miter joint between two ¼-in.-wide pieces of wood may be negligible, but the same error in joining two 1-in.-wide pieces can be a disaster. To minimize the errors, I recommend making all your drawings full-scale, and even larger when practical.

Splayed butt or miter joints—I'll use the simple knife box shown in figure 1 at right to explain the layout procedure developed in figure 2 on the next page. All of the tray's sides are splayed at the same angle and made from the same thickness wood. Also, no actual dimensions or angles are given. I haven't provided this information, because the method works equally well for any set of measurements or angles, and the simplification helps make the method easier to understand. The method is exactly the same for butt and miter joints, so I'll describe the procedure for the butt joint (see figure 2A), but I'll also show the result for mitered construction with equally and unequally splayed sides (see figures 2B and 2C).

For projects requiring only right-angle joinery, the top, front and side views give you all the information you need. This is not so when angled joints are used. For example, none of the three views shown in figure 1, taken individually or as a set, provides either a direct measurement of the angle between the tray's sides and ends or their true shapes. This is because the two-dimensional representation distorts the true shape of the sides. What you see is only a projection of the true shape on the plane of the drawing paper. You need to imagine the ends and sides as if they were laid flat, so when looked at from above, the true shape may be seen and measured.

Begin with the ends—The angle of the top and bottom bevels of the ends can be measured directly, because the side view (see the bevel angle S in figures 2A through 2C) gives the true cross-section

Fig. 2: Determining cutting angles for splayed joints

Instructions apply to these three examples and all other cases.

I: To determine true shape of outside face of end:
1. With A as center, rotate true height of end; line A-B to intersect bottom extension at C.
2. Drop vertical lines from A and C to intersect extension lines from corners of outside face (D, E, F, G) in top view.
3. Connect D, E, F, G to get true shape of outside face.

II: To determine true shape of inside face of end:
1. Project I and H (true length of inside face) onto line A-B.
2. With A as center, rotate projected length of inside face, I'H', to intersect extension at J and K.
3. Drop vertical lines from J and K to intersect extension lines from corners of inside face (L, M, N, P).
4. Connect L, M, N, P to get shape of inside face.

III: Set miter gauge on tablesaw (or rotate arm on radial-arm saw) to angle W. Measure with protractor.

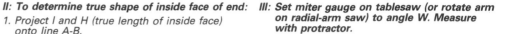

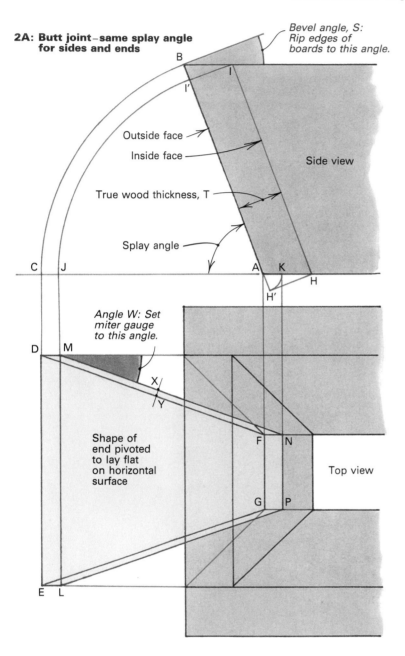

2A: Butt joint – same splay angle for sides and ends

Bevel angle, S: Rip edges of boards to this angle.

Outside face
Inside face
Side view
True wood thickness, T
Splay angle

Angle W: Set miter gauge to this angle.

Shape of end pivoted to lay flat on horizontal surface

Top view

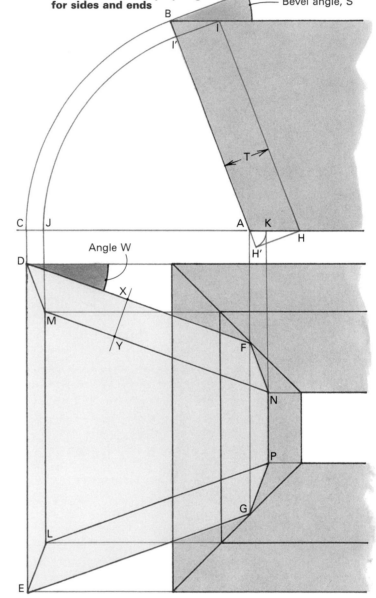

2B: Miter joint – same splay angle for sides and ends

Bevel angle, S

Angle W

---

shape of the end. Use this angle, measured from the vertical, to set the blade tilt when making these bevel cuts; otherwise, the end's shape is distorted. But if you imagine its outside, bottom edge (F-G) to be hinged, the end can be rotated (around point A) to lay flat in the plane of the paper, to reveal its true shape. It follows an arc centered on the bottom, outside corner (A), with a radius equal to A-B. The arc intersects the extended bottom line of the tray at C. Line A-C is the end's true height. Now, drop perpendiculars from C and A. These intersect with line continuations in the top view at D, E, F and G. When these points are connected as shown, the end's true shape, as if laid flat, is defined. More precisely, it is the true shape of the *outside* face of the end. To get the true shape of the

inside face, follow the same procedure, with one small wrinkle: The inner face must also be rotated about the same point (A) as the outside face, to ensure that the faces register properly in the true end view you're developing. To accomplish this, project H and I onto line A-B before doing the rotation. When the points are connected as shown, the end's true shape is fully developed.

The miter setting on your tablesaw (or the arm swing, if you have a radial-arm saw) to cut the sloped sides of the ends is measured directly from the true top view, as shown in figures 2A through 2C. Both faces are the same size, but because they are offset, the angle formed along the edge is not 90°. This angle determines the blade tilt necessary to make the compound-angle cut.

From *Fine Woodworking* magazine (May 1989) 76:65-67

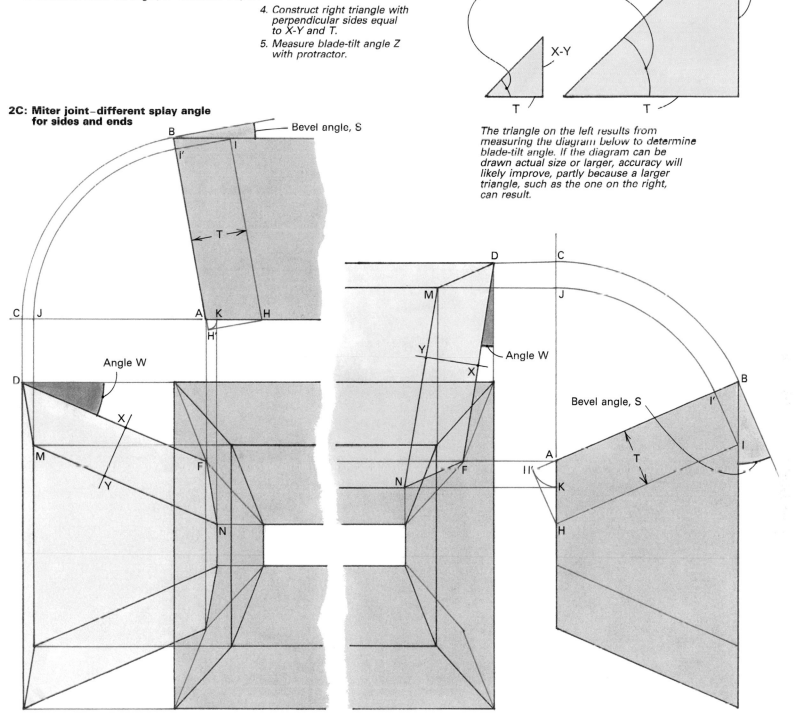

IV: To determine blade tilt:

1. Draw perpendicular line, X-Y, to side M-N.
2. Measure X-Y and divide by true thickness of wood, T.
3. Calculate blade tilt angle, $Z = \arctan X\text{-}Y/T$, or:
4. Construct right triangle with perpendicular sides equal to X-Y and T.
5. Measure blade-tilt angle Z with protractor.

The triangle on the left results from measuring the diagram below to determine blade-tilt angle. If the diagram can be drawn actual size or larger, accuracy will likely improve, partly because a larger triangle, such as the one on the right, can result.

2C: Miter joint—different splay angle for sides and ends

There are two ways to determine this angle: Measure the distance X-Y and divide it by the true thickness of the wood. Then use the arctangent (tan-1) function on your calculator (or use tables) to compute the angle. If you don't have the calculator or tables, carefully construct a right triangle with one perpendicular side equal to X-Y and the other equal to the thickness of the wood. Then use a protractor to measure the angle directly as shown in the drawing. As mentioned earlier, the accuracy of your measurement will be improved if you scale up your drawing as much as possible.

If, as in this example, the sides and ends are splayed equally, no further layout work is required: All of the dimensional information necessary to construct the tray is available from the top and side

views and from the true shape of the end you have just developed. But if the ends and sides are splayed differently, as in figure 2C above, or if you are using different thickness wood for the sides and ends, you have to repeat the process, this time using the end view in place of the side to determine the cutting angles for the sides.

Housed butt joints or splayed dovetails are handled in the same way. Once you have a true view of the ends, layout becomes a simple matter of adding the necessary construction lines. □

Graham Blackburn, author of numerous books on woodworking, is a furniture designer and maker in Soquel, Calif. He is also a contributing editor to Fine Woodworking.

Glueless Joinery

Furniture fastened with interlocking pins and wedges

by Russell Jason Beebe

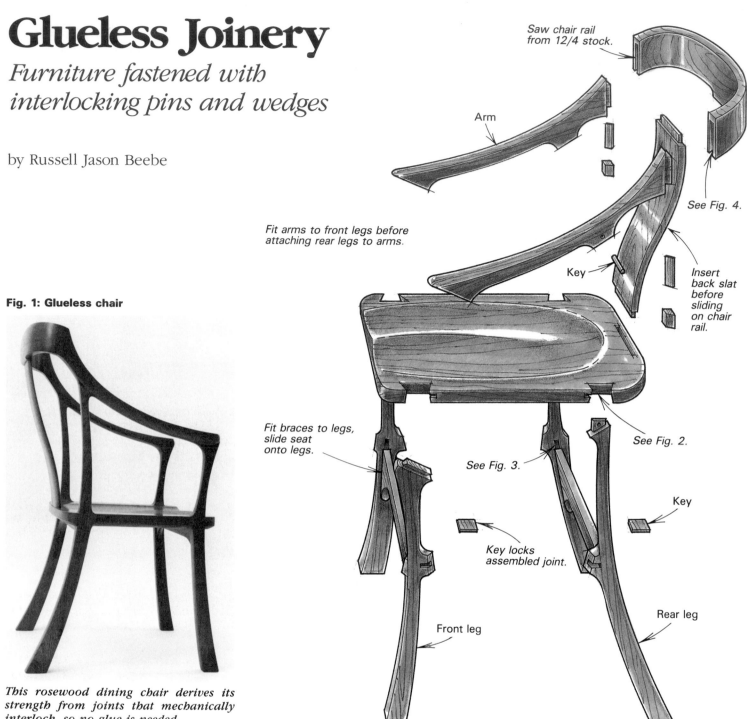

Fig. 1: Glueless chair

This rosewood dining chair derives its strength from joints that mechanically interlock, so no glue is needed.

Saw chair rail from 12/4 stock.

Arm

Fit arms to front legs before attaching rear legs to arms.

Key

See Fig. 4.

Insert back slat before sliding on chair rail.

Fit braces to legs, slide seat onto legs.

See Fig. 3.

See Fig. 2.

Key

Key locks assembled joint.

Front leg

Rear leg

A few years ago I had the good fortune to receive a crash course in woodworking from a Chinese master in Thailand. Old Jeng Yee showed me many things, some of which I'll never be able to do as well as he, and he forever changed the way I look at woodworking. Even though exposed joinery was popular in this country when I visited him in Thailand in 1981, he embraced the traditional philosophy that blind joints are stronger than exposed joints. Even if they weren't stronger, he maintained that the mechanics of exposed joints spoiled the esthetics of furniture.

Before I met Jeng Yee, the fanciest joint I knew was the dovetail. Generally I had used dowels and a lot of glue. The furniture looked good, but it lacked the qualities 70-year-old Jeng Yee valued most: a balanced design with structural integrity based on joints so well-cut they could be locked together without any glue or fasteners. Naturally, furniture built this well is beyond the

financial reach of many people, so Chinese master craftsmen often rely on glue to produce more inexpensive furniture. They use the same joints found on the highest quality work, but the holding power of glue can save time, and thereby cut costs, because the joints don't need to be cut so precisely.

Since I only studied with Jeng Yee a short while, instead of the full, five-to-seven year apprenticeship typical in China, my knowledge of joints and locks is limited, but my techniques are continually improving. Using the basic concepts he taught me, I have invented many of my own joinery techniques. My methods may not be exactly like those used in China, but they work. The goal is always to have the entire piece lock together in a logical sequence of assembly and always in consideration of function, strength of materials and appearance.

Besides being satisfying to cut, Jeng Yee's dry, locking joints offer several advantages. Joints that depend on glue tend to

Photo this page: Robert Jaffe

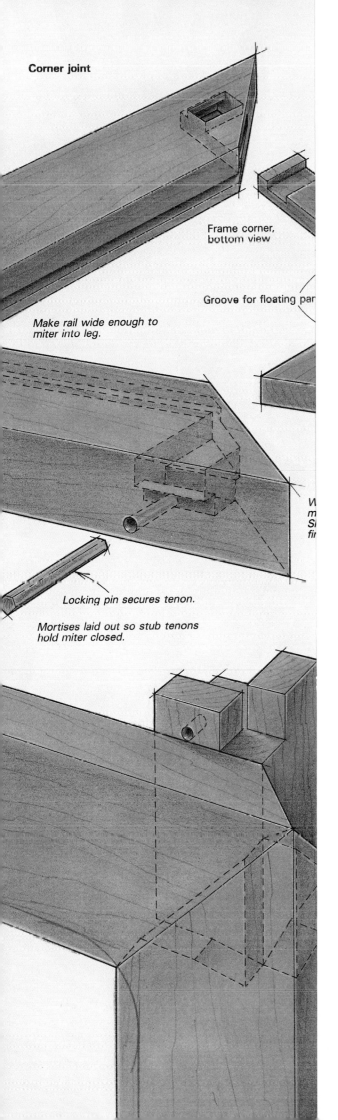

Corner joint

Frame corner,
bottom view

Make rail wide enough to
miter into leg.

Groove for floating par

Locking pin secures tenon.

Mortises laid out so stub tenons
hold miter closed.

weaken over the years as the glue shrinks or becomes brittle with age. Some might argue that point, but the fact remains that a serviceable dry joint must be cut perfectly and is, therefore, superior. Jeng Yee told me that when a student constructed one of these joints, his instructor would put it into a pot of boiling water long enough to get everything good and wet. Then he'd pull the joint apart. If any water seeped into the joint, the student's work was rated a failure.

The chair in figure 1 is a good example of what I learned from Jeng Yee. The design is my own with a few borrowed Asian characteristics. The structure is a product of some common knowledge and lots of imagination. The chair is quite comfortable and its light appearance is achieved by sculpting each part as much as possible, while leaving enough bulk at the joints for strength. After considering points of stress, compression factors and the strength of the wood to be used (East Indian Rosewood in this case), I guessed at a good structural design and built a prototype. The joints are several forms of the wedge, the sliding dovetail and the mortise and tenon. Miters are incorporated whenever possible because of the Oriental preference for converging grain patterns. You always have to plan the joint according to the strength needed at each point and the kind of wood. I used rosewood for the final chair, but built the first prototype with softer teak. The teak chair looks good, but the components were too delicately shaped to withstand hard use. The only American wood hard enough for joinery like this is hard maple.

When someone looks at the glueless chair shown in the drawing, the first reaction is "I can't even guess at how those joints are cut." Actually, if you're willing to experiment and practice, the joints aren't that difficult. Once you get past your initial hesitation and start cutting, you'll roll right along. My basic procedure is to rough out each joint with a bow saw or Japanese pull saw, then clean out the joint with chisels. Mating surfaces are progressively shaved during repeated trial fittings until a perfect fit is achieved. This is indicated by an increasing tightness without distortion as the pieces are forced together. To aid in the fitting of joints, I lightly sand the mating surfaces before each trial assembly. The pieces sliding together burnish away the sanding fuzz enough to clearly show the binding spots. If the joint is too loose, I glue shavings of the same wood to the mating surfaces and refit.

Before attempting to build the chair, I'd recommend you build a prototype as I did. The prototype will give you another opportunity to practice the Oriental techniques, then you can work from the prototype to develop full-size templates for every part. After tracing my templates onto 8/4 rosewood, I roughly cut out all the pieces. Joining areas are left well oversize and squared-off where possible to facilitate the cutting of joints. When cutting the pieces out, carefully consider grain patterns for maximum structural strength. Converging grain is always stronger than opposing. It's also a good idea to keep an eye on the moisture content. The wood should be thoroughly dry (6% is an acceptable moisture content in southern Oregon where I live).

Since the chair seat essentially dictates sizing and the basic framework, I start with the seat. I first chop out the mortise for the backrest, then cut the four leg wedge joints, as shown in figure 2. These wedge joints are like large dovetails cut into the sides of the seat. Again working from the prototype templates, saw, then chisel, the housings to shape. Remember they must be large enough to allow the seat to slide down over the legs into position. Now cut the corresponding wedge shape on the legs,

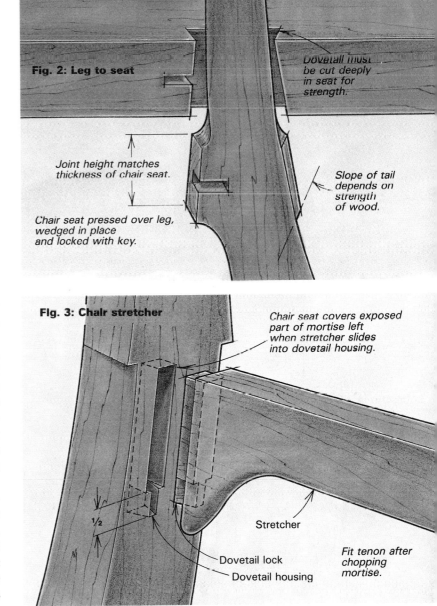

Fig. 2: Leg to seat

Dovetail must be cut deeply in seat for strength.

Joint height matches thickness of chair seat.

Slope of tail depends on strength of wood.

Chair seat pressed over leg, wedged in place and locked with key.

Fig. 3: Chair stretcher

Chair seat covers exposed part of mortise left when stretcher slides into dovetail housing.

1/2

Stretcher

Dovetail lock
Dovetail housing

Fit tenon after chopping mortise.

again with saw and chisel. Don't attempt to fit the legs to the seat yet, though. The legs must first be attached to the stretchers to ensure that the seat will be properly positioned.

The stretchers, figure 3, are fit into the legs with a straight mortise and tenon with an Oriental twist a ½-in. dovetail section that locks into the mortise. I saw out the tenon in the conventional fashion, then cut in the pin with a ¼-in. chisel. The mortise is pretty conventional too, except the bottom ½ in. is narrower than the rest of the mortise and the section's walls are sloped to act as the pin housing. The tenon on the rail can then be fit into the mortise, lowered down and locked into the dovetail as the seat is forced down over the legs. This sliding action means you can restrict the movement of the legs somewhat during assembly, and still have enough flexibility to make final adjustments. When the rail is locked into position, a ½-in. section of the mortise will be visible at the top of the joint, but this cavity will be covered by the chair seat when it's installed.

With the seat fitting flush on the braces, I chop out the mating slots for the keys that lock the legs and seat into place. The arms are next held in position so the joints attaching them to the legs can be laid out and cut. A blind, sliding dovetail is used on the front legs. The rear legs are attached with a beveled mortise and tenon. Since the arms are held by three joints the sliding dovetail at the front, the beveled tenon on the rear legs and the chair back itself—the arms must be fitted very carefully. Once the arms have

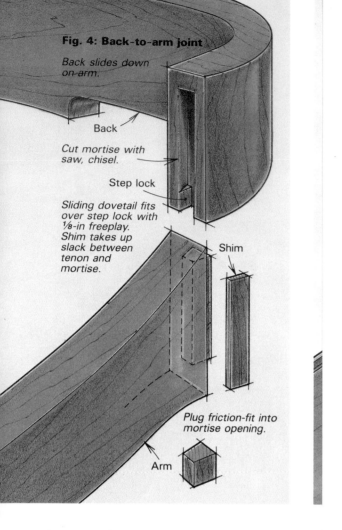

Fig. 4: Back-to-arm joint

Back slides down on-arm.

Back

Cut mortise with saw, chisel.

Step lock

Sliding dovetail fits over step lock with ⅛-in freeplay. Shim takes up slack between tenon and mortise.

Shim

Plug friction-fit into mortise opening.

Arm

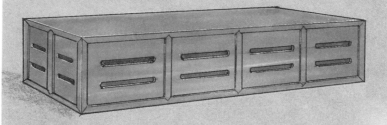

Fig. 1: Gustav Ecke's theory of the evolution of the box pattern

A. 1000 B.C.—mitered frame-and-panel sides

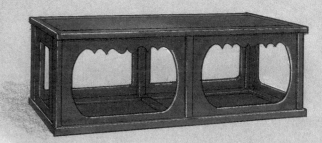

B. 9th Century A.D.—ornamental cut-out in panels

This rosewood table, left, built by the author, possesses the simplicity of form and under-stated decoration characteristic of Chineses domestic furniture. Not modeled after any one piece, this walnut bench, below left, demonstrates elements common to the post-and-rail method of construction, such as the apron that extends part way down the legs and the curved pieces on the ends of the top, known as 'bird's tails.'

been installed on the legs, the joining surfaces tc can be adjusted if needed. With the back held in ap tion, the sliding dovetail joints are laid out and the

These joints involve a step-lock to restrict vert To locate this lock, there must be approximatel play in the joint when the pieces are fitted. Th taken up by inserting a shim of corresponding thi joint at final assembly. The chair back is lowered so this joint must be blind at the top. The mortis rest can be cut at this time, then the arms and bad Now the length of the backrest can be adjusted cut according to the seat angles. With the back the backrest is fitted into the seat and the chair i

Rather than lock all the joints now, I leave the sembled, even if it means holding it together w mark out the areas that need to be carved or shape be done with the chair intact, but it is more easily d pieces. After the pieces are shaped, I assemble ther and fit the appropriate locking keys. I usually do the legs to the seat first. Here you have to make sur horizontally. Then the hole is drilled through blind tenon locating the rear legs to the arms, and a do wood is inserted. Lastly, the shims are cut extra long the sliding dovetail locating the back of the arms, a plug is inserted from the bottom. Now the keys a the chair smoothed and finished with a clear oil fi

Chairs are among the most difficult woodworkin you wish to try glueless joinery, you might begin joints used in the table shown in figure 5, which exercise in joint layout and cutting. It's fastene miters, locking mortises and tenons, and several

Learning from the Chinese
Decorative elements adapted to contemporary furniture

by Allan Smith

From *Fine Woodworking* magazine (November 1988) 73:52-55

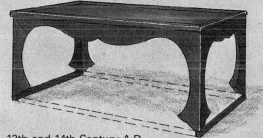

C. 13th and 14th Century A.D.–
Bottom frame members of side panel disappear, and vertical frame members end in foot-like projections, but outer edges are still straight.

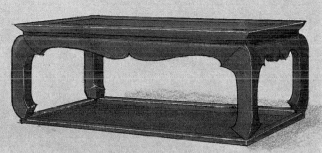

D. 15th Century A.D.–Legs are one solid-shaped piece, curved on outside. Bottom frame is still in use.

When I started designing furniture about 15 years ago, my plan was to make pieces of simple form, using oil-finished hardwoods to achieve a "natural" look. I rejected ornamentation such as carving, inlay and applied moldings. The beauty of the wood itself would be the main attraction. The result was austere but serviceable furniture, which I liked at first but eventually became bored with. The need to put more life into my designs sent me to the library on a quest for inspiration, where I discovered some masters of simplicity, including the Shakers, Gustav Stickley, Edward Barnsley and James Krenov. But when I came across *Chinese Domestic Furniture* by Gustav Ecke in the shop where I worked, I knew I'd found what I had been looking for: furniture of simple but highly refined form, beautifully proportioned, light, graceful and strong, enlivened by subtle shaping and unpretentious decoration.

Nowhere in *Chinese Domestic Furniture* is there any mention of the individual designers or makers of this exquisite furniture. The written records of China contain very little documentation of furniture or its makers. Some authorities infer from this that woodworking was held in low esteem compared to pottery or bronze work, even during the Ming period (A.D. 1368 to 1644), when much of the best furniture was built. It seems that furniture-makers were considered "tradesmen" rather than "artists," in spite of their high level of skill. For the past several centuries, Chinese furniture has been collected and analyzed chiefly by Westerners.

European appreciation of Chinese furniture began in the 18th century and was at first focused on the highly decorated furniture of the Chinese aristocracy. Although in form it often resembled more modest Chinese furniture, it was usually covered with colored lacquer, extensive carving or both. Only recently, as more austere furniture has become fashionable in the West, has the undecorated hardwood furniture of China become known here. This furniture, known as "Chinese domestic," demonstrates Chinese furniture design in its purest form and is now widely considered to be the highest achievement of their woodworking tradition. It was intended for the private households of the middle class, a relatively small group made up of merchants, scholars, artists and civil servants. It is distinguished from other Chinese furniture by the use of hardwoods of exceptional quality, finished with thin coats of clear resin and wax and brought to a high polish, but without other surface adornment, such as carving, inlay or painting.

It is not surprising that a simple, natural style of furniture with restrained decoration evolved where materials of exceptional quality were available. The tropical forests of Southeast Asia supplied Chinese furnituremakers with some of the world's most spectacular woods, including several species of rosewood (*Dalbergia*) and padauk (*Pterocarpus*), which are known for their rich colors and strong, often irregular figure. The peak of development in Chinese furniture design was reached at the time when the quality of lumber available to Chinese woodworkers was at its highest. As trade with the West increased and supplies of the best wood dwindled, a decline began to set in.

Traditional construction–Our knowledge of Chinese furniture is based on a relatively small collection of pieces that survive to the present day and on a few drawings and paintings depicting the furniture, so it is difficult to trace its historical development in detail. However, all the evidence we have points to a remarkably unbroken tradition in which a few enduring forms and decorative elements have been repeated for thousands of years.

This stylistic consistency is partially due to the limited, although highly developed range of techniques employed by Chinese woodworkers. Their method of furniture construction can be summarized in a few simple rules. First, panels must "float" in a frame to accommodate the wood's seasonal movements. The typical panel was planed very thin, fitted into grooves in a frame and braced with battens fitted into dovetailed housings in the back of the panel. Second, corners are mitered where any two furniture parts meet in the same plane. Thus, the mitered frame with floating panel is a fundamental building unit of Chinese furniture. Third, furniture is assembled with locking joints, which allow wood parts to move without cracking and permit disassembly for moving or storage. The basic joint was the mortise and tenon, with locking pins only where necessary. There was little, if any, use of veneer, lamination or any other technique requiring glue. Following these rules was, in part, a practical necessity in a place where changes in the weather could be severe, high-quality glues were not available and furniture was expected to last for generations. This limited range of techniques forced the creativity of Chinese furnituremakers into narrow channels. But the designs that ultimately emerged are renowned for their harmony of structure, line and detail.

Elements of design–In both furniture and room design, great stress is placed on balance and symmetry. Major furniture pieces stand alone, centered along a wall, or they are placed in pairs, two identical or complementary pieces side by side. The structure of most furniture conforms to one of a small number of basic patterns. Chests, benches and tables conform to either the "box" pattern or the "post-and-rail" pattern.

Box pattern–The low table pictured on the facing page shows the final evolution of the box pattern. According to a theory first presented by Gustav Ecke in the 1944 edition of *Chinese Domestic Furniture*, this pattern originally consisted of a low box or platform with mitered frame-and-panel sides. Figure 1 details how this "box" was modified over the centuries. In later pieces, legs made of one solid, shaped piece replaced the two frame members joined at the corner. After the bottom frame disappeared alto-

The mitered panel doors and the profile of the top edge give this ash buffet an Oriental flavor, even though the construction methods are those of modern plywood cabinets.

gether, the legs of all but the lowest tables were strengthened with connecting rails. Finally, the outside edges of the legs were made to follow the curves of the inside edges, resulting in the mature design shown. With the use of solid legs came one of the most influential features of Chinese furniture: the "horse-hoof" foot. European designers borrowed this detail, usually turning the foot outward and using it as the termination of a cabriole leg. Both orientations of the foot, inward and outward, are present in Chinese furniture.

Post-and-rail pattern—The bench shown on p. 44 exemplifies the post-and-rail pattern, which is familiar from Oriental temple gateways. This pattern's primary unit is a "rack" consisting of two upright posts (legs), often set at a splay, connected by a rail or rails and supporting a "yoke," which in this piece is the bench-top. Often an apron was run under the top and down the posts to strengthen the connection between these components on chests, tables and chairs. The curved pieces at either end of the top, known as "bird's tails," are a common decorative feature of post-and-rail tables. Tall chests were constructed from a pair of racks with solid panels in place of the rails, and with back, floor and doors hung between the posts. Drawers were often hung between the posts of altar tables.

Decoration—I think the most appealing aspect of Chinese domestic furniture is its harmony of structure and decoration. The Chinese used decoration to clarify structure and to make structural elements perform a decorative function. This can best be understood by distinguishing three broad types of furniture decoration: Formal decoration consists of the overall shape and proportions of a piece of furniture. Form is usually distinguished from decoration, but forms themselves can be decorative, especially when they depart from the conventional. Consider, for example, the bold curves of bentwood furniture, the exaggerated height of Art-Nouveau chair backs or the flowing "organic" shapes of stack-laminated furniture. Surface decoration includes anything that is seen or felt on the surface of a piece but makes little or no contribution to its form, such as inlay, painting or shallow carving. Structural decoration includes brackets, rails, latticework and moldings, which contribute to the strength of a piece without greatly modifying its form.

The forms of Chinese furniture are simple and fairly standardized, often falling back on the box or post-and-rail patterns. At the same time, the proportions of pieces are varied freely according to practical requirements. Tall chests, for example, come in many sizes, some with upper and lower levels, open shelves or drawers. Tables come in an even larger variety of sizes, with a

variety of aprons, rails and brackets. The chairs have rectangular seats and straight, sometimes slightly angled legs, with gracefully curving backs and arms. Although the proportions always seem to be carefully planned, I don't know of any formula governing them. Symmetry, however, is nearly always maintained. Any asymmetrical piece is normally accompanied by a mating piece of complementary asymmetry.

Surface decoration is minimal, limited to a little bit of carving or decorative hardware and the wood's rich color and figure. There is never any attempt to conceal the structure behind paint, veneer or carving. However, the construction method is not always clear. Through tenons, dovetails and locking pins are often apparent on early pieces, but concealed joints later became the norm.

Chinese domestic furniture excels in its structural decoration. Aprons, braces, brackets and rails are treated as opportunities for decoration. They are gracefully, sometimes even whimsically shaped, becoming the primary adornments of otherwise austere pieces. The subtle use of decoration that clarifies or emphasizes structure can be seen in the table on p. 44. The bead around the insides of the legs and apron helps define the leg-apron structure as a unit supporting the top. The transition between this supporting structure and the top is defined by the groove around the top of the aprons. The 45° jog in the otherwise straight line of the rails connecting the legs brings these rails into harmony with the other elements of the piece, each of which ends in a 45° miter. Even the horse-hoof foot ends in a vestigal miter where it would join the no-longer-existing bottom frame member.

The approach to design in Chinese domestic furniture can be summarized as follows: Take a traditional form and adapt it to the specific practical needs of the user, for example, for storage or for use in a particular setting; adjust the proportions of the piece to form a harmonious whole; select elements of structural decoration, such as brackets, moldings and aprons, from the traditional design vocabulary and adapt them to the proportions of the piece; and then shape them inventively within the canons of Chinese taste. Finally, add a small amount of surface decoration, such as the convex or concave rounding of surfaces, small carvings or hardware.

The buffet or sideboard pictured above, at left, shows my use of this approach in a piece designed for a light, airy modern interior. I used mitered panels for the top and the doors, together with the indented waist separating the top from the case, to create a distinctly Oriental feeling. The miters add a note of contrast to the rectangular facade of the cabinet and complement the angled edge of the top as well. There is much about this piece that lies outside the Chinese tradition: the recessed plinth, the overlay doors with wooden pulls and the blond wood (ash) with a white Formica top panel. However, I think a little of the Chinese domestic spirit still lives in it, in virtue of its symmetry, simple form and restrained decoration. □

Allan Smith builds custom furniture in Hopewell, N.J.

Further Reading

Chinese Domestic Furniture by Gustav Ecke. Charles E. Tuttle Co. Inc., Box 410, Rutland, VT 05701-0410; 1962 (a facsimile of original 1944 edition).

Chinese Household Furniture by George N. Kates. Dover Publications Inc., 180 Varick St., New York, NY 10014; 1948.

Chinese Furniture by R. H. Ellsworth. Random House, 201 E. 50th St., New York, NY 10022; 1970.

Chinese Furniture by Michel Beurdeley. Kodansha International USA, Ltd., c/o Harper and Row Publishers, 10 E. 53rd St., New York, NY 10022; 1979.

Chinese details; plate joinery

My interest in Chinese furniture is aesthetic, not antiquarian. I have not tried to reproduce Chinese originals, but to adapt Chinese design principles to my own furniture, which is built by economical modern methods. I employ plate joinery where appropriate on case pieces.

The design of this walnut bookcase is based on several Chinese two-section chests. These chests were often tapered narrower at the top than at the bottom, and the vertical frame members usually extended downward to form the legs. The originals were built entirely of solid wood with mortise-and-tenon joints. My bookcase preserves the look of these traditional pieces, with the narrower upper case and the legs formed by the vertical frame pieces, but the upper and lower sections are essentially plywood cases with solid trim. The mitered frames of the sides, which traditionally would have enclosed floating solid panels, are glued to plywood panels.

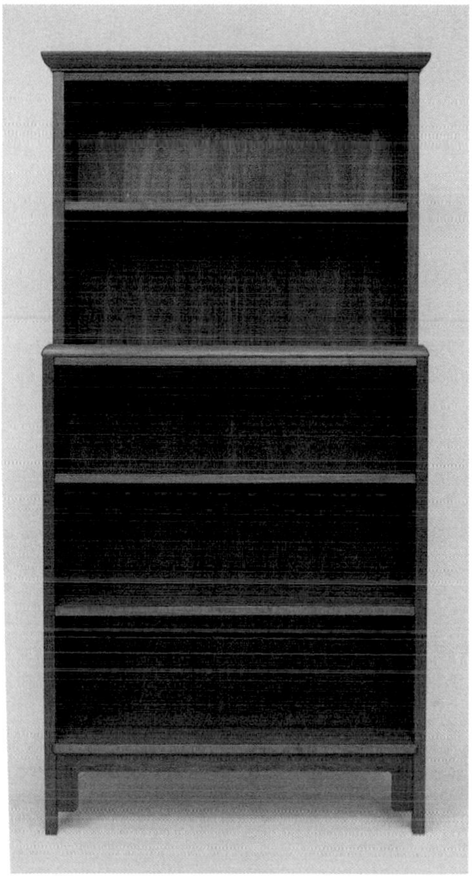

This walnut bookcase, constructed using plate joinery, shows a simple form enriched with Chinese details: mitered side panels, overhanging crown and an apron under the bottom shelf.

Fig. 2: Chinese-style bookcase

All panels are 3/4-in. plywood with solid edging.

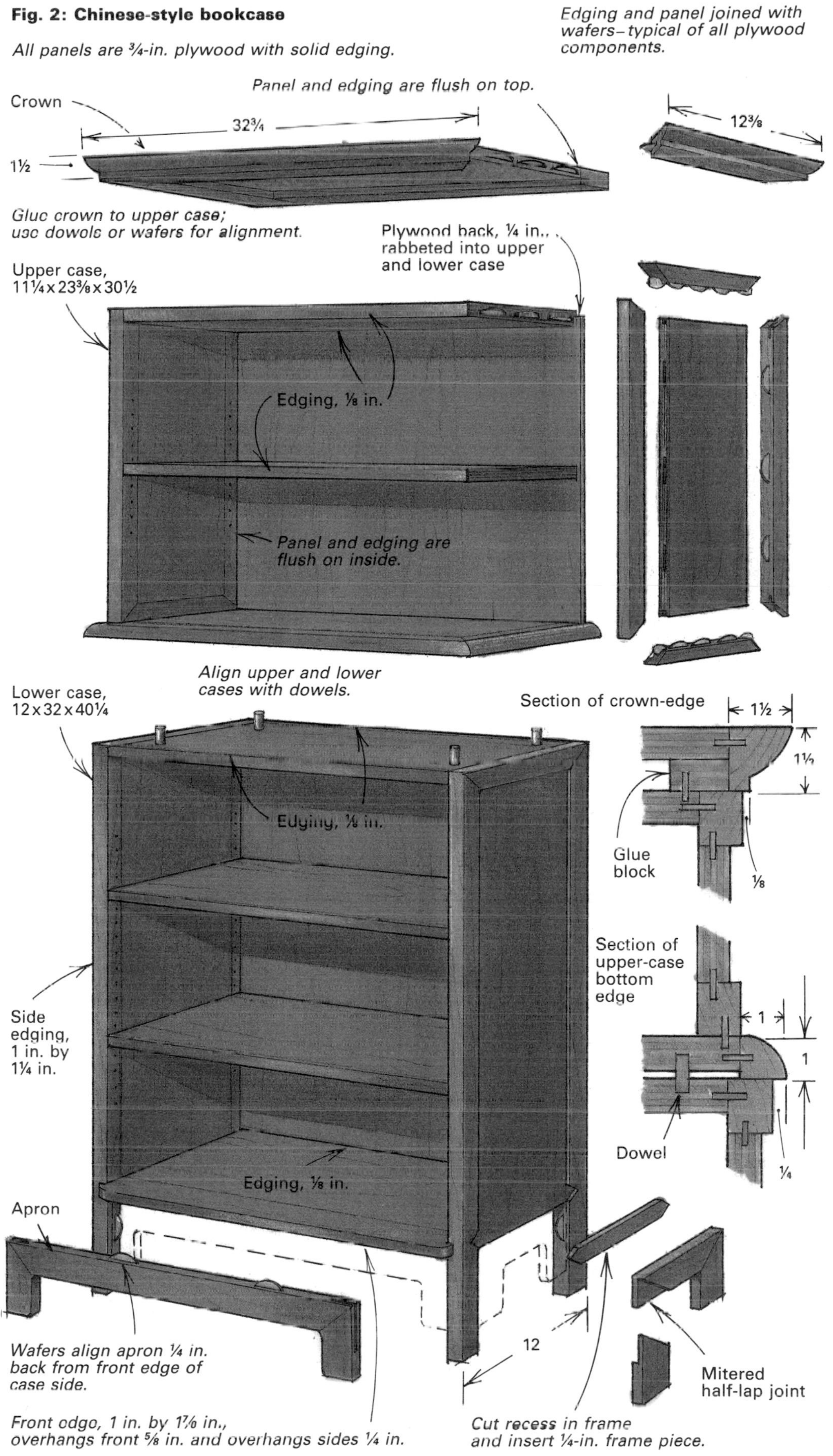
Edging and panel joined with wafers–typical of all plywood components.
Panel and edging are flush on top.
Crown
32 3/4
12 3/8
1 1/2
Glue crown to upper case; use dowels or wafers for alignment.
Plywood back, 1/4 in., rabbeted into upper and lower case
Upper case, 11 1/4 x 23 3/8 x 30 1/2
Edging, 1/8 in.
Panel and edging are flush on inside.
Lower case, 12 x 32 x 40 1/4
Align upper and lower cases with dowels.
Section of crown-edge
1 1/2
1 1/4
Glue block
1/8
Edging, 1/8 in.
Section of upper-case bottom edge
1
1
Dowel
1/4
Side edging, 1 in. by 1 1/4 in.
Edging, 1/8 in.
Apron
Wafers align apron 1/4 in. back from front edge of case side.
12
Mitered half-lap joint
Front edge, 1 in. by 1 7/8 in., overhangs front 5/8 in. and overhangs sides 1/4 in.
Cut recess in frame and insert 1/4-in. frame piece.

Plate-joinery machines offer furnituremakers and cabinetmakers a fast and accurate way of joining wood together. The plate joiners above, from left to right, are the Virutex 0-81, Freud JS 100, Porter-Cable Model 555 and Elu Jointer/Spliner 3380.

Plate Joiners

Comparing eight portable slot-cutting machines

by Allan Smith

Anewcomer to the field of woodworking techniques, plate joinery has won wide acceptance among American cabinet-makers. It is especially useful in small cabinet shops that lack sophisticated joinery equipment, like multispindle horizontal boring machines or computer-controlled mortisers. A plate joint is a species of spline or "floating tenon" joint: Slots are cut in both pieces to be joined, and precut plates or "biscuits" of compressed wood are glued into the slots. Plate joints let you bypass much of the layout work and cutting operations associated with traditional joints, such as dovetails, dowels and rabbets/grooves. They are fast, accurate and safe to produce, and they are suitable for all types of wood and wood-base materials, such as plywood and particle-board. As in the case of dowel joints, parts can be cut to final size prior to joining, but the slots for plates are easier to locate and more forgiving than dowel holes. Three different sizes of biscuits are available for use in stock of different widths and thicknesses.

The speed and convenience of plate joinery is due to a special machine called a plate joiner. The machine is basically a plunge-cutting circular saw with a guide for referencing the blade to the stock and with built-in stops, which set the cut to the correct depth for biscuits. Although all plate joiners cut slots in a similar fashion, there are differences between various makes and models worth considering before buying. To date, there are eight different machines on the market, shown above and at the top of the facing page, manufactured by six different manufacturers: Virutex, Freud, Porter-Cable, Elu, Kaiser, Lamello. I tried these machines for six months in my shop in New Jersey, where I build custom cabinets and furniture. While all the machines cut slots well, I found that some of the machines are easier to use than others. Also, there are special features that can make one machine more useful than another for particular applications, including operations other than plate joinery. Before I discuss my observations about the individual machines, let's look more closely at how plate joints are made, how a plate joiner is constructed and the features that distinguish various models. A chart summarizing the eight models is on p. 52.

How plate joinery works—The first step to creating a plate joint is to accurately cut mating slots in the two pieces of wood to be joined. Butt the two pieces together and strike a short pencil line on the face of the pieces across the joint to mark the location of each slot. Generally, a biscuit will be inserted every couple of inches along the joint. Next, the depth adjustment is set to locate the slot, generally in the middle of the edge. The pieces to be joined are separated and the center mark on the plate joiner is aligned with a pencil line. The machine is turned on and pushed into the wood to cut a slot. The operation is repeated until slots are cut at each pencil line. Glue is put into the slots, and a biscuit is inserted into one side of each mating pair. The biscuits are die-cut from compressed wood and should fit snugly into the slots (provided they are kept dry). When the joint is clamped, moisture from the water-base white or yellow glue causes the compressed fibers of the biscuit to expand, resulting in a joint that's remarkably strong. Although a plate joint registers the pieces to be joined parallel to the biscuit surfaces, the slots are slightly longer than the biscuits and allow the joint to be shifted a bit along its length—about 1/16 in. in either direction.

From *Fine Woodworking* magazine (May 1989) 76:60-64

Plate joiners are plunge-cutting circular saws that create slots for football-shape biscuits, glued into the slots like splines. The machines above, from left to right, are the Kaiser Mini 3-D and the Lamello Junior, Standard and Top 10.

While case construction is perhaps its primary use, a plate joiner is very versatile and can be used in making panels and frames, or for cutting grooves. You can use biscuits to join boards along their edges, say for a tabletop, as shown in the photo below, right, or you can join a leg and apron or rail and stile with biscuit-reinforced butt joints or miters. Partitions or shelves can be joined to cases by cutting slots for biscuits in the face of one panel and on the edge of another. In each case, the slots should be spaced evenly along the joint; use as many as needed for strength and alignment of the joint. Sometimes two plates are used side by side, to give more strength when joining heavy stock, say 8/4 or thicker. For other plate-joinery applications, check your machine's manual and use your imagination.

Like all other joining methods, plate joinery has its limitations: It cannot be used effectively on very small or very large parts, and it has no decorative value. Because slots allow some side-to-side shifting, a plate joint won't align parts perfectly along the joint the way dovetails or dowels will.

A plate joiner is probably one of the safest power tools in the shop. But, its whirling blade still deserves respect, and you should observe a few rules for safe plate joining: Never attempt to cut a slot in a small piece that's hand-held or can't be firmly clamped down, to prevent the plunging blade from grabbing and hurling it. Manufacturers recommend you always keep your hands behind the blade area when plunging, but many craftsmen prefer to press down on the fence, to stabilize the machine—a practice I've found safe because your hand is still away from the cutting edge. When plunge-cutting, a plate joiner can send a cloud of particles through its dust chute with considerable force, so keep your face away from the chute area and always wear safety goggles. Also, if you work for a long period of time, you should wear a dust mask or fit the machine with a vacuum hose. Most plate joiners are very loud—an unpleasant reminder to wear earplugs or earmuffs.

Plate-joiner construction—On most plate joiners, the blade, arbor and motor are mounted on a moving carriage that rides in the machine's baseplate. Pushing on the plate joiner's body and/or handle plunges the blade through the faceplate, which is part of the base, and into the workpiece. After the slot is cut, a spring retracts the blade behind the faceplate, out of harm's way. To plunge smoothly and accurately, the fit between carriage and baseplate must be precise: If the fit is too loose, the blade may make a sloppy cut, resulting in too large a slot; if the fit is too tight, plunging

will be difficult or jerky. The return springs, too, should provide just the right amount of pull, so the blade is retracted quickly but you don't have to fight the spring during plunging.

Fences and guides—Most plate joiners have adjustable, removable fences that attach to the machine's faceplate. With the fence held down on the face of the stock, both the angle of the machine and the placement of the slot on the stock's edge are determined. Adjusting the fence's height, relative to the blade, allows the slot to be centered on an edge, or placed as desired. Most machines have tracks or guides to keep the fence parallel to the blade while its height is adjusted, so that slots will also be parallel. The Lamello Top 10 and Kaiser Mini 3-D were the only machines I tried that had tracks machined accurately enough to allow setting the fence

The author uses the Lamello Top 10 machine to cut the slots for a simple edge-to-edge joint, such as would be used to join the boards for a wide tabletop. The adjustable-angle fence on the Top 10 is locked down so the face of the machine contacts the edge of the board squarely. Pencil lines on the board, which mark where the slots will be cut, are aligned to a centerline on the plate joiner's fence.

The adjustable fence on the Porter-Cable Model 555 flips over and positions the machine for cutting slots on a mitered panel's edge. Its 'D' handle design distinguishes it from other plate joiners, which must be grasped by the motor housing for plunge-cutting slots.

The stepped depth-stop on the Lamello Standard quickly sets to three positions that adjust the machine's depth of cut to make slots for different-size plate-joinery biscuits. Similar depth stops are found on most other models.

squarely without having to use a try square or painstakingly measure fence-to-blade distance. Most machines have hand screws or levers for locking the fences and for keeping the fence from moving during slot-cutting. The Lamello Standard, however, relies on two Phillips head screws for securing its fence, which is somewhat inconvenient.

In lieu of a fence, plate joiners can also be used by laying both the machine and stock flat on the bench, for plunging. The Elu, which lacks a front fence, must be used this way for edge-cutting slots. Most fences are reversible, the flip side allowing slotting on 45° edges, for mitered frames or panels. To locate the plate on a mitered edge, the fences on most machines reference to the inside edge of the miter. In contrast, the fences on the Elu and Porter-Cable reference to the miter's outside edge, so even if the pieces are of slightly different thicknesses, the tips of the finished miter will align. The Lamello Top 10 and Junior allow the miter to be referenced from either side of a mitered edge. In addition to 45° fences, the Lamello Top 10 and Standard and the Kaiser machines have fences that set at any angle from 0° to 90°, for plate joining odd-angle pieces. On machines without this feature, you must

make an angled wedge to shim the standard fence to the angle you need. Besides the standard fence, the Elu and the Kaiser come with edge guides for aligning slot cuts or grooves on a surface parallel to the edge—very handy for panel work.

Most plate joiners use some kind of device to keep the machine from shifting out of position due to the force of the blade entering the workpiece. Among the machines I tried, most have a pair of spring-loaded steel points that retract into the faceplate when it's pressed against the work. Some plate joiners allow points to be removed if the machine is used to cut continuous grooves. The Lamello Top 10 has a pair of rubber bumpers in lieu of points, but these aren't removable and I didn't find them any more effective than steel points. I found the best anti-slip feature on the Kaiser's faceplate, which has a ribbed-rubber covering that's very effective in preventing slipping, though it can't be removed for grooving operations. The Elu model I tried had no anti-slip feature, but I did not find this to be a problem during slot-cutting. Elu's newest models feature removable steel points.

Motor and blade—The universal motors used in plate joiners range in rated amperage from 4.6 amps to 6.7 amps (manufacturers don't rate them for horsepower output). Generally, the more-expensive machines come with more-powerful motors, but all the machines are adequately powered. Cuts in hard maple caused all the machines to slow, but the Kaiser and Lamello Top 10 slowed the least. The Porter-Cable and the Lamello Junior slowed down the most, but not enough to cause any problems.

Most plate joiners have the motor mounted horizontally and transfer the power to the blade via beveled gears. While this may be mechanically efficient, it seems to make the machines very noisy. Surprisingly, the least-expensive machine in the review, the Porter-Cable, was by far the quietest, probably because its vertically mounted motor drives the blade with a belt instead of gears.

Most of the blades on the machines are 6-tooth carbide blades approximately 4 in. in diameter, except the Elu, which sports a 12-tooth blade. Although blade designs varied, all cut smoothly. For grooving or trim work in veneers or plywoods, Elu offers an optional 30-tooth blade. Blade change requires partial disassembly of the carriage and baseplate on all plate joiners, and most use a pair of wrenches to loosen the bolt that locks the blade. In contrast, the Lamello Top 10 and Kaiser machines both incorporate blade locks, to make blade changes, however infrequent, easier.

Depth adjustment—The depth a plate joiner's blade plunges can be set anywhere from 0 in. to about ¾ in., and most machines have built-in stops for the three standard biscuit sizes: #0, #10 and #20. Depth of cut is set by turning a threaded stop rod conveniently located on most machines on the base aside the motor. Most of the machines have three stops, making it easy to change over from one biscuit size to another without fine-tuning the depth of cut. The exceptions are the Elu and the Lamello Junior. When setting the Lamello Junior, the adjustment rod must be screwed in or out and the depth of blade plunge measured. This makes changing from one biscuit size to another a matter of careful measurement or trial and error—a real hassle. The Elu's depth adjuster is slightly better, because it has a depth-of-cut scale calibrated in millimeters, but it has no markings to indicate plate sizes. The machines with stepped stops allow the depth of cut to be fine-tuned with a locking collar on the stop rod.

Handles and switches—Most plate joiners are designed to be held by the "barrel," or motor housing, and a handle on top during use. But two of the machines, the Porter-Cable and the Elu, are designed to be held differently: The Porter-Cable has a "D" handle with a trigger switch; the Elu works on an altogether-different principle from the other plate joiners—pivoting the blade into the work rather than plunging—and hence has a different grip.

Switches may be found on the top, side or rear of the motor housing, depending on the machine. I found it easy to get used to switching any of the machines on or off. The Virutex features a rubber switch cover, to keep dust from fouling the switch's electrical contacts. Most of the machines have locking switches, so you don't have to keep your finger on the switch during the cut. The exceptions to this are the switches on the Porter-Cable and the Elu, both requiring constant pressure. This can get tedious, but can add to the machine's safety: The motor switches off when the operator lets go.

Accessories—Standard accessories for plate joiners usually include wrenches for changing the blade, lubricating oil to keep the carriage sliding smoothly and an assortment of biscuits. All the models come with carrying cases (the Lamello Junior's is cardboard), which can be very handy if you do on-site work. Vacuum hoses are available for all the models (except the Freud and Porter-Cable). These attachments are especially great for left-handers, who stand on the dust-chute side of the machine while running it.

An accessory I consider indispensable is Lamello's glue applicator: It's a glue bottle with a tip that fits into plate slots and applies glue to both sides at once. It works well in positions that would be awkward to reach with an ordinary glue bottle. Several companies, most notably Lamello, manufacture a variety of tools for installing special hinges and knock-down fittings, which fit into the slots cut by all plate joiners.

Lamello Top 10, Standard and Junior—The Swiss-made Lamello was the first plate joiner introduced into the United States, and in some ways, Lamello has set the standards for the field. Their Top 10 recently replaced the "Top" as Lamello's best and highest-price model. It is an extremely well-made machine. The Top 10's powerful motor and blade unit slide on precisely machined runners with absolutely no play, and the firm yet not-too-strong spring tension makes plunging it a pleasure. The machine's adjustable-angle fence is calibrated from 0° to 90°, which makes cutting odd miters a breeze. The fence has a quick-set position that automatically centers slots in ¾-in. stock, and a clip-on plastic fence plate, which is provided, will center slots in ½-in. stock. The detachable, standard fence adjusts for height on an accurately machined track, and my only complaint is that the height scale on the fence is marked in ⅛-in. increments—too coarse for precise positioning. Optional accessories for the Top 10 include special defect-patching attachments, designed to cut out surface defects and replace them with football-shape patches, available in a selection of woods. Also, there's a stand for turning your portable machine into a stationary tool.

Lamello's Standard and Junior models exhibit the same high-quality construction as the Top 10, but lack some of its features. The Standard has an adjustable-angle fence, but it's uncalibrated except for a 45° mark, and its adjustable-height fence lacks the guides found on the Top 10. The Junior has no adjustable-angle fence, and I found the tracks that the fence rides on didn't keep the fence parallel to the blade when I adjusted its height. The Junior's greatest shortcoming is that its depth adjuster makes no provision for easy shifting from one size plate to another, as discussed earlier.

Elu Jointer/Spliner 3380—Distributed in the United States by Black & Decker, the German-made Elu is a high-quality machine that is so distinct in design that comparing it to other plate joiners is a bit like comparing apples to oranges. The machine's pivoting

The unusual design and pivoting-blade action of the Elu 3380 allows it to do more than just cut slots for biscuits: It plows grooves and does panel cutting, trim and cut-off work as well. Above, the author uses the Elu with a scrapwood fence to cut biscuit slots across a plywood panel so it can be joined to a partition.

Unlike most plate joiners, the Kaiser Mini 3-D has two separate fences: The one shown being adjusted pivots out from the face and adjusts to any angle for odd-angle miter joinery. The other fence, on the bench behind the machine, does only regular 45° and 90° joints. It slides up and down, for adjustment, in two vertical holes just behind the Kaiser's ribbed-rubber anti-slip face.

carriage is designed to allow the unit not only to cut slots, but to plow continuous grooves and to work as a small panel saw, with a maximum depth of cut of about ¾ in.

Standard equipment with the Elu includes an edge guide and a 45° fence with rods that slide into the faceplate. As mentioned earlier, having to screw and unscrew the depth adjuster to change between plates sizes is inconvenient.

The Elu doesn't have a front fence for doing regular slot cutting in square-edge stock; the machine's base and the stock must be laid on a flat surface for edge slotting. Instead, the Elu features a fine-adjustment screw that allows the blade to be raised or lowered relative to the base. By setting the blade height, the slot can be centered on the edge of ½-in.- to 1¼-in.-thick stock. Overall, I found the Elu somewhat less convenient than the other machines for general-purpose plate joinery. However, for the purpose of making grooves or panel sawing and cut-off work, no other machine is so versatile.

Kaiser Mini 3-D—This machine is based on a disc grinder manufactured by AEG in Germany, to which a moving carriage base and

Plate-joiners								
Manufacturer Model number	Distributor	List * price	Motor amps	Fence settings	Weight (lbs)	Accessories Standard, *Optional*	Switch-lock/ blade lock	Anti-slip feature
Elu Jointer/Spliner 3380	Black & Decker 10 N. Park Drive Hunt Valley, MD 21030	$485	5.0	90°/45°	7.9	Metal case, edge guide, tools *vacuum adapter and hose, 30-tooth veneer blade*	No/No	Steel points, detachable
Freud JS 100	Freud 218 Feld Ave. Highpoint, NC 27264	$285	5.0	90°/45°	6.2	Plastic carrying case and tools	Yes/No	Steel points
Kaiser Mini 3-D	W.S. Jenks and Son 1933 Montana Ave. N.E. Washington, D.C. 20002	$559	5.7	0° to 90° Adjustable	6.4	Metal case, edge guide, tools , *vacuum adapter and hose*	Yes/Yes	Ribbed rubber
Lamello Top 10	Colonial Saw 100 Pembroke St. Box A Kingston, MA 02364	$639	6.4	0° to 90° Adjustable	6.8	Wood case , *edge trimmer, defect-patching attachment, stationary stand, vacuum hose, glue bottle*	Yes/Yes	Rubber bumpers
Lamello Standard	Colonial Saw	$489	4.6	0° to 90° Adjustable	6.6	Same as Top 10, except plastic case	Yes/No	Steel points
Lamello Junior	Colonial Saw	$369	4.6	90°/45°	6.1	Same as Top 10, except cardboard case	Yes/No	Steel points
Porter-Cable Model 555	Porter-Cable Box 2468 Jackson, TN 38302	$270	5.0	90°/45°	6.1	Metal case and tools	No/No	Steel points
Virutex 0-81	Holz Machinery 45 Halladay St. Jersey City, NJ 07304	$305	5.0	90°/45°	6.5	Plastic case and tools , *vacuum hose*	Yes/No	Steel points

* Street prices are typically 20% to 45% lower

slot-cutting blade have been added. The AEG motor is of high quality, and the sliding action of the carriage is equivalent to that of the Lamello machines. Blade change is particularly convenient on the Kaiser. The machine comes with a standard fence, reversible for 45° miter work, and an edge guide for making slots on a panel up to 10 in. from the edge. Both the anodized-aluminum fence and edge guide mount on posts that slide in holes running through the machine's face. The posts keep the fence parallel to the blade and thumbscrews lock it positively. The face of the Kaiser has a separate adjustable-angle fence, shown in the lower photo on the previous page, that pivots out for odd-angle miter work. This pivot system works well, but there's a small amount of play in the locking mechanism, and the small fence itself felt a bit delicate. Initially, I found fine adjustment of the depth of cut to be very inconvenient, as it seemed to require partial disassembly of the machine. When I spoke to the Kaiser representative about this, he pointed out that there was an Allen wrench in the rear of the bottom plate for making such adjustments (which he assured me should rarely be necessary).

Virutex 0-81—The Spanish-made Virutex is a medium-price machine that's very similar in construction and features to the Freud and Lamello Junior. The fence on the Virutex is cast metal and has a 45° wedge on one side for guiding slot cuts on miters. The Virutex's fence locks with levers, which are easier to lock than many of the plastic knobs found on other machines. The sliding action of the carriage is not as smooth as on the Lamello machines—there is a small amount of play—but it is adequate for accurate slotting. The Virutex's main shortcoming is the inadequacy of the tracks for keeping the fence parallel to the blade, which makes setting the fence somewhat tedious. The Virutex is a decent-quality machine, considering its price is in the low half of the field.

Freud JS 100—The Freud plate joiner is made in Spain and comes similarly equipped to the Virutex, but sells for less money. It has a smaller base and fence than any of the other machines, but this is

not a significant disadvantage. The Freud's fence is practically identical to the Virutex, except it uses opposing thumbscrews to lock the fence height. There's more play in the Freud carriage than on any other machines I reviewed, and the blade had enough runout on the first machine I tried that the slots it produced were $\frac{1}{128}$ in. oversize. This blade wobble also seemed to make the blade more apt to grab the workpiece during plunging. Fortunately, a second machine I tried didn't have this problem. Overall, the Freud performed adequately, and it's one of the lowest-price plate joiners on the market.

Porter-Cable Model 555—Except for the Elu, the American-made Porter-Cable is the only plate joiner that departs from the standard horizontal-motor design pioneered by Lamello and adopted by all the other companies. The Porter-Cable's motor is mounted vertically, and the different type of drive mechanism associated with this arrangement no doubt accounts for the quietness of the machine. Those who have used tools with "D" handles, such as those found on most hand-held circular saws, will probably find this machine more comfortable to hold than any of the other machines. The handle was, however, awkward to grip when the machine was used vertically, say for cutting slots in the face of a panel resting on the benchtop.

The Porter-Cable I tried included a reversible fence for 90° and 45° work, but it lacked tracks for fence alignment, and the two small plastic knobs used to lock the fence were nearly impossible to tighten by hand. Since I conducted this review, Porter-Cable has remedied both of these shortcomings by adding tracks and larger knobs to the fence. I feel the carriage's return springs are too strong; I like the plunging action of the machine better with one of the two springs detached. Despite these few peeves, I think the Porter-Cable is a good value, especially considering it's the lowest-price plate joiner on the market. □

Allan Smith builds custom furniture in Hopewell, N.J.

Glued-up panels are essential for many woodworking jobs. The process seems straightforward, but care must be taken to ensure that the panel has an attractive grain pattern, is flat and free of excess glue. Above, the author removes glue squeeze-out with one of the small plastic tabs used to seal plastic bags in grocery stores. The narrow strips along the edges of the assembly are scraps that prevent the clamps from damaging the panel. Clamps are mounted both above and below the panel to keep it flat.

Edge Gluing Boards
Making flat panels with nearly invisible joints

by Christian Becksvoort

Many woodworking projects involve gluing together several narrow boards to make a large panel for a tabletop, carcase side or other large surface. The process seems fairly straightforward, but there are many factors to consider. Selecting the stock, matching and orienting the grain, jointing the edges, gluing and clamping all affect the outcome of the finished panel.

The process begins with proper stock selection. It is highly unlikely that you can get a finished ¾-in.-thick panel out of ¾-in. stock. Even if the glue-up was perfect and the surfaces were planed to perfection, some scraping, sanding or planing would be necessary. Rough ¼ lumber is a full inch, which gives ample thickness for machining out a ¾-in.-thick panel. Unfortunately, the surface of rough-sawn lumber is so uneven that it is difficult to match grain and color

or detect minor imperfections, such as surface checks. Thus, when I purchase ¼ stock, I have it milled on two sides to ⅞ in., hit or miss. This means that most of the faces will be planed (hit), although there will be an occasional patch missed by the planer. To me that's a good compromise; about 95% to 98% of the surface is visible, yet there is still ⅛ in. of stock for sanding or planing after the panel is glued. The result is a clean panel that is a full ¾ in. thick.

In general, avoid cupped or twisted stock. Bows and crooks are salvageable. The more careful you are in selecting stock, the easier the glue-up and the flatter the panel. When possible, cut all the pieces out of a single board to ensure similar grain and color throughout. Remember, it is virtually impossible to get three 4-ft. pieces out of a 12-ft. board. Most boards must be trimmed from 1 in.

In gluing up narrow boards, the goal is to produce a panel of uniform color, with a fairly continuous grain pattern across its width, as shown in the photo above, left. A poorly matched panel, shown in the photo above, right, looks more like an assemblage of separate boards.

to 6 in. on each end to remove checked sections. Individual panel pieces should be 1 in. to 2 in. longer than the finished panel to allow for gluing, clamp "sliding" and final trimming. Also, allow ample width for jointing, especially if the pieces are crooked or have rough edges.

Matching grain and color—When all the panel pieces are cut, match the grain and color. The goal is to produce a panel that looks as if it has continuous grain across its width, as opposed to separate boards glued together. Parallel grain along the edges of boards is fairly easy to match to parallel grain of the next board. Wide-face grain is a bit more difficult, while grain that runs out at an acute angle is extremely difficult to match up. The photos above show good and poor matching in a panel. With a little time, effort and practice, matching grain becomes almost second nature. The result of a well-matched panel is quite subtle. On the other hand, a mismatch is glaringly obvious. Experiment with different patterns: Remember that even with only two boards there are 16 different combinations of matching them!

Another aspect of matching is growth ring orientation. Here there are two schools of thought. The first holds that every other board in a panel should have its growth rings reversed. Thus, as each board cups, a slightly wavy panel results. The other theory is to have all the growth rings face the same direction. Then, if the boards should warp, they form one large curve. Generally, I hold with the second theory; I use cherry almost exclusively and it is a relatively stable wood. But I would follow the first method if I was working with wood that was prone to cupping or to excessive movement throughout the year (such as oaks or hickory). A second factor would be the amount of bracing or support attached to the panel. A tabletop with little overhang and rails under its full width will usually stay flat. So will a chest side that has locked corners and divider supports. On the other hand, large free-floating or unsupported panels, such as pedestal tabletops or slab doors, should have their growth rings reversed.

Finally, don't let rules stand in the way of common sense. If you have only three boards, and each has one good face and a minor defect (knot, worm hole, sap or chipped grain) on the other face, then obviously the defects all go on the underside. Nobody wants them on a tabletop or the outside of a cabinet, no matter what the

rules say. Once the boards are selected and their positions in the panel are determined, I mark the panel with a triangle, like the one shown in the above, left photo. The triangle makes it easy to instantly reconstruct all the careful matching you've just completed.

Next, true up the edges with a jointer or a long handplane. Either way, the edges of all boards must be absolutely perpendicular to the faces, otherwise the panel will be cupped. Some older texts recommend leaving a ¹⁄₆₄-in. gap in the center of each joint. This works only if the wood has recently come out of the kiln and has picked up some moisture at the ends. The theory is that eventually the rest of the board will pick up moisture, thereby relieving the stress caused by the gap. When I join boards, I aim for a tight joint along the full length. Undoubtedly there will be slight gaps now and then. If hand pressure can close the gap, I don't worry about it. However, if full clamping pressure is required to close the joint, there will be too much stress on the panel and the pieces must be rejointed. I always dry-fit my panels before gluing, so I can check if all the joints are tight, and identify potential problems, such as misalignment. For instance, two adjacent bowed boards may align properly, but result in a bowed panel. In this case, it's necessary to flip one board over so the bows counteract each other. Even though this makes aligning the joint more difficult, it results in a straighter panel.

There are several ways to make aligning boards easier. In furniture factories, a "glue joint" is used. This is usually a modified tongue-and-groove joint along the edges. I should stress that this joint is merely for alignment, not for extra strength. A fresh, well-fitting butt joint with good glue is more than adequate. Old timers used dowels on their glue joints, but I don't care for them. In fact, if they are too long, they can actually work to weaken the joint, since the grain of the dowels runs across the grain of the boards. I find these devices unnecessary. If an unexpected misalignment occurs during glue-up, lay a piece of scrapwood on the high area and persuade it down with a mallet before the clamps are fully tightened.

Glues are a matter of preference. There are specific glues for special circumstances: resorcinol and epoxy for exterior use, plastic resin for water resistance and hide glue for possible future disassembly. I use an aliphatic resin glue, Titebond, almost exclusively. It is relatively inexpensive, has a reasonable assembly time, requires no premixing, possesses a long shelf life, sets fast, has very little creep and makes an exceptionally strong joint. It's ideal

Fingers make fine glue applicators. Here the author runs a bead of glue along the length of the joint and spreads it over the entire edge. A brush or narrow paint roller could also be used.

Rather than rely on dowels or other devices to align boards during glue-up, Becksvoort simply uses a mallet and a piece of scrap to hammer on the joint until the boards lie flat.

for panel work. Clamp time is 20 minutes under ideal conditions (over 75 degrees F, low humidity) to two hours if the panel will be subjected to stress (planing or sanding).

Clamps are another item to take into account. Bar clamps come in standard lengths, from 1 ft. to 10 ft., while pipe clamps can be made from any length pipe. Although pipe clamps are cheaper, they bend easier. The steel I-clamps or flat bar clamps last several lifetimes. My favorites are Hartford clamps, no. 5, available from the Hartford Clamp Co., Box 8131, E. Hartford, Conn. 06108; (203) 528-1708. These have a ¼-in. by 1½-in. steel bar, and a sliding L-vise handle, which is a joy to use in close quarters.

If you glue panels on a regular basis, a glue table or rack is indispensable. Pipe clamps have "feet" or flat bases that allow them to be set directly on the floor or workbench. Bar clamps are more likely to tip over, so they should be supported by a rack or glue table. The table consists of a sturdy base, a top at a convenient height and two ¾ in. by 2-in. rails about 24 in. apart to accept clamps. After you clamp the rails together, cut slots about 6 in. apart with a dado blade. The size and shape of the slots depend on the style of clamps you have. Then, attach the rails opposite each other. When setting up the table, place clamps in the end slots and sight along the length of the table to be sure the clamps are parallel, that is, in the same flat plane. The table may need to be shimmed, otherwise you might introduce twist into the panels being glued. A glue rack is a little simpler—merely two rails on a frame or, better yet, on a braced plywood sheet to catch glue drops. The rack can be put on sawhorses and stored upright if space is at a premium, but it will have to be leveled each time you use it.

Tightening clamps—On most panels, I space the clamps about 2 ft. apart on the glue rack. As the glue-up proceeds, other clamps will be put on the top of the panel between the bottom clamps to equalize the pressure and keep the panel flat. Spacer sticks inserted on each edge keep the clamp heads from compressing the grain. Now it's time for a dry run. Does everything line up? Are there any major gaps? Can you align the joints? If all checks out, it's glue time.

I prefer a thin glue film on each surface of the joint, but one thick film per joint works too. Run a bead of glue the length of the joint and spread it over the entire surface of the edge. Fingers work fine as applicators, as shown in the above, left photo. Then, lay the boards back down in order and proceed clamping. I usually start at the area of worst alignment and force the boards up or down as needed by pushing, prying ends up or down or persuad-

ing high spots with scrapwood and a mallet, as shown in the above, right photo. After the first bottom clamp is tight, set a clamp on top, midway between the bottom clamps. Never tighten all the bottom clamps first, as this causes the panel to buckle and explode. Finally, go back and tighten up the clamps as much as possible. If necessary, clamp the ends, as shown in the photo on p. 53. Having "glue-starved joints" is nothing but an excuse for dirty (oily), ill fitting joints or inappropriate glue. The clamp pressures recommended by glue manufacturers for automatic clamp presses far exceed any pressure you can apply by hand. The key is to keep the pressure even on the top and bottom so the joints are tight and the panel flat. A certain percentage of glue is forced into the grain; only the excess squeezes out. Have you ever noticed that when using very thin glue films there is little, if any, squeeze-out? Even so, the joint holds.

Excess glue should be removed since it introduces moisture into the panel, causes swelling and slows drying. It also clogs sandpaper and gums and dulls planer knives when dry. A cloth or scraper will do, although recently I've started using the little flat plastic tabs used to seal plastic bags in grocery stores. They do an excellent job and can be reused by flexing them and popping off the dried glue. Be sure to remove glue from both sides of the panel. When doing a run of several panels, scribble the time on the panel so you'll know when you can free up the clamps for the next round.

Cleaning up squeeze-out—As a general rule of thumb, I never glue up wide panels in one piece, but in two halves. A 48-in.-wide tabletop made up of many narrow boards can provide a real wrestling match. Four or five boards is all I usually do at a time, unless they are very well behaved.

When the panels are dry, the clamps can be removed. Again, alternate between the top and bottom clamps so that the pressure can be released evenly. Planing or sanding is the next step, which you can do in your shop if you have a wide planer or belt sander. I find it is more cost-effective to take several panels to a large cabinet or mill shop and use the wide belt machine. Five or six panels can be sanded, all the same thickness, flat and smooth to 120-, 150- or even 180-grit, in about one-half hour at a cost of $20 to $30. These machines can handle 24-in.-, 36-in.-, 48-in.- or 56-in.-wide panels. Look in the yellow pages and call for an appointment. ☐

Christian H. Becksvoort builds custom furniture in New Gloucester, Maine, and is a Contributing Editor to Fine Woodworking.

Fastening Tabletops

How to cope with wood movement

by Christian Becksvoort

I remember the first table I built in the junior high school wood shop: Philippine mahogany, carefully mortised and tenoned. When it came time to attach the top, I went whole hog; glue all around and black, round-head screws. I took the table home, put some plants on it and parked it directly over a hot-air outlet. Needless to say, the top did not survive the winter. It bowed and cracked. Thus ended round one in a continuing battle of wits between wood movement and my efforts to cope with it.

What it comes down to is this: When relative humidity goes up or down, so does the moisture content of wood, and it expands and contracts in width, across the grain. It doesn't change in length (actually it does, but so little that it can safely be ignored). The problem is how to attach a solid-wood tabletop that shrinks and expands across the grain to rails that don't change in length.

When designing a table, there are ways to minimize wood movement. In general, let the grain of the top run in the longest dimension. For example, a 3-ft. by 7-ft. tabletop should be glued up from 7-ft. boards, so there's only the movement of the 3-ft. width to contend with. On a round or square top, glue up the top from quartersawn stock, if possible, because it's likely to move about half as much as plainsawn stock.

Even using quartersawn stock won't eliminate wood movement problems, so I use one of the four methods shown in the drawing to accommodate movement. All of these require screws in some form or another. No matter which method I use, I anchor the tabletop at each end with a screw through each rail, skirt, brace, or support where it intersects the centerline of the

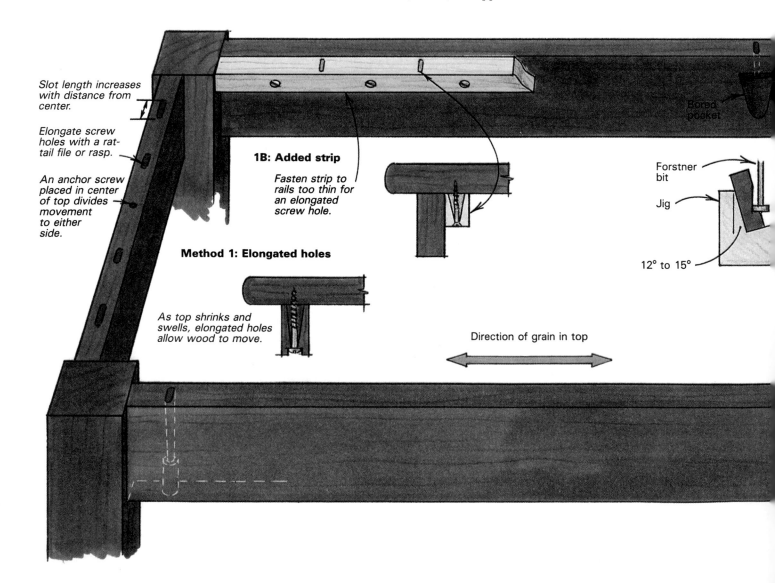

Slot length increases with distance from center.

Elongate screw holes with a rat-tail file or rasp.

An anchor screw placed in center of top divides movement to either side.

1B: Added strip

Fasten strip to rails too thin for an elongated screw hole.

Method 1: Elongated holes

As top shrinks and swells, elongated holes allow wood to move.

Bored pocket

Forstner bit

Jig

12° to 15°

Direction of grain in top

top. This screw divides potential wood movement into halves, 50% to the left of center and 50% to the right.

Method 1, the one I use most often, is simply screws through the table rails into the top. Except for the anchor-screw hole at each end, the holes are slotted or "ovalized" in the direction of potential movement with a rat-tail file or rasp. In the end rails that run across the grain of the top, the farther these holes are from the center, the longer the slots. In the side rails that parallel the grain of the top, the slots are all the same length. Use an awl to mark the actual location of the screw in the slot. To ease the actual movement I sometimes use round-head screws and washers.

On a table with relatively thin rails, the slots would break through the side rails. In this case, I glue or screw strips to the inside edges of the side rails, as shown in drawing 1B.

Drawing 1C shows a variation of the slotted hole technique which allows screw access through pocket holes on the inside surfaces of the rails. On antique tables these pockets were three-sided holes chiseled into the rail. A faster alternative is to use a Forstner bit in a drill press. Make a jig, as shown, with a 90° rabbet tilted about 12° to 15°. Rails can be set into the jig, drilled with the Forstner bit, then re-drilled with a ¼-in. bit for the screw shank.

Method 2 involves grooves and fingers (sometimes called buttons). Before assembling the table base, run grooves along the inside upper face of the rails, then cut wooden fingers to fit the grooves. These are best cut in quantity from wide endgrain cutoffs, such as the trimmed end of the tabletop. An alternative is to use metal fingers (available from Craftsman Wood Service

Co., 1735 West Cortland Ct., Addison, Ill. 60101).

Method 3 uses the "figure 8" or desk-top fastener (the best are Knape and Vogt #1547, but less expensive ones are available from The Woodworkers' Store, 21801 Industrial Blvd., Rogers, Minn. 55374). The fasteners are installed in shallow, blind holes flush with the tops of the rails. This method is ideal for fastening rails or cleats running across the top grain because the fastener pivots as the wood moves. If set in slightly oversize holes and positioned at a 45° angle to the rails that parallel the grain, a desk-top fastener will allow a bit of movement, though not as much as a finger will.

I use the sliding dovetail shown in method 4 as a last resort for extreme amounts of movement or for a trestle tabletop, where there are no long-grain rails. For example, I recently completed a 4-ft. by 24-ft. conference table made in three 8-ft. sections. The architect specified that the grain run in the 4-ft. direction, so each section had 8 ft. of moving wood to contend with. In this case, I routed a dovetail groove along the length of each 2-in.-thick rail running across the top grain (stopping just short of one end). I fastened 20 2-in.-long dovetail blocks along each long side of the top with a dab of glue and two screws. I waxed the dovetail grooves and slid a rail over each line of dovetail blocks. I put a heavy screw through the rail at the centerline of the top to anchor the two firmly and divide potential movement in two. □

Chris Becksvoort, a professional furnituremaker in New Gloucester, Maine, is the author of In Harmony With Wood _(Van Nostrand Reinhold Co., 1983)._

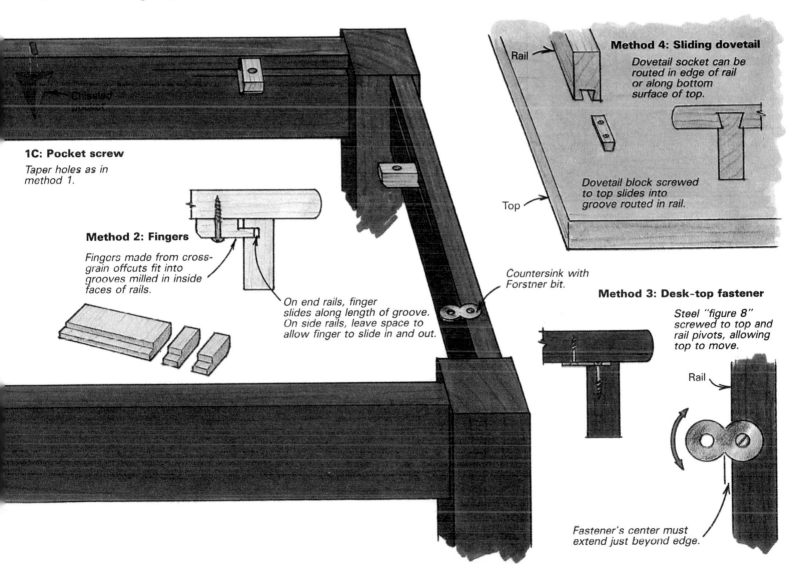

1C: Pocket screw
Taper holes as in method 1.

Method 2: Fingers
Fingers made from cross-grain offcuts fit into grooves milled in inside faces of rails.

On end rails, finger slides along length of groove. On side rails, leave space to allow finger to slide in and out.

Countersink with Forstner bit.

Method 4: Sliding dovetail
Rail
Dovetail socket can be routed in edge of rail or along bottom surface of top.

Dovetail block screwed to top slides into groove routed in rail.

Top

Method 3: Desk-top fastener
Steel "figure 8" screwed to top and rail pivots, allowing top to move.

Rail

Fastener's center must extend just beyond edge.

The two semicircular ends of this 10½-ft.-long dining table can be used as pier tables against a wall, or fastened together to make a separate round table. The top is maple veneer on particleboard, with banding, aprons and legs of solid purpleheart with ebony inlay.

Solid Banding on Round Tabletops
A three-section racetrack table

by Graham Blackburn

The commission was for a large, maple-veneered dining table with a broad, solid banding of purpleheart, and inlaid with ebony—a very striking color scheme. Eventually I'll make a set of chairs to match, but that's in the future, as my shop is too cramped for space to tackle both projects at once.

The initial problem was how to design a table that would be big enough for the occasional dinner party of 12 without dwarfing the three or four people who would use it the rest of the time. A table that expanded and contracted by means of leaves was out of the question because in its contracted state it would look far too small for the room it was to occupy.

The solution was a large table with removable ends that, when not required for the maximum number of diners, might stand as pier tables against a wall. This would leave a smaller center section to seat three or four more intimately, and still leave the room filled comfortably. The full table is a form known as a "racetrack" table—that is, an oval table with straight sides. Besides maintaining comfortable spatial relationships between the

room and the table, this arrangement also makes possible a variety of seating opportunities, as shown in figure 1.

I made up the veneered sections using a large press belonging to a friend. Not only does veneer make the construction of a large flat surface easier than using solid wood, it also allows the use of patterned figure, and avoids problems of expansion and contraction that would otherwise destroy the solid-wood banding.

Using a standard-density particleboard, I laid up fiddleback-maple in the pattern shown in figure 2. This pattern ensures that the two end sections join the center section and each other with a book-match that's balanced from the very center of the whole table. The underside was simply slip-matched with plain maple. As shown in the drawing, I faced the joining edges of the sections with ½-in. maple. The alternative would have been to veneer these edges later, after the panel had been veneered and trimmed. This is not a bad practice, but it does leave an extra line of veneer showing.

It's worth noting that, for a table this size, ¾-in. particleboard

Photo: Woody Packard

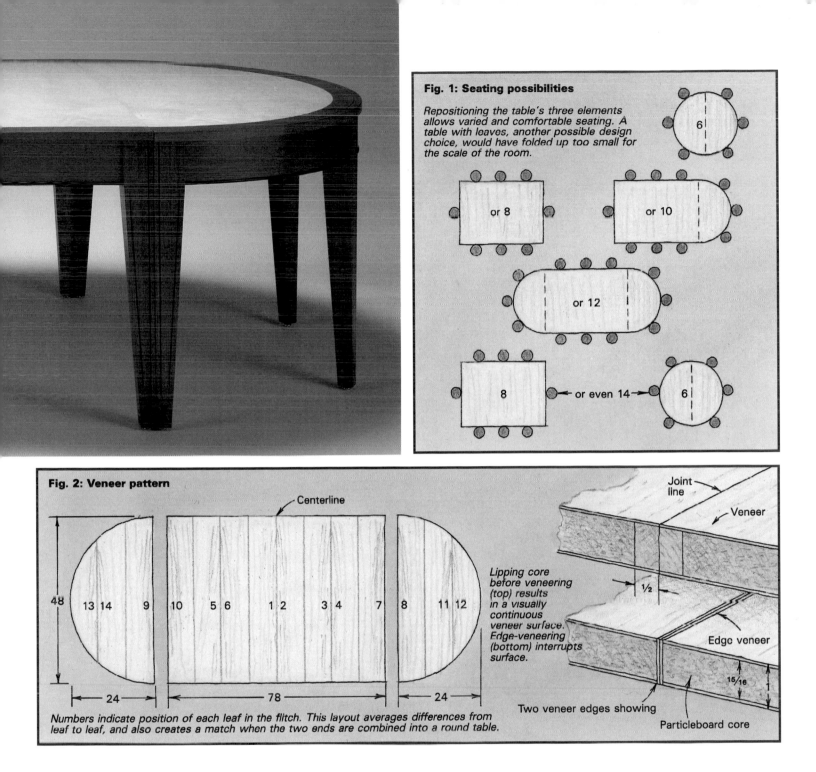

Fig. 1: Seating possibilities

Repositioning the table's three elements allows varied and comfortable seating. A table with leaves, another possible design choice, would have folded up too small for the scale of the room.

6

or 8

or 10

or 12

8 ← or even 14 → 6

Fig. 2: Veneer pattern

Centerline

48

| 13 | 14 | 9 | 10 | 5 | 6 | 1 | 2 | 3 | 4 | 7 | 8 | 11 | 12 |

← 24 → ← 78 → ← 24 →

Numbers indicate position of each leaf in the flitch. This layout averages differences from leaf to leaf, and also creates a match when the two ends are combined into a round table.

Joint line

Veneer

Lipping core before veneering (top) results in a visually continuous veneer surface. Edge-veneering (bottom) interrupts surface.

1/2

Edge veneer

15/16

1

Two veneer edges showing

Particleboard core

would have looked too thin. I custom-ordered a sheet of particleboard, thicknessed to 15/16 in., from the Eagle Door and Plywood Co. (450 Oaktree Ave., South Plainfield, N.J. 07080), so that when the top was veneered on both sides it would be a full inch thick.

Banding is frequently veneered cross-grain on solid or veneered stock. This has its advantages—the grain is always perpendicular to the edge, there's little waste, and the pieces are often small enough to minimize any problems related to wood movement. However, solid banding has advantages, too—the edge doesn't have to be separately veneered or previously faced, and it's easier to work any desired molding in a solid edge than in a veneered or composite edge.

To cut the ends to shape, a router was mounted in the circle-cutting jig shown in figure 4 (p. 61) and the jig carefully positioned on the panel at the center mark. With a ⅛-in. double-flute helical bit, I took four increasingly deep passes to cut out the semicircle. As a precautionary measure, I had first drawn the outline on the panel with a pair of trammel points (with pencil at-

tachment), and set the circle-cutting jig to cut ⅛ in. outside this line. Then, when the semicircle had been cut out, a light finishing cut, running the router the "wrong" way, clockwise, brought the panel to size and left a perfectly square edge.

There's always the question, when making a jig, of how refined it should be. If I know I will be using a jig over and over, I rarely resist the temptation to make it a visual and tactile pleasure—I am very fond of varnished mahogany and polished brass. But for a one-off job, I usually settle for a jig that will simply get the job done. This attitude sometimes makes me feel I'm a cog in a Rube Goldberg cartoon, but it has the advantage that when the job is done I can dispose of the contraption without remorse. If I'd saved every jig I've ever made, I wouldn't be able to walk through my shop.

The number of segments making up the edgebanding is a matter of choice, depending partly on how well you can match the grain, but for a two-part circular top the number must be even. I chose 12—six a side—since I would be able to get all the seg-

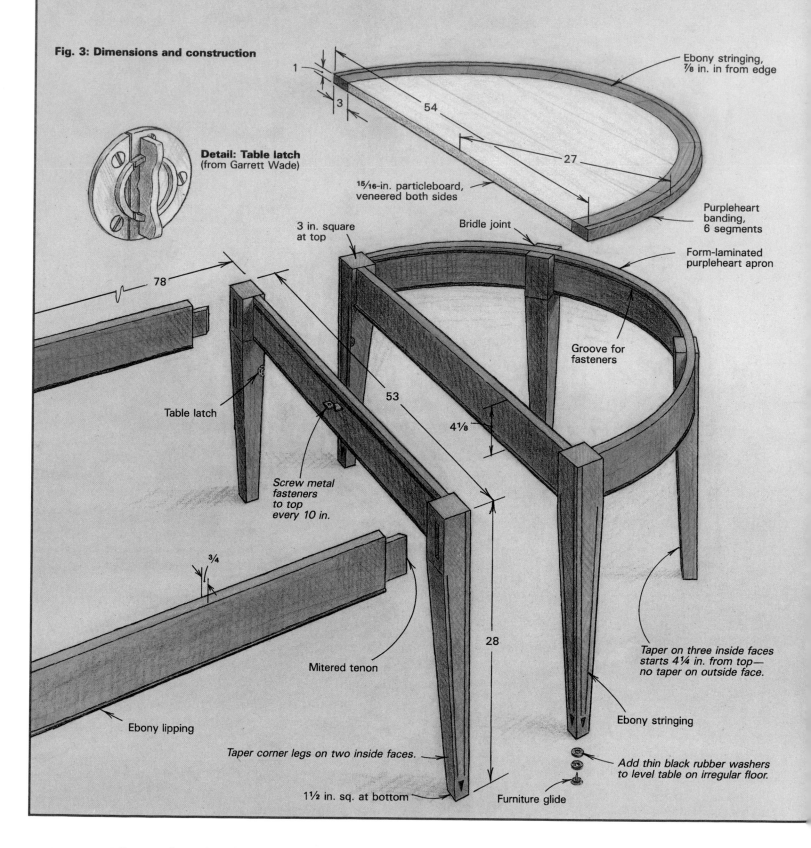

Fig. 3: Dimensions and construction

Detail: Table latch
(from Garrett Wade)

1

3

54

27

Ebony stringing,
⅞ in. in from edge

¹⁵⁄₁₆-in. particleboard,
veneered both sides

Purpleheart
banding,
6 segments

Bridle joint

Form-laminated
purpleheart apron

3 in. square
at top

78

Groove for
fasteners

53

Table latch

4⅛

Screw metal
fasteners
to top
every 10 in.

¾

28

Mitered tenon

Ebony lipping

Taper on three inside faces
starts 4¼ in. from top—
no taper on outside face.

Ebony stringing

Taper corner legs on two inside faces.

1½ in. sq. at bottom

Furniture glide

Add thin black rubber washers
to level table on irregular floor.

ments sequentially out of one length of purpleheart I had on hand. Figure 5 shows the general arrangement of the banding and also how to work out the angles for the banding segments. The width of the banding is a matter of choice, in this case I thought 3 in. looked nice. If you have a board somewhat longer than the circumference you intend to band, then all the segments can be marked on it in a straight line and numbered so the grain can later be matched.

Having done this before, I had a template on hand that I used to indicate the segments on the chosen board; you can make a template exact enough for this purpose by marking the position of the six segments around one of the semicircles—the distance

between marks will give you the inside measurement of the segment and you trace the inside curve directly from the panel.

I used a protractor and a straightedge to produce the lines to the circumference. Even though I did this as carefully as possible, measuring between each point on the circumference gave me 12 slightly different lengths. So, I averaged out the distances and marked and measured again (and again) until each segment measured exactly the same.

Thickness the banding stock to a dimension ¹⁄₁₆ in. thicker than the veneered panels; I'll discuss the reason for this a little later. Then, using the template as a guide, carefully cut the stock into lengths and rip the pieces to uniform width. Next, cut the miters

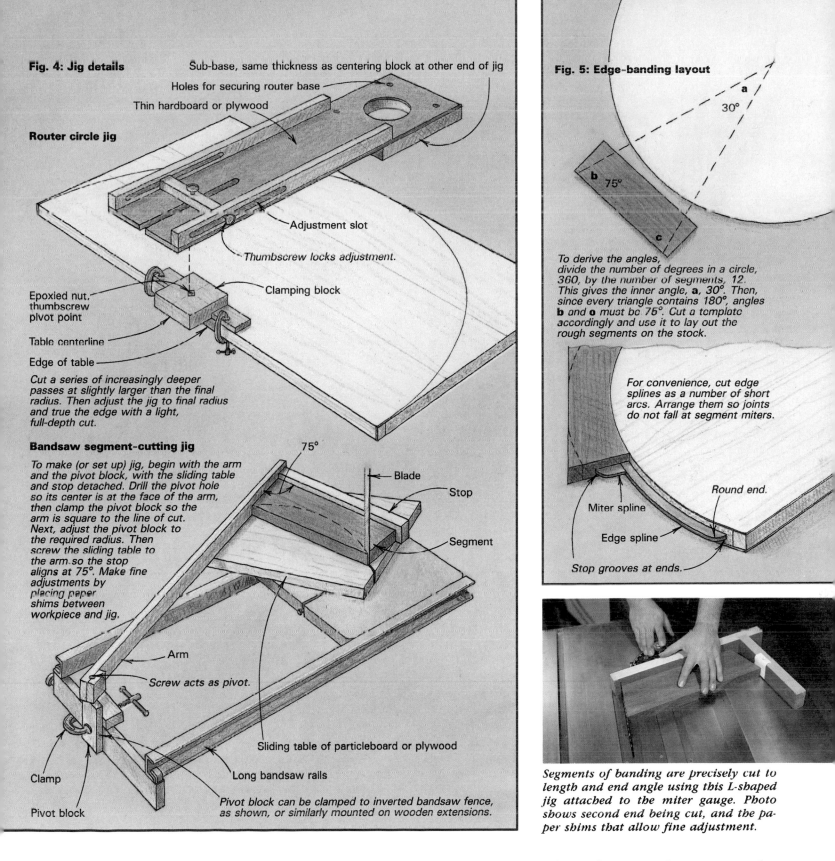

Fig. 4: Jig details

Sub-base, same thickness as centering block at other end of jig

Holes for securing router base

Thin hardboard or plywood

Router circle jig

Adjustment slot

Thumbscrew locks adjustment.

Clamping block

Epoxied nut, thumbscrew pivot point

Table centerline

Edge of table

Cut a series of increasingly deeper passes at slightly larger than the final radius. Then adjust the jig to final radius and true the edge with a light, full-depth cut.

Bandsaw segment-cutting jig

To make (or set up) jig, begin with the arm and the pivot block, with the sliding table and stop detached. Drill the pivot hole so its center is at the face of the arm, then clamp the pivot block so the arm is square to the line of cut. Next, adjust the pivot block to the required radius. Then screw the sliding table to the arm so the stop aligns at 75°. Make fine adjustments by placing paper shims between workpiece and jig.

75°

Blade

Stop

Segment

Arm

Screw acts as pivot.

Sliding table of particleboard or plywood

Clamp

Pivot block

Long bandsaw rails

Pivot block can be clamped to inverted bandsaw fence, as shown, or similarly mounted on wooden extensions.

Fig. 5: Edge-banding layout

a

30°

b 75°

c

To derive the angles, divide the number of degrees in a circle, 360, by the number of segments, 12. This gives the inner angle, **a**, 30°. Then, since every triangle contains 180°, angles **b** and **o** must be 75°. Cut a template accordingly and use it to lay out the rough segments on the stock.

For convenience, cut edge splines as a number of short arcs. Arrange them so joints do not fall at segment miters.

Round end.

Miter spline

Edge spline

Stop grooves at ends.

Segments of banding are precisely cut to length and end angle using this L-shaped jig attached to the miter gauge. Photo shows second end being cut, and the paper shims that allow fine adjustment.

on the tablesaw using a stopped fence attached to the saw's miter gauge, as shown in the photo on this page.

When making this jig, position the stop so that the first miter is cut a hair oversize. When the workpiece is turned to cut the miter on the other end, paper shims stapled to the stop can be folded down to bring the second miter to exactly the right place. Adjust the number of paper shims until the distance on the short side is *exactly* the same as the distance between the segment-length marks on the rim of the semicircle. This is absolutely critical if all segments are to join perfectly and completely encircle the top. So make as many trial cuts as necessary to ensure that the angle and dimensions are correct.

The next step is to cut the inside curve on the segments so that they fit against the edge of the semicircles. I accomplished this with the help of a shopmade jig for the bandsaw. The basic construction and the important pivot and adjustment details are shown in figure 4.

Here are a few less obvious points to bear in mind. First, make sure that the table, the jig, and the segment are all perfectly perpendicular to the blade, or the segments will tilt when butted up to the tabletop. Second, for a perfect arc to be cut, the leading edge of the blade's teeth must be exactly perpendicular to the *very center* of the jig's pivot point. And third, the distance between the center of the pivot point and the inside edge of the

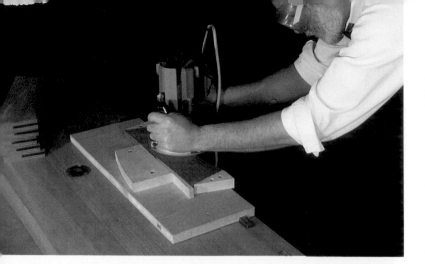

Blackburn routs slots for splines with a slotting cutter whose pilot bearing rides along the work's edge (top photo). The clamping jig holds the work securely by means of wedges and movable blocks that can be screwed down where needed. When slotting the miters (lower photo) the screw shown acts as a length stop.

blade must be the same as the radius of the tabletop. Having set everything up to these specifications, increase the radius by ⅟₃₂ in. and, once again with the use of paper shims, make a trial cut on a piece of scrap (cut to the same size as the segments) to ensure that the blade enters and leaves the segment exactly at the corners. With a perfectly sharp bandsaw blade, it's possible to make a finish cut good enough to glue onto the table edge, but I prefer to make the cut ⅟₃₂ in. larger, then individually fit each segment at the proper place on the circumference using a compass plane. If you don't have a compass plane, you could true the curve by adapting the router setup used to cut the semicircles, or by using a shaped sanding block.

At this point you can lay out the segments around the two semicircular tops, arranged as one circle, to check for correct miters, closeness of fit, and overall length.

Cutting the grooves for the splines that attach the segments to the tabletop and each other is the next operation. This used to be done with a hand router with a curved sole, but is now more easily accomplished with an electric router, a slotting bit and a small holding jig, as shown in the photos above. The reason for having cut the segments ⅟₁₆ in. thicker than the tabletop now becomes clear—to ensure that the segments, when attached, will be a little proud of the table's surfaces (both top and bottom). This makes planing and cleaning up the banding easier and safer than dealing with a surface that could possibly be lower than the central veneer. The easy way to achieve this fit is to cut the groove in the tabletop first, and then lower the bit ⅟₃₂ in. before cutting the grooves in the segments.

Splines may be made from Masonite or plywood—just choose

a slotting cutter of the same thickness. For a 3-in.-wide banding, a 1-in.-wide spline is adequate. You can lay out the curved strips with trammel points and cut them on the bandsaw. Be sure to check that the spline is not too wide anywhere—it would be disastrous to discover this in the middle of gluing up.

The assembly order is as follows: First glue the edge spline into one of the halves, then glue the first end segment and attach. Glue and insert the miter spline and then attach the next segment, and so on. When both halves are banded, clamp them together with a band clamp around the whole circle, pulling opposite pairs of segments into position, where necessary, with a long bar clamp. To ensure that the end segments on both halves line up with the ends of the halves, insert a strip of batten between the two halves. Wax the batten so the glue doesn't stick to it.

Gluing-up a top of this size is quite a lot of work, and white glue might give you a little more time than yellow glue, but even so you'll have to work fast and carefully. Position each segment exactly, for it will not want to move much horizontally when all of its neighbors are in place. As soon as you have made sure that all the segments are tight against the veneered panels, and all the miters are closed, make one more circuit before the final tightening of the band clamp, to check that the top surface of each segment is flush with its neighbor. Any discrepancy here can be rectified with a smaller clamp directly over the joint.

To cut the outer circumference, separate the two halves and reattach the router circle-cutting jig as explained earlier, but this time increase the radius by 3 in. (or by whatever width banding you have decided on). Slowly, in small increments to avoid tear-out, trim the outside edge to a semicircle. This is a critical step since you have invested so much time by now. You might even first cut close to the line with the bandsaw, or even a saber saw, and then merely trim to the finished size with the router.

Final treatment of the edge can be achieved in various ways. I prefer a few light passes with the compass plane, but this must be set very finely and be very sharp because of the alternating grain direction on each segment. Another choice would be to make a curved sanding block from scrap.

The top and bottom surfaces of the banding can now be planed flush with the veneer and then the whole surface gone over with the scraper.

The other construction details are shown in figure 3. When making my table, I edgebanded the center section with two straight pieces cut to the same width as the curved banding.

Legs were cut and mortised to receive the aprons, which, for the semicircular ends, were form-laminated. The two central legs at each end were attached with bridle joints, all others with mortise-and-tenon joints.

Before the legs and skirts were glued up, the legs were tapered, and the skirts slotted at the top of the inside to receive the metal fasteners that hold the top down.

Finally, the tabletop and legs were inlaid with ebony stringing. I had left the inlay design to the end, as a sort of insurance policy, thinking that if any of the joints in the banding did not fully close up, I could position the stringing to cover the gaps. I am pleased to report, however, that this consideration did not materialize. In fact, the glue lines were all so clean, I decided they should be left to be seen. When the fates are kind, why not go with the flow? □

Graham Blackburn is a furniture designer and maker in Woodstock, N.Y., and author of numerous books on woodworking.

Shattered Glass

A novel approach to designing a tabletop

by Spider Webb

Glass can add visual impact to many different pieces of furniture. As a glazier, it was only natural that I began to experiment with ways to combine various types of glass with my woodworking. Eventually, I included the interesting textures created by shattered tempered glass. In my tabletops, the shattered pane is sandwiched between two ¼-in.-thick pieces of glass and the entire assembly is framed with 2x3 oak. The table, shown in the photo below, is 13 in. high, 24 in. wide and 54 in. long, and is made from quarter-sawn white oak with snakewood splines. I used clear glass in the top, bronze-tinted glass in the center and LOF golden vertical #208 glass (one-way mirror), available from most glass wholesalers, in the bottom.

Building the table—After determining the size of your coffee table, cut the front, back and side rails to length. For the table in the photo, I cut two ¼-in.-wide by ¼-in.-deep rabbets, ½ in. apart, on both ends of all the rails to accept the ½-in.-long snakewood splines. To hold the ¾ in. of glass, I cut ¹³/₁₆-in.-deep dadoes the length of all the rails. This leaves ¹/₁₆ in. on all sides so the glass can move once it is inserted into the frame. After cutting the rails, test-fit the frame for accuracy.

Next, cut the four legs to the desired length, and then measure and drill holes in the legs and underside of the frame for 1-in.-long, ½-in.-dia. dowels to join the legs to the frame. I cut ¼-in. by ¼-in. slots, ¾ in. down all sides of the legs and 1¼ in. from the end of the underside of the frame to receive ½-in.-thick triangular braces. Mill ¼-in. tenons to fit into the legs and bottom of the table.

Dry-assemble the frame, and then drill a ⅛-in. hole in one side rail so you can later shatter the center glass. I center this hole in the dado in the middle of one side because I like the pattern created when the glass shatters: the lines branch out like a tree.

Before glue-up, I round the corners of the legs with a ¼-in. roundover bit in the router. Then, I disassemble the frame and sand all the pieces. The next step is to glue up the table. I use G-2 slow-curing epoxy, available from The Wooden Boat Shop, 1007 N.E. Boat St., Seattle, Wash. 98105. After cleaning the squeeze-out with acetone, I let the frame dry for several days and then stain the oak with Benite sand-and-fill stain, available from Daly's Inc., 3525 Stone Way N., Seattle, Wash. 98103. Although it's a bit more expensive than most, I think it's four times as good.

Then, use a sandstone lubricated with plenty of water and grind the glass to fit the frame. After cleaning and dry-fitting the glass in the frame, I run a thin bead of clear silicone caulking around the inside of the top dado, and then glue up the frame around the glass. The caulking seals the top piece of glass so coffee and other liquids don't leak into the middle of the table.

The final step is to shatter the glass through the ⅛-in. hole previously drilled in the center of the side rail dado. When I first began making these tables, I tried using a nail to break the center glass, but usually ended up breaking the top or bottom glass because the nail bent too easily when hit with a hammer. From all my trials and errors, I've found that a flat, hardened punch works the best because it doesn't bend. To shatter the glass, lightly hit the punch with a hammer; be careful not to chip the glass, however, because it won't shatter from that spot and you'll have to make another hole. When the center glass has shattered and branches out like a tree, your table is complete. □

Spider Webb is a hobbyist woodworker who owns University Glass in Seattle, Wash.

The author has made shattered-glass tabletops from many types and textures of glass. Here, bronze-tinted glass was sandwiched between two other panes of glass, framed with oak and then shattered from a single point on one edge so the cracks branch out like a tree.

Furniture from the Lathe

New forms from traditional techniques

by Dick Burrows

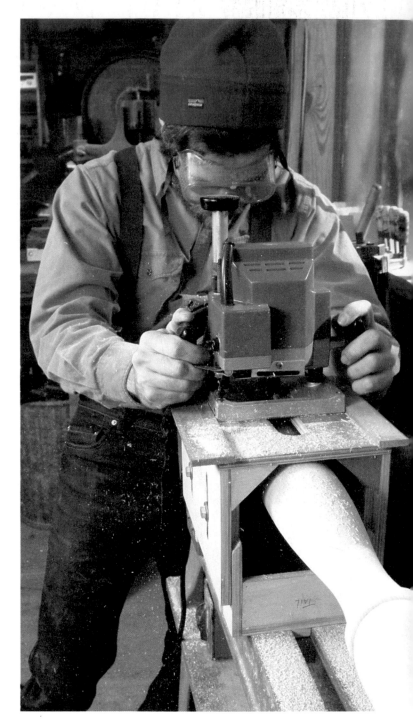

Years ago, when I was traveling from craft fair to craft fair selling turned and carved bowls, I was continually surprised by the contempt some people had for lathe work. Perhaps it was because they remembered how easy it was in junior high school to produce an ash tray or candlestand—the machine did all of the work and most of the designing. And, lathes have been around forever, filling our lives with bats, bowls and brush handles.

Bowl turners have grabbed most of the publicity in recent years for changing the image of turning, proclaiming themselves artists in search of the perfect shape, the perfect finish, the ultimate art object. But, what about all those other woodworkers to whom the lathe is still just another tool, no more glamorous than any saw or chisel hanging from their tool racks. After visiting furnituremakers across the country who rely heavily on lathe-turned furniture parts, I found they are more attuned to the new wave bowl turners than to the old-time production turners or those who think lathe work is a synonym for junior-high-school clunky. The last thing they want is for their furniture to look as if it popped off a lathe.

Actually, none of the furnituremakers I talked with considered himself primarily a turner—some were almost deferential toward the skill of the bowlmakers—and none wanted to be limited to the round or cylindrical forms traditionally associated with turners. Pennsylvania woodworker Mark Sfirri, for example, uses a lathe to carve and raise panels for cabinet doors; Californian Lewis Buchner combines stacking techniques with turning to

produce top-of-the-line cabinets too large to fit on any lathe. Another Californian, Robert Leung, does massive faceplate turnings up to 56 in. in diameter, then bandsaws them apart and reassembles them into sculptural tables and desks.

Speed is what makes the lathe special for this group of furnituremakers. The lathe can produce cylindrical and curved shapes almost as fast as a planer can flatten stock. It can transform an idea into a scrapwood mockup so quickly that it virtually makes wood a three-dimensional sketchbook. If your idea doesn't work out, you can redraw the shape with gouge or skew, or just start over with a new blank of wood, again and again if you want, until you get it right, then you can quickly turn your refined idea into a finished product. With a lathe, a clever worker can almost mass-produce parts for cabinets, tables, chairs, benches, as well as for a variety of mirrors, boxes and other decorative items. And the tool itself is fairly simple, easy

From *Fine Woodworking* magazine (July 1986) 59:34-40

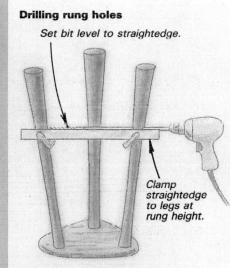

Drilling rung holes

Set bit level to straightedge.

Clamp straightedge to legs at rung height.

To align rung holes, Kopf runs a bit extension between legs so the first hole is the drill-guide for the second hole.

Bob Kopf

The curly maple and mahogany game table (29 in. by 36 in. by 36 in.), left, is a good example of Kopf's efforts to make functional furniture with a minimum number of joints and wood elements. The legs are assembled by boring through the maple block that will become the ball, turning a tenon on a mating mahogany piece, then gluing the two pieces together and turning them as a single piece. Kopf, far left, mortises table legs with a plunge router and a box-like jig mounted over the lathe bed. Runners on top of the jig guide the cut. Bolts and wingnuts in the side slots set the jig height. The mahogany and ash buffet (36 in. by 16 in. by 60 in.), above left, has tapered breadboard ends and chamfered edges that blend with the angled legs to create a sense of motion. Kopf shapes the tops with a block plane, which he says cuts a very shallow curve. This curve is a very personal trademark because it depends largely on the distinct way his arm and hand move and twist during each plane stroke. Kopf sometimes relies on wood grain to convey a sense of visual unity, as shown on the three stools, above center, cut from a single plank of bird's-eye maple.

to maintain, relatively inexpensive, and doesn't require a cabinet full of cutters and gouges to be versatile.

One of the first woodworkers I visited was Bob Kopf, who works in an airy shop decorated with camouflage paint, a real standout amid the chestnut brown sheds of the neighboring tobacco farms in the tiny community of Walnut Cove, N.C. I first became interested in Kopf's work about 10 years ago when I was living in Charlotte, N.C. At a time when many of us were making tables and stools that resembled those our grandfathers made, Kopf was incorporating elongated knobs, swollen feet and other unconventional forms in his turnings as he tried to make elegant furniture with the minimum number of joints and wood elements. His later experiments with balance points, carving stools and tabletops, and combining parallelograms, rhombuses, and architectural forms would lead to tables with tapered breadboard

ends, chamfered handplaned edges and legs turned and angled to draw the eye toward the motion of the table. Some of his more recent works include tables with legs that look like segmented cones, almost insect like, and dining room sets where the spindles and balls seem to be growing out of each other to form legs.

Kopf is passionate about his explorations in design and about the lathe being an incredibly fast way to make furniture, but he's laid back about the mystique of the machine and its tools. When asked what lathe tools he favored, he replied one big one and one little one. The big one turns out to be a 1⅛-in. roughing-out gouge, the smaller one a ¾-in. gouge. He sums up his turning technique simply as a "whole sense of working, producing a smooth feeling and a smooth shaving."

Self-taught, Kopf relishes methods of work that are practical and logical. Rather than make a big production of boring rung holes, he uses a drill extension and lets the first hole be the drill guide for the second, as shown in the drawing on the preceding page. Mounting the rungs in the legs is equally low-tech, Kopf glues the legs into the top then springs the legs apart enough to jockey the rungs into place. The maneuver is simple—he puts his hand on one leg, then wedges his elbow against the next leg to push the two apart. For joinery, he relies heavily on his plunge router, which he uses with a simple box-like jig that fits over the lathe bed, as shown on p. 64. With this setup, he can cut up to eight mortises in ten minutes. A favorite joint is the wedged mortise and tenon, which he considers almost foolproof.

His old Crescent lathe doesn't even have a faceplate, but he doesn't miss it, concentrating exclusively on spindle turning. "You really have only two shapes to work with—the cove and the bead, everything springs from those two shapes. We've all studied the old ways, now we're trying to do newer interpretations of the cove and bead, explore shapes, trying to come up with something new and current."

Kopf does about 20 major pieces of furniture a year, most of them commissions for tables and chairs, benches and sets of stools. He says his work has been strongly influenced by the work of Wharton Esherick, Brancusi and the Shaker prohibitions against excessive ornamentation and decoration. In the thirteen years that he has been a full-time furnituremaker, he says he's been constantly experimenting to refine his designs. One of the most significant changes in his work is that his components have been getting lighter. "I've learned how to make things just strong enough. The pieces are also structures—stronger than the sum of their parts. I used to really overbuild things."

I contacted furnituremaker and designer Lewis Buchner in San Francisco after seeing an intriguing picture of his lacquered armoire and table shown below. The piece was so symmetrical it had to be turned, but since it was more than 6 ft. tall and hollow, it was difficult to imagine how. Buchner told me both the 78-in. armoire and the 18-in. table were simply stacks of 32-in.-diameter rings glued together with yellow glue. Buchner assembled each ring from six bandsawn segments of western red cedar, then glued four of the rings together, staggering the joints between segments for maximum strength. Each four-ring unit was then mounted on a faceplate on a large patternmakers' lathe and turned inside and out until the walls were about ½ in. thick. A set of oversize, homemade calipers was used to ensure that the inside and outside diameters of the rings were identical. The top and bottom of the armoire were also turned on a faceplate.

Sets of the ring units were then glued and butt jointed together to form three sections: the upper cabinet, the waist and the lower cabinet. He cut the doors by mounting the cylinders in a cradle and running the pieces over the tablesaw, as shown below. After the three major segments were glued together, the doors were remounted using custom-made wooden hinges of goncalo alves, the same wood used for the turned door handles.

Buchner uses a lathe for many of his designs. It's also an efficient tool for making joints—turn a tenon on one piece, fit it into a bored hole and wedge the tenon—and it works well in combination with other tools in the shop. "I use a lathe like a bandsaw, shaper or any other tool in the shop. I often like to

Photo: Phil Toy

Lewis Buchner

This lacquered armoire and matching table were constructed from stack-laminated rings of western red cedar. Buchner assembled each ring with six bandsawn segments, then glued the rings together in groups of four. The four-ring segments were turned down to ½-in. thick, 32-in. diameter cylinders which were, in turn, glued together to make the 78-in.-high armoire and 18-in. table. Lights shining on the white textured gesso and copper leaf interior create a soft-glow in the stained-glass-like windows.

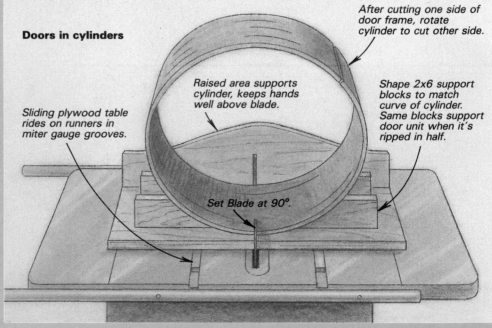

Doors in cylinders

After cutting one side of door frame, rotate cylinder to cut other side.

Raised area supports cylinder, keeps hands well above blade.

Shape 2x6 support blocks to match curve of cylinder. Same blocks support door unit when it's ripped in half.

Sliding plywood table rides on runners in miter gauge grooves.

Set Blade at 90°.

Robert Leung

This koa and African padauk hall table is contructed almost entirely with lathe-turned parts. The cleverly-designed top and drawer assembly is made from one large faceplate turning. First, a series of troughs is turned in the middle of a square blank. By cutting that turning apart, reassembling and re-turning it, as shown at right, Leung simultaneously makes the top and pigeonholes for the drawers.

Photo: Robert Leung

Semi-circular table and drawers

A. Glue up 36-in. block of 8/4 koa. Square and joint sides, then turn section shown in the middle of the square.

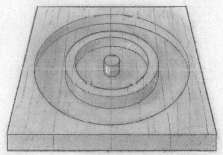

B. Bandsaw disc in half and reassemble.

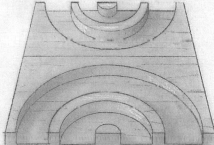

C. Saw off corners and turn blank round before sawing the two halves apart.

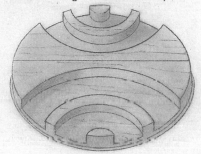

D. Flip two halves together and glue to 3-in.-wide band of ¼ in. padauk.

Carve padauk band to match curve of turning. Small handsaw separates banding sections to make drawer pulls.

E. Trough-like drawer bodies and mirror frame bandsawn from second turned disc.

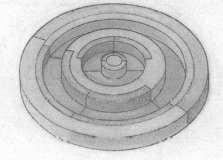

---

incorporate round forms in my designs, and the lathe is just the right tool for certain processes."

Another Californian, Robert Leung, also relies heavily on faceplate turnings in his work. Leung works in a large shop in what used to be a paint factory in one of Oakland's industrial areas. The factory is now being divided and renovated into studios for woodworkers, potters and other artists. Leung, a woodworker for seven years, was running a movie theater when he started making his own furniture with a coping saw and a file. He was soon hooked on wood and enrolled in the woodworking program at Cal. State (San Bernardino). There, he worked with Leo Doyle, an RIT graduate who got him started in turning. Leung says he stuck with it because he liked the curved forms that were possible on the lathe, he was excited by the possibilities of combining stacking techniques with lathe work.

Smooth, rounded forms are a favorite motif for Leung in all his work, from small boxes to large tables. He says he prefers imported hardwoods, like pau ferro and koa, because they have more color than domestic species. Many of his large forms could be carved with a router, but he says the lathe permits more detailing. Much of his work is done on faceplates made from large plywood discs, ranging from 12 in. to 56 in. in diameter. Some of the larger ones are propelled by the coving action of a body grinder, rather than the lathe motor. The rotation of the grinder bit cutting the wood keeps the faceplate spinning.

One of his best known designs is a coffee table made from a 30-in. to 34-in. disc of 8/4 koa that's turned, then bandsawn into three wedge-shaped pieces. The bottom of each piece is grooved to fit over a Y-shaped frame welded from ½-in. square steel. The grain of each wedge seems to be cascading down each curved edge, creating an impression of both restfulness and tension. "When you deal with curves, there is always implied tension," says Leung.

The koa and African padauk hall table shown above is almost entirely lathe-made. The drawers for this table are shaped on the lathe using the procedure outlined in the drawing, but for many of his smaller works Leung waxes the three edges of the carved or assembled drawers before sandwiching them into the large disc. The tension from clamping when the rest of the disc is glued up holds the drawers securely while the disc is being turned. Once the piece is taken from the lathe, the waxed drawers can be pulled out.

When I visited Mark Sfirri at his home in New Hope, Pa., a popular tourist town with a rich resource of woodworkers, including George Nakashima and Robert Whitley, he laid out a series of

Turned raised panels

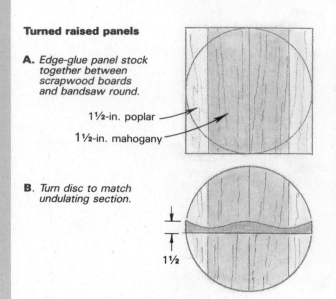

A. Edge-glue panel stock together between scrapwood boards and bandsaw round.

1½-in. poplar

1½-in. mahogany

B. Turn disc to match undulating section.

1½

C. After bandsawing away the scrap poplar, joint panel edges and crosscut the ends to make large rectangle. Rip the rectangle down the center to separate the door panels.

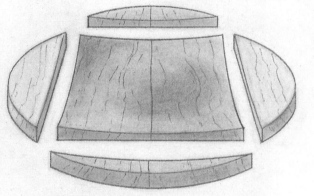

D. Raise panels on table saw with blade set at 90° and the fence cocked for a cove cut. Do the cross-grain cuts, then long cuts to prevent tearout.

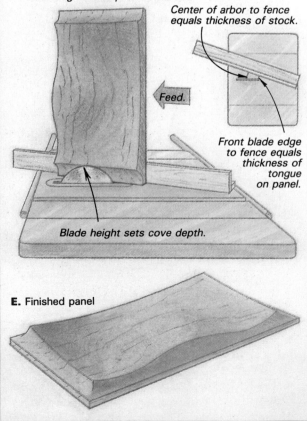

Center of arbor to fence equals thickness of stock.

Feed.

Front blade edge to fence equals thickness of tongue on panel.

Blade height sets cove depth.

E. Finished panel

Mark Sfirri

Sfirri combined a tablesaw and lathe to come up with a machine-made panel with a handcarved look, above. The cove cut used to raise the panels on the tablesaw continues the shaping begun on the lathe because the blade cuts more deeply into the thickest area of the turnings, but takes less wood from the thinner areas. Split turnings are a good way to make mirrors, especially if you don't mind making two at a time. The sides of the 52-in.-high walnut mirror are two quadrants of a cylinder formed from four pieces of walnut joined together with glue-and-paper joints. After the pieces are separated, they can be tapered on a tablesaw, since the two straight, unturned sides of each quadrant form a right angle that can be run against the saw's rip fence. The pieces are joined at the corners with a beveled miter and spline.

Photos: Mark Sfirri

slides on his dining room table to show how his furniture had changed since 1970 when he began working with Tage Frid at the Rhode Island School of Design. "Frid often pointed out that there were numerous, untapped possibilites for the lathe in furnituremaking, but we didn't do much with it." In addition to Frid, Sfirri said he was inspired by the work of Canadian Stephen Hogbin, one of the first contemporary turners to cut turnings apart and reassemble them into sculptural forms.

"I originally used the lathe for speed," Sfirri told me. "I don't think I was in any way compromising on my designs, but it was faster than making everything by hand. I didn't want to make something that looked as if it had come off a lathe." After turning the pieces, he then shapes, carves and assembles them into more complex forms that can't be readily related to the original cylindrical or round form that spawned them. Sfirri always enjoyed carving with traditional handtools—chisels, gouges, files and rasps—but knew nobody would be able to afford his work unless he could do carving on a production level. The lathe gave him a way to do just that.

One of his early lathe experiments involved producing a set of dining room chairs with only turned parts. Even the contoured arms and curved slats were turned on large faceplate jigs. He's still using the chairs in his home, and although they are quite attractive and comfortable, he's reluctant to go into too much detail about how they were made because he remembered how easily the parts flew out of the jig when he was turning them. His other experiments included a series of sculptured raised panels, and a large, turned disc which, when bandsawn apart, became little, tapered wooden race cars. Adding scrap to widen an assembly for turning, as was done with the raised panels shown at left, is a technique Sfirri also likes for making bowls and other objects where an oval or oblong, rather than circular form is needed.

Sfirri, who teaches woodworking and design at Bucks County Community College in Newtown, Pa., was trained as an artist before becoming a furniture designer, so he feels comfortable with sketching out ideas. But he still likes the spontaneity offered by the lathe and the flexibility it gives him to see and work out possibilities. Even with this freedom to explore, though, he was Frid's student long enough to understand the need to work out every step of the construction process before work begins. On complex assemblies, he always provides some means for holding the work, bearing surfaces for sawing, or a way to clamp the piece while joints are being cut. When he turns mirror frames, for example, he uses paper and glue to make a 4-piece spindle, turns the shape he wants, then splits the turned quadrants apart. Each quadrant has a 90° angle and two straight sides that can act as reference surfaces for further machining, such as tapering the piece or cutting the rebate to house the mirror glass.

Composition and interrelation of parts, not turning, is the main focus by Christopher Weiland, a designer and furniture-maker in Penn Run, Pa. Turning was just the natural way to develop a beautiful shape that would bring together the planes, shapes and lines of his design, as in the mirror and jewelry box shown above. After seeing the mirror in a turning show, I called Weiland to ask how it was made. He told me the base of the mirror is a faceplate turning rabbeted to hold a mirror which is secured with ebony pins. Both the bottom and the top, a resawn and bookmatched pear plank turned on the faceplate, are grooved to accept the horizontal supports, which are finger jointed together with brass pins and ebony spacers. The jewelry box bottom and lid are faceplate turned discs that were cut down the middle then jointed to strips of maple and a thin, flat piece of padauk.

Christopher Weiland

The pear mirror, above, is two faceplate turnings joined by maple supports that hinge together with brass pins and ebony spacers. The bottom and lid of the jewelry box, right, are cut in half, then joined to strips of maple and a thin padauk slide.

Photos: Christopher Weiland

A few hundred miles south of Pennsylvania, deep in the Blue Ridge Mountains, I visited David Scott, a woodworker who likes turning so much that a lathe was his first major power tool purchase when he went into business for himself five years ago. Scott came to North Carolina to attend the production crafts woodworking program at Haywood Technical College in Waynesville. He liked the area so much he stayed, and now works in a small one-man shop behind behind Waynesville's Museum of North Carolina Handicrafts, where he and his wife, Kathy, are caretakers.

Almost everything Scott makes includes lathe parts from clocks and yo-yos to stools, tables, beds and benches. All of his work is functional, has a light, airy feel, clean lines and a highly polished, clear finish. The variety of products is essential to his business, since he sells most of his work directly through craft shows. Living in a rural area with few galleries, he relies on the craft shows to generate both commissions and a good portion of his income.

I asked him why he was drawn to the lathe. "It would be a cliché to say quickness of results, but it must be a factor for everybody who turns. Just the ability to form something quickly. But it's something more difficult to explain, too. From the start I felt that so many turners did round forms, especially bowls, that it was important to do something different, to alter the form, to find a fresh approach in an area that had been heavily mined for years."

When you make furniture from the lathe, Scott says you're starting the design process by setting limits—you're restricting the number of flat parts you can use, you can only produce a limited number of shapes, and there are often no natural relationships between the parts. It isn't long before you begin carving the lathe-turned parts, or splitting them apart and reassembling them.

Although he doesn't do mechanical drawings, Scott invests a lot of time generating ideas with a sketch pad and pencil. Then, rather than developing the idea fully with more drawings, he goes right to the lathe and turns a quick study piece from scrap

David Scott

For production work, Scott, above, relies on a Hegner duplicating attachment. The duplicator follows the prototype shape and a V-shape cutter brings the blank to a nearly finished shape. Scott likes to combine the colors and textures of wood. He emphasized the lines of his rocker, above right, with mahogany and maple laminations and curly maple arm rests. On the table, right, he blended the laminated ash and Maccassar ebony braces into the turned bands on the legs to soften the lines of the piece. This walnut and curly maple bench, far right, is one of Scott's first pieces where function is secondary to appearance. The bench itself is fairly plain—the energy is in the turning—the random pattern of spindles and the playful back rail.

wood. "I'm a real seat-of-the-pants person. I rely on the educated guess, trial and error. I prefer straightforward, simple solutions, clean lines, nice proportions, with one piece relating to another and to the whole in an understandable way, rather than having just an array of pieces." Often he ties his designs together by laminating woods of contrasting color. When he was in school, he worked hard to make sure the laminations didn't show, but soon realized he was missing a good way to emphasize the lines of a piece. On small, glass-topped tables like the one shown above, he marries the diverse elements together by repeating the turned shapes and bands thoughout the piece, then connecting the turnings with laminated braces. For the table, he laminated the braces from ⅛-in. strips of ash and ⅟₃₂-in. thick Macassar ebony, then blended the braces into the turned leg bands and coves to soften the lines of the piece. Recently, he has been

extending this type of interplay by machining tusk tenons to match the shape of the turning supporting the tenon.

From top-of-the-line designer furniture to a bare-bones stool, from the eminently functional to the purely whimsical, a lathe can be an efficient, useful tool for all sorts of work. The main danger in relying on the lathe harkens back to those people who contemptuously relegate it to the junior-high-school kids. Things made on the lathe all too often look as if they were made on the lathe. The tool can overpower the craftsman, quickly obliterating a thoughtful design into a stack of Tinker Toy parts. But, if the designer's eye controls the process, the lathe is a versatile workhorse that can improve the products of any shop. □

Dick Burrows is an associate editor of Fine Woodworking.

Thirty-Two-Millimeter Cabinets

A one-man shop adapts the European system

by John Masciocchi

For six years, I've had my own small shop and made everything from custom furniture to *shoji* screens. Cabinets have been the mainstay of my business—especially Euro-style cabinets with their characteristic clean lines, continuous facades and concealed hinges. Until recently, I constructed my cabinets with traditional face frames and standard dado and rabbet joinery—processes that were cumbersome and unprofitable.

In hopes of finding a better way to make these attractive cabinets, I visited the Charles Grant Company, a large shop in Portland, Ore., that employs a German-developed cabinetmaking process known as the 32mm system. The beauty of the 32mm method is that it completely standardizes cabinet construction and hardware mounting, and it allows you to do all the work—from cut out to installing hinges and drawer guides—*before* the cabinet is assembled. The flat panels of 32mm cabinetry are easier to machine, handle and store; they can even be shipped flat for assembly on site. Furthermore, the cabinet materials are processed by machines expressly designed for 32mm cabinetry. I watched with glee as a small crew in the 30,000-sq.-ft. shop turned out as many precisely made, high-quality cabinets in a day as I might make in a month.

I was even more excited to learn that employing the 32mm system doesn't necessarily demand exorbitantly expensive machinery or a grand scale of production. By adapting the same construction practices used in large cabinet factories to my limited resources, I've found that I can profitably use 32mm's advantages in my 1,800 sq. ft., one man shop. These streamlined methods, coupled with the subcontracting of some of the more involved processes, mean that each cabinet job requires less time, allowing me to invest my energy in the design details that ultimately sell my work.

Much of the 32mm system's efficiency comes from the highly economical way in which Euro-style cabinets are constructed. Traditional American-style cabinets consist of a simple plywood box, joined by dadoes or tongue-and-groove joints, with a solid-wood face frame nailed and glued to the front edges of the plywood. The face frame does three things: it stiffens the carcase against racking; gives the plywood a finished look; and provides a mounting surface for door hinges. Some shops make the face frame after the carcases are built; some make it before. In either case, however, face-frame cabinets require two distinct stages of construction; normally, doors and drawers come last and are made only after the cabinets themselves are assembled.

Euro-style cabinets, on the other hand, don't have face frames. A typical case is built of cabinet-grade plywood, veneered particleboard or fiberboard covered with plastic laminate; normally,

Clean, fully overlaid doors and drawer fronts give Euro-style cabinets an austere, seamless look that accrues from the efficiency of 32mm construction methods.

the edges are banded with the same material that covers the panel. Instead of using dadoes or tongue-and-groove joints, the top and bottom panels of European cabinets are doweled into the carcase sides and/or fastened with special knockdown fittings. To keep the frameless cabinets from racking, a plywood panel is then let into grooves at the back of the cabinet.

The 32mm system was developed in Germany about 50 years ago to streamline cabinet production. Incidentally, there's nothing mystical about 32mm as a dimension: it's simply as close together as the spindles on the multiple-drill boring machines would go. In place of conventional joinery, the 32mm system depends on a series of accurately placed holes—8mm-dia. "construction" holes for the dowels and knockdown fasteners that

Photo this page: Jim Piper; drawing: Joel Katzowitz

hold the cabinets together, and 5mm-dia. "system" holes for drawer slides, hinges, shelf pins and any accessories to be installed inside the cabinets. European manufacturers make an amazing assortment of hinges, drawer slides, pulls, mounting brackets, knockdown fasteners, slide-out baskets and so on (see "Euro-style hardware," right), all designed to conform to the diameter and spacing of these holes.

In its most refined form, 32mm cabinetry requires a huge investment in specialized equipment. A thoroughly equipped shop might have a sliding-table panel saw, an automatic edgebander, a computer-driven multiple-spindle boring machine, a hinge-boring and setting machine and a pneumatic case clamp. But some makers here and abroad have introduced smaller, less expensive machines that can make 32mm accessible to even a one-man shop. You don't have to employ the entire system to reap many of its benefits: My investment in special equipment and tooling—basically a multiple-spindle boring attachment for my drill press and a hinge-boring and setting machine—totaled less than $2,000.

Since I don't have a fully equipped shop, my 32mm methods aren't entirely orthodox. Instead of the usual stretchers at the top of base cabinets (see figure 1), I find it more efficient to use a solid-plywood top for the carcase. Some 32mm shops rely entirely on dowels for case construction, using pneumatic case clamps for assembly. In these shops, construction holes are bored by a machine whose multiple spindles first bore the cabinet sides and then pivot to the horizontal to bore the ends of cabinet tops and bottoms. Fixed stops and fences ensure perfect hole alignment. Since my shop lacks this equipment, I subcontract the boring on larger jobs, then assemble the cabinets with assembly screws that are basically knockdown fasteners specially designed for plywood and particleboard carcase work. If I need to add a partition, a stretcher or a fixed shelf later, I bore construction holes myself with a special 5mm/7mm stepped drill, then drive in an assembly screw. On smaller jobs that aren't worth subcontracting, I use a nail gun to tack the cabinet parts in place, then drill for and drive in assembly screws.

After designing a set of cabinets, I begin by preparing a complete cutting list for each cabinet, including all of the carcase parts, doors, drawers and kickplates. I note boring instructions for each part, then map the parts out for best yield. Next, each part is marked with a cabinet number, cutting list part number and dimensions. The cutting list also provides accurate information for estimating costs and purchasing materials.

Next, I cut the panels into cabinet parts on a 12-in. sliding-table panel saw with a scoring blade that neatly cuts through delicate surface veneers or composition materials without much tearout. As parts are cut, they're numbered and labeled for edge-banding and boring. I label the parts on their edges—that way, the marks won't need to be sanded off later and they can also be read when the panels are stacked.

Edgebanding comes next. For a small shop with neither the space nor the capital for an edgebander, subcontracting this operation is an alternative. I don't have an edgebander, so I almost always farm out the work to a shop that glues, applies, flush-trims and bevels the edgebanding of my choice. Transporting the cut panels takes time, but automatic edgebanding is five to ten times faster than work done by hand.

The all-important tasks of layout and boring are next. Here again, systemic advantages of 32mm come into play. European companies make jigs and fixtures for laying out parts and positioning hardware. One of the most useful is the Blum "Magic

Euro-style hardware

Cabinet suspension fitting **(1)** mounts to the inside of upper cabinets with two screws and hangs on a metal rail attached to the wall. Adjusting screws on the front of the fitting allow for up-and-down and in-and-out motion, enabling adjacent cabinets to be accurately aligned. Fasteners such as those shown left to right in **(2)**—assembly screws with snap-on cover caps, two-part system hole connector screws and cam-locking knockdown fasteners—help make cabinet assembly fast and precise. The concealed hinge **(3)** has a compound action that simultaneously lifts doors out and away from the cabinet face. Different models are designed to open to 90°, 120° or 180°, or to accommodate special situations, like 45° corner cabinets. Adjustable plastic feet **(4)** allow a cabinet installed over an uneven floor to be accurately leveled; a screwdriver hole at the top allows each foot to be raised or lowered, and a plastic clip snapped into a kickplate kerf provides quick mounting. Smooth-operating metal drawer guides **(5)** ride on nylon-rimmed ball-bearing wheels and come in lengths from 12 to 24 inches. With regular guides (bottom), the carcase half mounts on the system holes while the other half lines up with the bottom of a drawer and screws into the side. New models (top) combine drawer sides and guides, and need only be fitted with a front, back and bottom. —*J.M.*

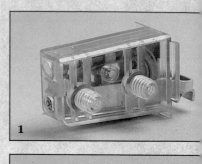

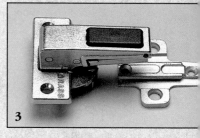

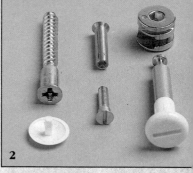

From *Fine Woodworking* magazine (November 1987) 67:57-61

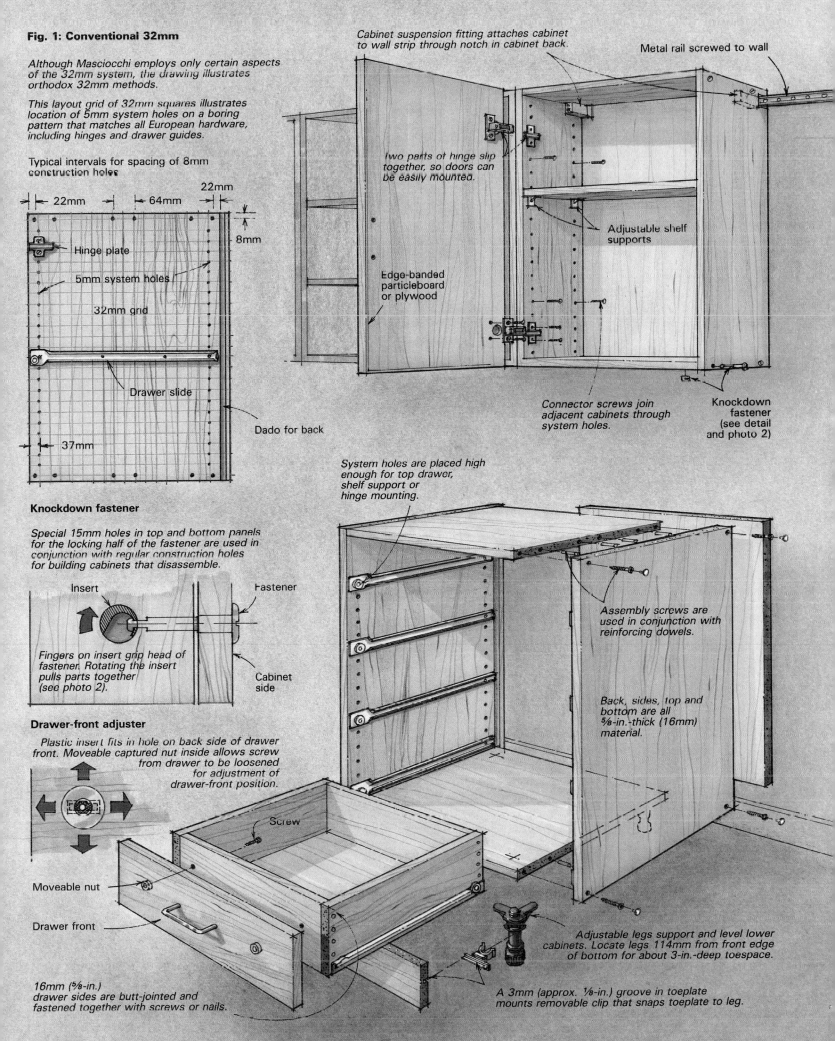

Fig. 1: Conventional 32mm

Although Masciocchi employs only certain aspects of the 32mm system, the drawing illustrates orthodox 32mm methods.

This layout grid of 32mm squares illustrates location of 5mm system holes on a boring pattern that matches all European hardware, including hinges and drawer guides.

Typical intervals for spacing of 8mm construction holes

22mm
64mm
22mm
8mm

Hinge plate

5mm system holes

32mm grid

Drawer slide

37mm

Dado for back

Knockdown fastener

Special 15mm holes in top and bottom panels for the locking half of the fastener are used in conjunction with regular construction holes for building cabinets that disassemble.

Insert

Fastener

Fingers on insert grip head of fastener. Rotating the insert pulls parts together (see photo 2).

Cabinet side

Drawer-front adjuster

Plastic insert fits in hole on back side of drawer front. Moveable captured nut inside allows screw from drawer to be loosened for adjustment of drawer-front position.

Screw

Moveable nut

Drawer front

16mm (⅝-in.) drawer sides are butt-jointed and fastened together with screws or nails.

Cabinet suspension fitting attaches cabinet to wall strip through notch in cabinet back.

Metal rail screwed to wall

Two parts of hinge slip together, so doors can be easily mounted.

Adjustable shelf supports

Edge-banded particleboard or plywood

Connector screws join adjacent cabinets through system holes.

Knockdown fastener (see detail and photo 2)

System holes are placed high enough for top drawer, shelf support or hinge mounting.

Assembly screws are used in conjunction with reinforcing dowels.

Back, sides, top and bottom are all ⅝-in.-thick (16mm) material.

Adjustable legs support and level lower cabinets. Locate legs 114mm from front edge of bottom for about 3-in.-deep toespace.

A 3mm (approx. ⅛-in.) groove in toeplate mounts removable clip that snaps toeplate to leg.

Computerized cabinetry

by Sandor Nagyszalanczy

Practically everything about the 32mm system of cabinetmaking is tailor-made for automation and computer-assisted manufacturing. So when I visited the Kochman Brothers' partially automated cabinet shop in Boston recently, I wasn't too surprised when we spent more time looking at a computer screen than at cabinets or machines.

Bill Kochman, formerly a computer troubleshooter, and his brother Jim, an experienced woodworker, set up shop about 11 years ago to make 32mm-system cabinetry. They were reasonably successful, but things didn't really take off until they invested in the kind of sophisticated 32mm machinery that makes it possible for even a tiny shop to build an enormous volume of casework. While 32mm will work at any level of involvement, the Kochmans believe that a shop shouldn't bother getting into the method unless the owners are willing to automate.

The Kochmans started with a basic ensemble of 32mm machinery to complement their regular equipment. For about $35,000, they bought: a sliding-table panel saw; a horizontal/vertical, 21-spindle boring machine; an edgebander; a hinge-boring and setting press; and a hydraulic case clamp. Later, they added a seven-spindle automated milling machine and a small network of computers to perform both computer-aided design (CAD) and computer-aided manufacturing (CAM). In the first year of computerized operation, the shop's productivity doubled. Last year, the Kochmans' business grossed close to

$1 million—a prodigious output for a shop of only 3,000 square feet and five people. I found it hard to reconcile the Kochmans' success with the fact that their shop had fewer machines than the average one-man furniture studio.

Computers connected to machines clearly improve productivity, but they also fundamentally alter the way work is done. Rather than handling the design and construction of each cabinet separately, the computer is programmed with all the possible cabinets and cabinet parts the shop produces, standardized and stored in digitized memory. Employing a complement of off-the-shelf and custom-programmed software and six personal computers (IBM PCs and an Apple Macintosh), Bill Kochman simply enters general information, such as choice of wood and style of doors, on a keyboard. He then specifies the type of cabinet and the dimensions of each. Moments later, the computer spits out finished drawings and plans, an itemized cut list and a cost estimate. If any specs change, he can produce an entirely revised plan—while the client waits.

The fun begins when the CAM system feeds all this data to "Big Al," the Kochmans' Italian-made, seven-tool Alberti computer-numerically controlled (CNC) milling machine. This machine handles all panel-boring and routing tasks with flawless accuracy, maintaining 0.5mm tolerances and allowing for minute variations in plywood thickness. Kochman says the computer can handle layouts and machining

that are "so complex to do normally, you wouldn't bother." He also advises anyone planning to do 32mm cabinets without CNC control to buy boxes of 5mm and 8mm plugs "to cover up all the system holes you'll drill in the wrong places."

Kochman's dependence on computers eliminates tedious layout work, but it places a burden on him to be dead-accurate with his initial dimensions and measurements. The computer won't specify cabinet parts that won't fit together into a finished case, but the manufacturing process is so devoid of manual setup that mistakes turn up only at the very end of the process, when the cabinet won't fit into the kitchen. In fact, the only task in the shop that requires human regulation and measurement is setting the rip fence to cut plywood and particleboard panels to size. Even that will change when the shop gets its new CNC vertical panel saw, now being custom-built in Japan.

Although all of this automated efficiency reduces labor costs and makes a 32mm shop potentially more profitable, it doesn't result in inexpensive cabinets. When all is said and done, the high cost of 32mm equipment must still be recouped.

After seeing John Masciocchi's and the Kochmans' shops, I was impressed but also sensitized to the shortcomings of 32mm construction. Specifically, the *process* of making 32mm cabinets is more exciting and intriguing than the cabinets themselves. The system does one thing, and does it extremely well, but at the cost of aesthetic variety and individuality. The Kochmans have addressed this issue by designing a line of cabinets with frame-and-panel doors and curved carcase sides, trading some efficiency for aesthetic variation.

Bill Kochman says another failing of 32mm cabinets is the complex concealed hinges that swing the closely mounted doors. The hinges make the seamless look possible, but they often sag and need to be adjusted to keep the doors from banging into each other. Kochman told me about one furnituremaker he knows who employs some 32mm methods, but who uses standard barrel hinges instead of concealed ones to avoid this problem.

Is the woodworker of the future destined to become a digitized craftsman, spending more time running a computer than making sawdust? I expect to see a lot more of the kind of woodworking automation that the Kochmans are using, though I don't think CAD/CAM technology will force the traditionally minded, one-of-a-kind woodworker to trade in his or her tablesaw for a PC. Still, if you can stand the pace, it's one way to build a profitable woodworking business. □

The key to automated 32mm production is the CNC milling machine. Its computer memory stores the complex patterns that allow the machine to perform hundreds of different boring and routing operations on cabinet parts.

Sandor Nagyszalanczy is an assistant editor at Fine Woodworking.

Wand" (part number 65.400.01), a jig for laying out holes. With it, I'm assured that all of the holes are correctly positioned so the hardware fits and the shelves don't wobble on their pins. The Magic Wand also accepts snap-on fittings that aid in accurately positioning hinge plates and drawer slides.

I bore the long rows of 5mm system holes (set 32mm apart, of course) with my linear, multiple-spindle drill-press attachment (see photo, right). I set the drill-press fence so the system holes are set back 37mm from the edge—a dimension that corresponds to the mounting requirements of the drawer slides and the concealed hinges for the doors. Before mounting any hardware, the panels are finished—either by spraying them with lacquer, or by brushing finish on the solid-wood edgebanding I sometimes apply to plastic-laminate panels.

Doors and drawers come next. An essential component of 32mm cabinetry is the concealed hinge. These rather complex devices mount inside the cabinet and allow door edges to almost touch when the doors are closed, giving Euro-style cabinets their seamless look. Concealed hinges have a compound opening action that pivots each door away from its neighbor, thus providing plenty of clearance as the doors are opened. The best thing about these hinges is that they're adjustable via screws that move the door in all three planes. Each hinge consists of two parts: a mounting plate that fastens to the carcase, and a cup-and-arm arrangement that fits into a round 35mm mortise bored into the door. The mounting plate screws right into the system holes bored during the drill-press operation, speeding along the otherwise time-consuming process of positioning each hinge on the cabinet individually. On cabinet sides that don't otherwise need system holes, I use a separate jig to locate the hinge plates individually.

Now it's time to bore the mortises in each door for the hinges' cup-and-arm assemblies. First, I first transfer the centerline from the carcase side to the door and use it to set the stops on my Blum hinge-boring and setting machine, which mounts on a second, smaller drill press in my shop (see bottom photo, right). This clever machine bores a 35mm hole for the hinge itself and a pair of 10mm holes for the screws that hold the hinge in place. Then, a pivoting insertion ram automatically sets the hinge in place. The hinge screws are fitted with plastic inserts similar to plaster plugs that allow the ram to push—not drive the screws into the door.

To mount the drawers, I use Blum bottom-mount slides (part number 230E) that require a ½ in. clearance on each side of the drawer. Thus, the drawers are 1 in. narrower than the inside width of the carcase; a separate drawer front, made of the cabinet's show wood, is screwed on later. The drawers themselves are simple boxes joined at the corners by nailed butt joints with a glued and nailed plywood bottom. Installing the slides on the carcase involves nothing more than locating the correct holes vertically and screwing the slide into the system holes. On a small job where it isn't economical to drill all of the system holes, I use another jig made by Blum ("Minifix," part number 65.220) to align the slides while I screw them in.

No matter how carefully the drawers are made and the slides are installed, minor adjustments must be made to align the drawer fronts after the cabinets have been assembled. This otherwise frustrating job is easily accomplished with the drawer-front adjuster shown in figure 1. This coupling device friction-fits into a hole bored in the drawer front. The front is then attached by screws driven from inside the drawer into the coupling, where a captured nut permits the front to be repositioned

The author uses 12 of the 18 drills on his line-boring drill press attachment to quickly bore rows of system holes on cabinet sides. The drill press's ingenious band drive rotates alternating drills clockwise and counterclockwise, thereby eliminating the need for elaborate gearing to drive the multiple spindles.

A low-cost drill-press attachment does double duty by boring three screw holes simultaneously and then pressing the hinge in place on the cabinet door.

and properly aligned before it's tightened down to final fit.

The real joy of 32mm is that all of these steps are done with the panels lying flat on the workbench. As soon as the hardware is installed, the carcases can be assembled, the doors hung, the drawer fronts attached and the final shop adjustments made. Since the panels are already finished (and have been since before the hardware was mounted), the cabinets are now ready to be hung. True to form, there are gadgets to speed installation, too, including leveling feet for lower cabinets and metal hanging rail systems for uppers. □

John Masciocchi is a furnituremaker, cabinetmaker and 32mm consultant in Portland, Ore.

Sources of supply

The following is a partial list of suppliers for 32mm hardware (H), machinery (M) and consultation (C):

Amcrock Corp., P.O. Box 7018, Rockford, IL 61125-7018 (H).

Julius Blum, Inc., Blum Ind. Park, Highway 16—Lowesville, Stanley, NC 28164 (H, M).

Jon Elvrum, Woodworking Technology & Training, 10052 Gravier, Anaheim, CA 92804 (C).

Grass America, Inc., 1202 Highway 66 South, Kernersville, NC 27284 (H, M).

Häfele America Co., P.O. Box 1590, High Point, NC 27261 (H).

Hettich America Corp., Box 7664, Charlotte, NC 28217 (H, M).

Holz-Her U.S., Inc., Box 240280, Charlotte, NC 28224-0280 (M).

Holz Machinery Corp., 45 Halladay St., Jersey City, NJ 07304 (M).

Mepla Inc., P.O. Box 1469, High Point, NC 27261 (H, M).

Ritter Manufacturing, 521 Wilbur Ave., Antioch, CA 94509 (M).

SCMI Corp., 5933 Peachtree Ind. Blvd., Norcross, GA 30092 (M).

Vacuum Jigs
Holding the work with thin air

by James L. Kassner, Jr.

Furniture manufacturers and short-run production shops are constantly searching for new, efficient ways to hold workpieces of all sizes and shapes for machining. Air clamps and lever-lock hold-downs are often slow and clumsy—they frequently get in the way while machining, making it necessary to reclamp the part several times. An alternative that's rapidly gaining wide acceptance in production workshops (although it's still rarely considered in smaller shops) is vacuum-pressure workholding. With these systems, the holding force is sufficient to solidly lock down a piece for routing, shaping or turning. Vacuum systems can be turned on and off quickly for part changes. They also flatten thin, warped material, and leave the top and edges of the workpiece exposed for machining, obstruction-free. Often, you can completely machine a part without reclamping it, thus eliminating a source of error in machining.

Vacuum jigs are fairly simple to make. They're also durable, and can be adapted to a home shop. A typical system (see figure 1) consists of a vacuum pump connected by a hose to a plywood or particleboard jig outfitted with an assortment of holes, grooves and gaskets. A groove is routed into the face of the jig, just inside the periphery of the area where the workpiece will rest. A special soft-rubber gasket (channel seal) fits into this groove to form an airtight seal between the workpiece and the jig. The workpiece is placed on the jig, and the pump is turned on to suck the air out from under the part. The force exerted by atmospheric pressure on top of the part locks it firmly to the jig.

A vacuum jig usually carries the work into a blade or cutter, or locks the work in place while the cutting tool comes to it. The jigs tend to have low profiles, since the suction is applied to the back of the workpiece. We use vacuum jigs with computerized routers on production runs of wooden clock parts, but the jigs also work well with low-tech machines: shapers, drill presses, lathes or pin routers.

Building a vacuum system is expensive—you need a vacuum pump, plumbing, fittings and related hardware. However, your work volume may be sufficient to justify the expense—especially since the system can be used for other operations, such as vacuum-veneering panels (see pp. 100-101).

From *Fine Woodworking* magazine (September 1987) 66:72-75

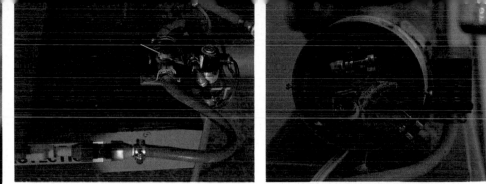

Left, the vacuum system is supplied by a 30-gal. tank and a 6.2 cfm pump driven by a 1½-HP motor. The large Bourdon pressure gauge is seen on the front of the tank, with the vacuum pressure gauge below it. The inlet filter is mounted near the tank's back, above the pump. The oil lubricator is positioned above the pump, and the exhaust filter is mounted to the right. The check valve is barely visible behind the inlet filter. The vacuum dump valve (above, left) applies or releases vacuum to the jig. The valve connects to both the pump and the jig with ½-in. ID radiator hose. A close-up of the Bourdon gauge (above, right) shows the needles that read the high and low setting for the vacuum pump. The pump is activated and switched off as vacuum rises above and falls below prescribed levels.

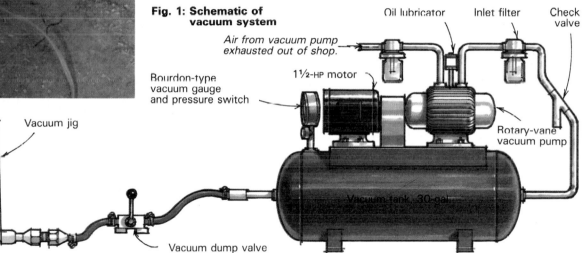

Fig. 1: Schematic of vacuum system

Air from vacuum pump exhausted out of shop.

Oil lubricator Inlet filter Check valve

Bourdon-type vacuum gauge and pressure switch

1½-HP motor

Rotary-vane vacuum pump

Vacuum jig

Vacuum tank, 30-gal.

Vacuum dump valve

Vacuum pumps are classified by the manner in which they move air: rotary-vane, piston, diaphragm and blower models are common. Rotary-vane pumps—either lubricated or oil-less—are best-suited for vacuum-holding work. All vacuum pumps are rated in two different ways: by the maximum vacuum they can create under zero air flow, and by the vacuum they produce at a specified air flow. The vacuum attainable from any vacuum pump is steadily reduced as the air flow in cubic feet per minute (cfm) increases.

Within the scope of your budget, my advice is to buy a vacuum pump with as high an air-volume-handling capability as possible. Rotary-vane vacuum pumps can range from 1 or 2 cfm to hundreds of cfm. Remember that wood is porous, so air will leak into the vacuum system through the pores in the workpiece. Additional air is drawn through leaks in the jig itself. In order for the pump to sustain a fairly high degree of vacuum under the workpiece in the presence of substantial air leakage, the pump must be rated for a reasonably high vacuum at a substantial air-volume flow rate. Our pump is a Gast, Model 2565, rated at 6.2 cfm at a vacuum pressure of 20 inches of mercury, or about 9.5 psi of vacuum-gauge pressure. This capacity enables us to handle four or more vacuum forms simultaneously on our computerized router. For the average small shop, a pump in the 3-to-6 cfm range should be sufficient. These pumps cost roughly $400 new, but they can be purchased used for $50 to $150 and then be reconditioned.

I think lubricated-type pumps are better than oil-less pumps for woodworking applications because they handle more air and generate slightly higher vacuum pressure. Lubricated pumps are also better able to handle the dusty air that's inevitably sucked into the vacuum system.

Like air compressors, vacuum systems work better when they're equipped with a tank (see photo, above left) that provides reserve capacity so the pump doesn't have to run full-time. The tank's extra capacity also helps handle the air-flow surge when the vacuum is turned on and the part is sucked down tight. We use a 30 gal. tank, but a smaller tank would undoubtedly work just as well on a less elaborate system.

A word of warning: Ordinary compressor tanks should *not* be used on vacuum systems. Tanks under vacuum may collapse if they're slightly out of round, so they must be made of heavier-gauge metal than compressor tanks. Air tanks rated for 400 psi or more should be suitable for vacuum applications.

Almost any kind of piping can be used to connect the system's components. I've had good results from ¾-in. ID galvanized steel and copper pipe. Seal all of the threaded joints with Teflon tape, which makes the joints easier to disassemble than when standard joint cement is used.

We install an ordinary brass, water-type flapper check valve (available from any plumbing-supply shop) to separate the pump from the reservoir tank. The valve prevents the reservoir from being bled down due to back leakage through the pump when it isn't running. The valve also allows the pressure to equalize across the pump so, once the pump is turned off, it doesn't have to start again under full load. The check valve should be positioned so its flapper hangs vertically. Grease applied around the

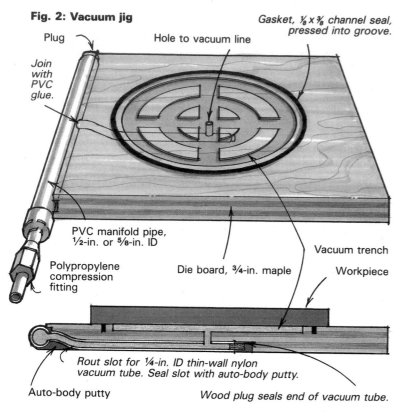

Fig. 2: Vacuum jig

Plug

Join with PVC glue.

Hole to vacuum line

Gasket, ⅛ x ⅜ channel seal, pressed into groove.

PVC manifold pipe, ½-in. or ⅝-in. ID

Polypropylene compression fitting

Die board, ¾-in. maple

Vacuum trench

Workpiece

Rout slot for ¼-in. ID thin-wall nylon vacuum tube. Seal slot with auto-body putty.

Auto-body putty

Wood plug seals end of vacuum tube.

Fig. 3: Universal vacuum jig

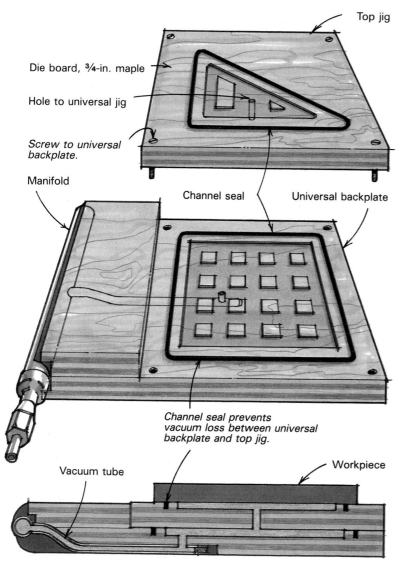

Top jig

Die board, ¾-in. maple

Hole to universal jig

Screw to universal backplate.

Manifold

Channel seal

Universal backplate

Channel seal prevents vacuum loss between universal backplate and top jig.

Vacuum tube

Workpiece

flapper helps seal it against leakage, but also necessitates frequent maintenance, since the grease collects wood dust.

The inlet filter located between the tank and the pump (see figure 1) also helps keep dust out of the pump. Due to the low pressure in the vacuum tank, wood dust that enters the system through pores in the workpiece during machining rapidly settles out in the tank. However, it's advantageous to use different tank outlets for the vacuum pump, the line to the vacuum jig and the pressure control. This gives the dust an even better chance to settle out in the tank, and lets the pressure control do its job more reliably. The filter on the exhaust port or muffler helps trap and collect lubrication oil mist in the glass jar. Venting the muffler's output outdoors via a garden hose keeps oil mist out of the shop air and greatly reduces workshop noise.

The most important routine maintenance item on the lubricated-type vane pump is to maintain the oil level with #10-weight detergent oil in the lubricator. Each filling should last for around 25 to 60 hours of operation. More rapid oil consumption does no harm; it simply exhausts more oil mist into the air.

As woodworking goes, making vacuum jigs is relatively simple. There are two different types of jigs. The simplest—designed to hold a specific workpiece—is shown in figure 2. If you need to hold several types of workpieces, I suggest you build the universal jig shown in figure 3. The beauty of this jig is that you can build one or two of the bases, then make as many custom formboards to fit on top as you want. You remove the formboard by loosening a screw or two, then replace it with another board that's shaped to the requirements of a different workpiece or a different operation. This eliminates the problem of building the more complicated base for each workpiece or operation. If I had to build my jigs over again, I'd build more universals and fewer single-purpose models.

If you were able to create a perfect vacuum under the workpiece (impossible to do, because of inevitable air leakage), the full weight of the atmosphere would bear down on it at 14.7 psi at sea level. The difference in the pressure above and below the work is described as ''differential'' or ''gauge'' pressure and is expressed in psi or inches of mercury. Vacuum pumps and gauges are most often rated in inches of mercury, not psi. However, psi is easier to convert into pounds of holding force, using this equation: Holding force (lb.) = area (sq. in.) × gauge pressure (psi). (In preparing your calculations, consider 15 psi roughly equivalent to 30 in. of mercury.)

As an example, assume the air pressure is about 15 psi, which—give or take a pound or two—will be the case in most parts of the world. A typical high-volume vacuum pump will remove enough air from behind the workpiece so that about 9.5 psi of air is bearing down on it. Multiply this gauge pressure by the area inside the gasket sealing the workpiece—let's say 10 sq. in.—and you have about 95 lb. of force holding the workpiece.

A typical jig setup is shown in figure 1. A trench cut into the top of the jig distributes the vacuum over the area of the part, and the vacuum dump valve serves as a ''switch'' to apply vacuum to the jig or to release it.

I recommend the use of ¼-in. nylon or rigid PVC tubing on these jigs. Polyethylene, polypropylene, Teflon and Tygon tubing can't be glued to anything, but nylon and PVC can be fastened to the formboard with epoxy, PVC cement or auto-body putty. Before assembly, sand the outside of the tubing so the body filler can grip it. Apply PVC pipe cleaner on the ends of the tubing, on the tubing's connections to the manifold and around the holes bored in the manifold. Then, glue the tubing to the manifold with PVC glue. Build up three or four layers of the glue so that it forms a substantial connection between the tubing and the manifold. Cement the manifold and the tubing in place with body filler after the glue has dried. The last step is to sand the bottom of the jig to make it as flat as possible. After all, it's the reference surface for your work.

Also, use ½-in. ID (or smaller diameter) automotive radiator hose to connect the jig to the vacuum system. This hose is flexible enough to allow the jig to move freely.

The best materials for jig bodies are Baltic birch plywood, hard maple die board and medium density fiberboard (MDF). The main requirements are that the material remain flat and be dimensionally stable. This rules out solid wood, which is prone to cross-grain expansion and contraction with the rise and fall of humidity. MDF is suitable for formboards subject to moderate wear and tear. It has relatively little adhesive binding the wood fibers together, so it tends not to retain threaded inserts very well when they're used frequently. Also, intricacies in the formboard tend to crumble with heavy use. MDF is extremely porous. After the vacuum trenches and the gasket grooves are cut, seal the whole jig with shellac to minimize vacuum leakage. Shellac plugs the pores thoroughly, while even multiple coats of other finishes don't. You can also buy ¾-in. MDF that's veneered on both surfaces. The veneered surface is pretty tight, but the interior remains porous.

A word of caution: MDF contains grit that quickly dulls ordinary high-speed steel bits, so cut the gasket grooves in it with a ⅛ in. solid-carbide bit. Cut the grooves in one pass, moving the bit in one direction. Don't backtrack, or you're liable to make the groove too wide for the gasket. The gasket groove should be at least ³⁄₁₆ in. from the edge of the vacuum trench. If not, the space between the trench and the groove might crumble.

Finnish or Baltic birch are good choices for jigs because both woods stay flat—even after machining to make the form. These birch plywoods are sold through hardwood supply houses and often through local lumberyards. Die board is a specially laminated hardwood plywood, the bulk of its veneer being hard maple. It's the most expensive, but it's also the most durable and it machines almost as cleanly as aluminum. Use only die board with five or more laminations. Jigs made from die board and most other plywood substrates are relatively nonporous when compared to particleboard. Thus, vacuum loss is less of a problem.

Die board can be drilled and tapped to accept coarse-thread machine screws, largely eliminating the need for threaded inserts. The direction of tapped holes should be perpendicular to the face of the board; threads tend to crumble in the endgrain. Use a standard metalworking tap and blow the chips out of the hole frequently during tapping. The threaded portion of the hole should be two or three times the diameter of the screw in length to provide adequate grip.

Even if vacuum loss in plywood jigs is minimal, it's a good idea to seal them with wood sealer, such as those available through the "Sources of supply" listed at right. These thin sealers penetrate deeply and help harden wood threads, making them more durable (although the hole may need rethreading after the sealer has dried). For ease of operation and to save the threads, wax any screws that will be inserted and removed often. If there's a danger of running a cutting tool into the screw, use brass, nylon or at least unhardened cadmium-plated steel screws. Carbide router bits will cut through unhardened screws, usually without damage. Never use hardened-steel screws or hard-steel dowel pins on formboards. A router bit will shatter if it hits a hardened metal, throwing steel and carbide fragments around the shop at high velocities.

The author built a lathe and vacuum chuck to handle clock parts that need to be turned. The principle of the chuck is the same as for jigs: sufficient vacuum is applied through it to lock down the workpiece. However, the setup requires a ball-bearing fitting to allow the vacuum line to remain stationary while vacuum is applied through the spinning headstock.

All stops or components that might easily be damaged or need to be replaced should be held in place with screws. For maximum accuracy, use mild-steel or brass locating pins in addition to the screws. Wax the pins to make them easy to remove. Parts may slide horizontally on the jig when heavy cutting forces are applied by a router or shaper. Prevent this movement by gluing 100-grit, A-weight, open-coat sandpaper to a large area inside the gasket with Titebond glue (contact cement would be too flexible). The sandpaper will grip the part when it's pulled down on the form by the vacuum. If the completed part has one or more holes in it, these can be drilled first, and mating wood dowels can be positioned on the formboard to engage the holes. (It's not usually necessary to install a gasket around the dowel if it fits its hole well.) In addition to preventing slippage, this doweled construction provides accurate location.

Vacuum workholding need not be restricted to flat objects; curved surfaces can also be machined. Holding curved pieces simply requires a bit more ingenuity on the part of the craftsman in designing and making the jig. □

James Kassner, Jr. builds and sells wooden-clock-movement kits at Kassner Woodcraft, Inc., in Tuscaloosa, Ala.

Sources of supply

Occasionally, surplus pumps, vacuum gauges and assorted electrical control relays can be obtained through:
Arbce Sales, 313 North Morgan St., Chicago, IL 60607.
Herback & Rademan Co., 401 E. Erie Ave., Phila., PA 19134.

Complete vacuum systems, dump valves, vacuum gauges, rotary couplings and channel seal are available directly from:
Magna-Lock U.S.A., Box 7012, Rockford, IL 61125.

Die board:
Lenderink, Inc., Box 98, Belmont, MI 49306.

Baltic birch plywood:
Allied International, Box 56, Charlestown, MA 02129.

Sealer:
Nelsonite Chemical Products, Inc., 2320 Oak Industrial Dr. N.E., Grand Rapids, MI 49505.
Prillaman Co., Box 4024, Martinsville, VA 24112.
Guardsman Chemicals, 1350 Steele Ave. S.W., Grand Rapids, MI 49507.

Lift Cabinets

Remote-control devices open the possibilities

by Scott Peck

People have always been fascinated with electronic gadgets that at the push of a button make things happen. At my shop, Masters Furniture and Design, we capitalize on this fascination by creating remote-control, electric-power lift cabinets that raise their tops to reveal what's inside. Lift cabinets offer a challenge for the woodworker and a dramatic presentation for televisions, video and projection equipment, stereos and small bars, and for displaying collectibles, like the guns in the cabinet we built, which is shown on the facing page.

The principle of a lift cabinet is simple: A remote-control device, like the one used to open your garage door, sends a signal to a receiver that activates an electric motor. The motor drives the lift mechanism mounted in the cabinet, which raises an inner case and whatever's inside it. Concealing precious items within such a controlled-access cabinet has a variety of advantages: It offers excellent security for valuables and protection from children, as well as protection from the adverse effects of light and dust. In its closed position, a lift cabinet can function as a hall table, chest or credenza. Lamps, photos or small sculptures can be left on the top continuously, provided you have ceiling clearance when the lift opens. Because of the many possible variations of lift cabinets, I won't describe how to build a particular cabinet in this article, but rather will describe the basics of lift mechanisms, cabinet design and wiring considerations, to help you design your own remote-control lift cabinet.

Lift mechanisms—There are lots of different ways to raise and lower a cabinet vertically, using scissor lifts, electrically driven screws, or air or hydraulic cylinders. After searching the catalogs to see what's commercially available, we discovered several units that are specifically designed for lift cabinets. These electric lift units are light and compact, and run on regular 110v household power. Depending on which brand and model you buy, lifts can raise cabinets weighing from 175 lbs. to 2,000 lbs. from 8 in. to 21 in. high. Most models are available with or without a remote control. The biggest drawback of lift mechanisms is their expense, which ranges from about $300 to more than $5,000, depending on the weight capacity and maximum height of lift.

We buy most of our lift mechanisms from two West Germany cabinet hardware companies: Hafele America Co. (Box 4000, 3901 Cheyenne Drive, Archdale, N.C. 27263; 800-334-1873 or 800-672-4853 in North Carolina) and Hettich (Box 7664, Charlotte, N.C. 28217; 800-438-5939 or 704-588-6666 in North Carolina). Their lifts operate on a scissor-action principle, lifting a cabinet much as a scissor jack lifts an automobile for tire changes, but using an electric motor instead of muscle power. The Hafele unit is built with angle iron and is somewhat lighter and less expensive than the Hettich lift. The Hettich unit features strong, rectangular steel tubing, and its added weight and rigidity give it a great deal of stability in the raised position. This led us to choose a Hettich unit for the gun cabinet and other large-scale lift cabinets we've built.

Case construction—A lift cabinet requires two separate cases: an exterior shell, which is the visible exterior of the cabinet; and an interior case that can be raised and lowered by the lift mechanism. The basic components of a lift cabinet can be seen in the drawing on p. 82. The design of the inner case depends on its function. For example, it may house a television, stereo system, bar or display cabinet. It may also have shelves, drawers or storage spaces, as needed. This case may be any size, as long as its weight, plus the material it's designed to hold, doesn't exceed the lifting capacity of the mechanism. Also, the case must be laid out to distribute weight evenly over the lift mechanism, to avoid stability problems and vibration when the lift operates. This means that heavy items should be centered over the lift, and the lift should be centered inside the exterior shell. The inner case shouldn't be shorter than the maximum distance the lift mechanism will rise; otherwise, the mechanism will show when the case is raised all the way up.

The exterior shell should be proportioned to allow at least ¼-in. clearance all the way around the inner case. The height of the exterior shell must be great enough to house the inner case as well as the closed lift, which is about 5 in. high. The goal is for the top of the inner case and the exterior shell to be level on the assem-

Remote-control lift mechanisms, like the one shown here by Hettich, are compact, yet powerful enough to lift heavy cabinets for pop-up televisions, display cabinets and home-entertainment centers.

From *Fine Woodworking* magazine (May 1989) 76:76-79

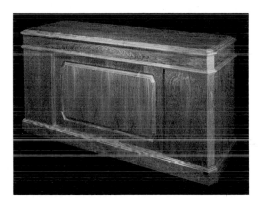

Disappearing gun display

The cabinet pictured above and right was designed to hold a matched set of shotguns. Its exterior shell is Honduras rosewood solids and panels veneered in Brazilian rosewood; the inner case is honeycomb panels veneered in Macassar ebony. Doors on the ends of the inner case allow access to the leather gun cases stored inside, and there are two flip-down shelves below the guns on the sides.

The cabinet holds four Holland-and-Holland double-barrel shotguns, two displayed on each side of the freestanding case. The guns, magnetically suspended from the mirrors, are engraved by Ken Hunt, with scenes depicting highlights of the Napoleonic era. The set includes more than 80 lbs. of leather, gold and ivory accessories, and is valued at $500,000. The cabinet was designed by myself and built by shopmate Jeff Reed at a cost of $16,000.   —S.P.

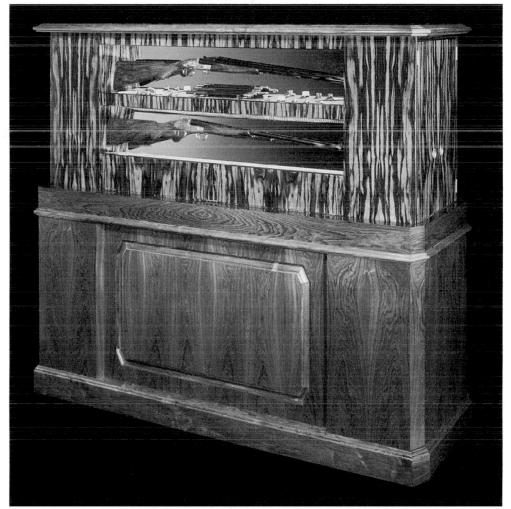

The author's custom gun cabinet is based on a remote-control lift mechanism, shown fully open above. When the cabinet is closed, above left, it hides and protects the expensive guns it was designed to house and display.

bled cabinet. The cabinet top attaches only to the inner case and raises along with it. By making the top overhang the shell by 1 in. or 2 in. on all show sides, slight misalignment between the top and shell won't be apparent when the top is shut.

Weight is probably the most important consideration when building a lift cabinet. A lift mechanism will raise the maximum load it's rated for, but the greater the load, the slower the lift. On smaller cabinets, we avoid heavy hardwoods and rely on strong frame-and-panel construction, reducing the thickness of case parts wherever possible. However, a larger case built this way is more subject to racking and lift-stability problems. We've found the best solution is to build the inner case and top with the veneered, honeycomb panels described in the sidebar on p. 83. These panels, which are similar in construction to torsion boxes and hollow-core doors, help the case retain its strength and stability while reducing its weight. You may use any materials or building methods you wish for the outer case, but on large cases, I've found it advantageous to use honeycomb-panel construction here as well. This weight reduction won't improve the performance of the lift, but it will save your back when the cabinet is moved.

Lift guides—Most commercial lift mechanisms tend to lack stability in the raised position. The extended scissor supports have very little lateral strength or resistance to wobble. The mechanisms may also vibrate while lifting or lowering. To prevent these problems,

especially in a large cabinet, you should build a guide system to stabilize the inner case. The system we came up with, shown in detail A on the next page, uses two nylon bearings that ride in tracks in the exterior shell. It works well and is not difficult to make or install. The guide bearing is a short section of ¾ in. nylon rod with one end chamfered and its center drilled with a stepped hole. You could instead substitute a short hardwood dowel lubricated with wax. A shoulder bolt secures this bearing to an angle-iron section screwed to the underside of the inner case. The bearing rides in grooves dadoed on the inside of the shell. The dadoes are about .010 in. to .015 in. wider than the diameter of the bearing and are stopped so they won't show when the inner case is raised. We leave two of the mounting holes on the angle iron bracket slightly oversize, to allow for lateral adjustment. Also, be sure the bearing bolt is fastened with a locknut: Lift vibration has amazing screw-loosening capabilities. To allow access for installing the guides on the inner case, cut out openings or trapdoors on the bottom or back of the shell. The openings also allow a malfunctioning lift to be serviced without removing the inner case (and its heavy contents).

After I began writing this article, the Auton Co. (Box 1129, Sun Valley, Calif. 91353-1129; 213-659-1718) sent me literature on a lift mechanism with geared tracks on each corner of the platform. I haven't tried the mechanism yet, but the manufacturer claims it eliminates the stability problems of scissor lifts and will support uneven loads of up to 600 lbs. (or more if custom-ordered).

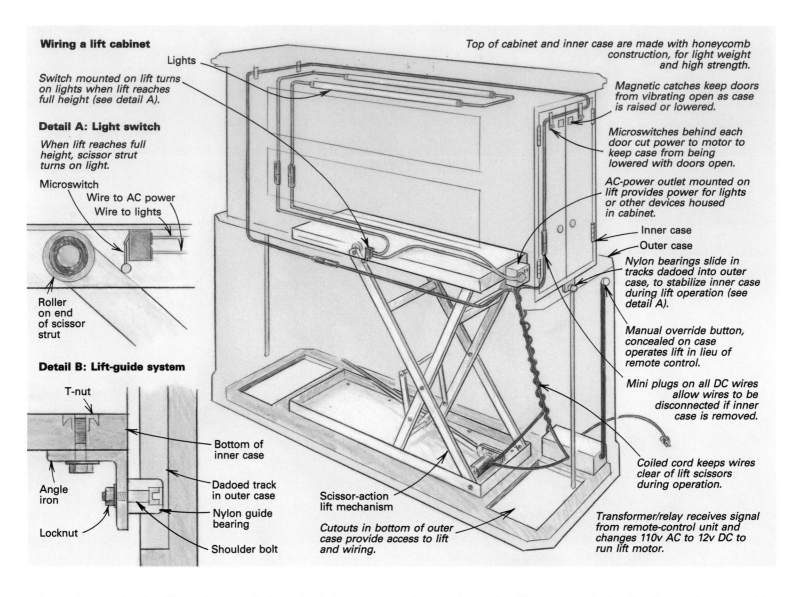

Wiring a lift cabinet

Lights

Switch mounted on lift turns on lights when lift reaches full height (see detail A).

Detail A: Light switch

When lift reaches full height, scissor strut turns on light.

Microswitch
Wire to AC power
Wire to lights

Roller on end of scissor strut

Detail B: Lift-guide system

T-nut

Angle iron

Locknut

Bottom of inner case

Dadoed track in outer case

Nylon guide bearing

Shoulder bolt

Scissor-action lift mechanism

Cutouts in bottom of outer case provide access to lift and wiring.

Top of cabinet and inner case are made with honeycomb construction, for light weight and high strength.

Magnetic catches keep doors from vibrating open as case is raised or lowered.

Microswitches behind each door cut power to motor to keep case from being lowered with doors open.

AC-power outlet mounted on lift provides power for lights or other devices housed in cabinet.

Inner case
Outer case

Nylon bearings slide in tracks dadoed into outer case, to stabilize inner case during lift operation (see detail A).

Manual override button, concealed on case operates lift in lieu of remote control.

Mini plugs on all DC wires allow wires to be disconnected if inner case is removed.

Coiled cord keeps wires clear of lift scissors during operation.

Transformer/relay receives signal from remote-control unit and changes 110v AC to 12v DC to run lift motor.

Wiring—The wiring for lift mechanisms isn't particularly complicated, but should be carefully planned before you start building. Following the drawing above, you'll see that there are really two kinds of wiring in a lift cabinet: 110v AC wiring and 12v DC wiring (drawn in orange). The lift motor runs on DC power delivered via a transformer/relay box, which receives AC power through a power cord plugged into a regular receptacle. Mounted next to the lift inside the shell (close to the openings, for replacing blown fuses), the box relays the signal to raise or lower the cabinet from either a remote-control unit or from a DC-wired, manual override button or key switch mounted in a discreet location on the exterior shell. An AC-power receptacle is attached to the lift itself, to supply power to appliances or lights in the inner case. This receptacle is connected to the power source by a heavy coiled cable designed to take up slack as the unit is retracted. The power cord from the relay box can be led out the back of most cabinets, but if the cabinet is free-standing, you'll have to consider how you're going to supply power to the cabinet. Two of our clients have ordered cabinets to go in the middle of a room, which required the electrical supply to be brought up from under the floor.

Interior lights can be installed inside the cabinet, provided you allow ventilation for bulb heat and follow safe practices for installing lights inside a wood enclosure (refer to building codes regarding enclosed fixtures). You can install regular on/off light switches inside the inner case, but our favorite trick is to use a hidden switch to turn the cabinet lights on and off automatically; the effect is very dramatic. Mount a microswitch, available from electrical-supply

houses, inside the lift as shown in the drawing, so the strut of the lift engages the switch only when it's fully open. Wire the switch so that when it's on it completes the power circuit to the lights.

Safety—A lift that's powerful enough to raise a big load is also powerful enough to cause potential harm, so there are a few precautions you should build into any lift cabinet. First, never bolt the inner case directly to the top of the lift. Instead, bolt a subbase to the lift with holes bored in it to receive short dowels on the bottom of the inner case, which keep the case in position. Next, if the inner case has doors or drawers, mount microswitches at each and wire them so that when they're open they break the circuit and cut power to the motor. These precautions are needed, because the force of an accidentally lowered lift is capable of crushing either a hand or a door that's left ajar. Also, anything that opens, such as a drawer, should have a magnetic or bullet catch to keep it closed, because vibration can cause things to open as the lift is rising.

The wires from the door and drawer switches all need to be run to the base. We've found tying these together and running them down the center of the coiled cable works well. Another trick is to have these switch wires connected with miniature plugs, available from electronic-supply houses, so you can still remove the case or power supply without having to remove both. □

Scott Peck is a furnituremaker and owner of Master's Furniture and Design in Denver, Colo.

Drawing: Roland Wolf

Honeycomb-panel construction

Honeycomb panels are incredibly strong, despite their light weight. We make ours by fitting a paper honeycomb into a frame, then gluing on a particleboard, fibercore or smooth hardboard skin. The panel is then veneered and edgebanded. The honeycomb core held in tension by the skin increases the panel strength tremendously, without significantly increasing its mass or weight. Honeycomb panels are not only ideal for lift cabinets, but for any big furniture, such as executive desks and conference tables, where weight, strength and a perfectly flat surface are a concern.

Industry has long used honeycomb construction as a weight-reduction technique for a variety of products, from hollow-core doors to featherweight aircraft parts. And, the technique isn't outside the reach of most craftsmen with access to some sort of press. Here I'll briefly outline the materials and procedures involved in making a honeycomb panel and point out some ways a small shop can produce high-quality panels.

Materials: Honeycomb cores are available in many materials, including paper, plastics, foams and metals. I've found corrugated-paper honeycomb to be economical and more than adequate for cabinet and furniture-making purposes. Paper honeycomb is available from The Norfield Corp., 36 Kenosia Ave., Danbury, Conn. 06810; (203) 792-5110, and from Verticel Inc., 4607 S. Windermere, Englewood, Colo. 80110; (303) 789-1844. The material comes in large sheets of plain or resin-coated paper in a variety of specifications. We've found that the higher the cell density, the stiffer the panel. The resin-treated paper yields the strongest, premium panel, but the less-expensive, untreated paper is fine for most applications.

For skin material, we prefer to use medium-density fiberboard (MDF). Although we occasionally use smooth hardboard, we typically use ¾-in.-thick honeycomb and face both sides with ¼-in. to ½-in. MDF, depending on the final desired panel thickness. For thicker panels, you can double or triple the honeycomb as long as the layers are separated by another skin layer. Skin materials thinner than ¼ in. are not recommended, because the honeycomb core will tend to telegraph through. Veneers glued to both sides of the panel provide the final surface and can be of whatever type of wood suits the project.

Because honeycomb panels receive edgebanding, you can use particleboard

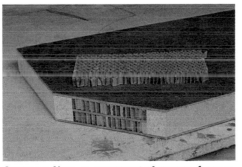

Surrounding a corrugated-paper honeycomb material with a particleboard frame and sandwiching it between layers of MDF, smooth hardboard or particleboard creates a strong, rigid and lightweight panel.

or any kind of wood for the panel's frame, as long as you make sure the stock is dry and dimensionally stabilized to your climatic conditions.

Construction: The first step in making a honeycomb panel is to build a frame that will surround the core material. The thickness of the frame members equals the honeycomb skin thickness. Frame width should be proportional to panel size and thickness: For a panel 2 ft. by 4 ft., we typically make a 2-in.- or 3-in.-wide frame. We prefer plate-joining the frame together, but you can use any joinery you like. Make the frame slightly oversize, so you can trim the panel to final size after it's been glued up. Besides an outer frame, you must add crossmembers to your frame that span the hollow parts wherever joinery will attach the panel to other panels or frame members. Also, add crossmembers in large panels every few feet, for additional strength and stiffness.

Because the strength of honeycomb construction depends on the edge of the paper bonding perfectly to both interior faces of the skin, close tolerances in frame thickness are crucial for a successful glue-up. If the outer framework is even slightly thicker than the honeycomb, you'll have little glue bond between the skin and the honeycomb near the frame, seriously weakening the panel. If the frame is thinner, the fragile edges of the paper honeycomb will bend when the skin is pressed on, again weakening the panel.

After the wooden framework is ready, the honeycomb is pieced into the frame to a friction fit. We usually cut the pieces we need from sheets we keep in stock, and if larger or irregular-size pieces are needed, we just fit in additional pieces. Edge-gluing the pieces together or into the frame is un-

necessary, because the panel gains rigidity through the honeycomb's vertical corrugations, not its horizontal stiffness.

Glue-up: The filled framework is now ready to be sandwiched between the outer skins, which have been trimmed to the same size as the frame. Coat the inside surfaces of both skins with a film of aliphatic-resin (yellow) glue applied with a short-napped roller. The sandwich is then assembled and placed in a veneer press until the glue dries overnight. If you are using a hydraulic or air-powered press, the pressure should be set a lot lower than if you were laminating a solid panel of the same size. This is because the actual surface area of the paper corrugations being bonded to the skin is relatively small.

Before applying the face veneers to the panel, you need to true up the skin to remove any surface distortion resulting from thickness variation in the different layers. We do this with a large thicknessing panel sander equipped with an 80-grit belt. If you don't have or can't rent time on such a sander, a high-speed orbital sander, such as the Porter-Cable 505, is capable of sanding a near-perfect, true surface…if you replace its sole. To do this, remove the felt pad and replace it with a square of ¼-in.-thick double-tempered hardboard cut to the same size. Scribble all over the surface of your panel with the side of a pencil. Then, lightly sand the surface with 100 or 120 grit, and you'll quickly see if you have any low spots. If you do, sand until true. This trick also works well for the first stage of final-sanding any veneered panel.

Veneering: The trued panel is now ready for veneering, which can be done anyway you choose, though our shop uses a large veneer press. After the veneering, the panel is trimmed to final size with a jointer, router or tablesaw. The edgebanding is then glued on and shaped as needed. All that remains is to cut the slots or mortises, or to bore the holes for the joints that attach the panel to the cabinet. It's best to keep a drawing or some record of where the crossmembers are, in case you need to cut joinery or mount hardware somewhere in the center of the panel. Finally, make sure to finish the honeycomb panel as you would any veneered panel—the same way on both sides. You'll enjoy working with the reduced weight of honeycomb panels, and they'll add a more high-tech element to spice up your work. —*S.P.*

Coopering
Curved panels from solid wood

by Skip Sven Hanson

C oopering, the creation of part or all of a cylinder from flat wooden staves with beveled edges, is most often associated with the art of barrel making. But for centuries, the techniques of the cooper have been used for the construction of lids, doors, and curved panels in fine furniture.

There are other methods for making curved panels. Thick timber can be carved to shape, but this method is wasteful, limits the choice of woods, and yields a potentially unstable panel. Laminating veneers over a curved form is a great improvement, offering precision, stability and repeatable results. But, what if the panel edge is to be molded? What if you prefer (as I do) to work in solid wood? Now the first choice is coopering.

Coopered panels, framed and unframed, make fine chest lids and cabinet doors. The simple chest with framed, coopered lid, shown at right, is a good coopering project for the novice. It is built from the coopered panel out, because of the unpredictability of the finished panel's radius. A small error in the bevel, repeated in each of the 20 or so strips, can result in a panel wildly different from the original drawing.

Because of the many glue joints, a grainy wood, like oak or ash, is a good choice for the first-time cooper. The labor-to-materials ratio is very high, so save your motorcycle crates for another project and use the finest piece of wood you can afford for this panel. A lid is such a prominent feature of a chest that you should also consider bookmatching boards resawed from a thick plank. Coopering can be safely done with stock as thin as ⅝ in.

Begin by drawing a full-scale section, showing the panel's arc and finished thickness. When selecting wood, add 25% to the panel height and 50% to the width, measured on the arc, for waste. Lay out the stock for the best match of grain and figure, then cut the boards to length and joint all edges. Reassemble the pieces and draw a large triangle that bridges all the pieces. This serves as a witness mark for keeping the pieces in order. Check again to be sure the stock is still at least 25% wider than the finished arc.

The width of the strips should be between 1 in. and 1½ in. The exact width should be chosen to maximize use of the boards and, this is very important, so the grain matches at the edges. Strips less than 1 in. wide are more work, more waste and more dangerous to machine. Strips much wider than 1½ in. require removal of a lot of stock to create a true arc. Draw chords equal to the strip width onto the panel section (figure 1), to make sure the width you've chosen gives you a panel approximately the size you want; if not, adjust the width accordingly. Remember that the actual panel will probably vary somewhat from your drawing.

Rip the strips to the chosen width plus ¹⁄₁₆ in. allowance for jointing, then place each in order on a workboard. With a soft

Coopered panels are a useful solid-wood alternative to laminated panels for curved work. They can be mounted directly, or they can be framed, as Hanson did for this chest lid.

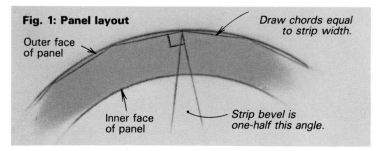

Fig. 1: Panel layout

Outer face of panel

Draw chords equal to strip width.

Inner face of panel

Strip bevel is one-half this angle.

pencil, number the ends of the strips and draw a line below each number to indicate the inside surface of the panel. At this point, it's best to sticker the strips for one or two weeks in a warm, dry spot, to let the wood's moisture content equalize with the atmosphere. If you skip this step, I recommend that you move like a bat out of Hell all the way through the glueup.

After stickering, reassemble the strips on the workboard, then joint a face of each and surface them to the same thickness. Do this one-at-a-time off the workboard and you won't waste a lot of time finding the pattern again. Then redraw the triangle on the face.

Next, at the intersection of two chords on the drawing, draw two lines, one perpendicular to each chord, as shown in figure 1. Measure the angle between the perpendiculars, as carefully as you can, with a protractor. Divide this angle by two to get the bevel angle.

To bevel the strips, set the jointer fence tilting into, not away from, the tables. Tilting the fence in permits you to joint strips already glued-up by running the outer, convex face against the

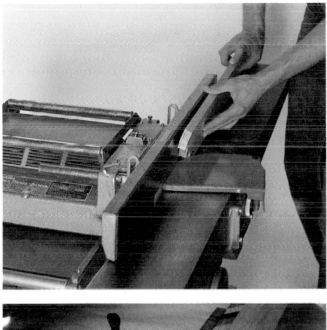

Tilting the jointer fence in toward the tables to bevel the strips allows you to joint glued-up segments (top left). When jointing narrow single strips, brad awls make good push sticks. After beveling, glue up pairs of strips, then pairs of pairs, and so on. As the glued-up segments get larger, use larger clamps to assemble them, as shown at bottom left. Dark strips are clamping cauls, which protect the strip edges. The final glue joint is on the panel's center-line. A combination of clamps and weight is usually necessary to draw the joint tight on both the inner and outer faces of the panel (right).

fence, as shown above, left. Bevel both edges of each strip, as well as about eight clamping cauls, 1-in. by 1-in. strips of scrap, the length of the strips. For safety, I push single strips across the jointer using two brad awls, one in each hand, as push sticks. Check the fit of each pair of strips, pairing them either side of the centerline.

The strips are glued in pairs, then groups of four (two pairs), and so on, with the final assembly on the center joint. Apply yellow glue to the edges of a pair of strips and clamp with C-clamps. Protect the edges with cauls, then clamp evenly, carefully, and with medium pressure. Scrape off squeezed-out glue and inspect the joint immediately, altering pressure as needed to eliminate gaps on either face. When the glue has set, place the pairs in order on the workboard. Glue any odd strips onto an already glued-up adjacent pair.

Next, glue pairs into fours and, after the glue has set, glue the fours into eights. Rejoint the edges if a dry fit shows a gapped joint. When C-clamps won't fit, use bar or pipe clamps, as shown

above, bottom left, scraping squeeze-out, inspecting and adjusting pressure as necessary. With a highly arched group of eight or more, you may need to weight the pieces in the middle or stretch a band clamp across, anchored to the center bar clamp, to get a tight joint. As you proceed, avoid gluing a small unit onto a larger group—say, a pair onto eight—so glue on odd segments as soon as the even segments have set up.

To glue the center joint, I use bar clamps, quick-action or C-clamps and weights if necessary. First check the fit dry, rejointing and adjusting the clamps until the two halves are positioned perfectly. Use a mirror and flashlight to see that the joint is tight, both inside and out. If it's not perfect now, it won't be later

I roll a medium coat of glue onto both edges with an engravers' brayer. I put the halves back in position on the clamps, pin the ends with 2-in. C-clamps if necessary, add the smallest amount of pressure on the bar clamps, and place the other clamps or weights in a way that will still allow me to inspect the joint, as shown above, right.

Plane panel edges, then use a squared-up piece of flexible material to scribe a line on the panel end square to the good edge.

Getting the joint tight on the outside is easy. If you want the inside perfect, too, you've got to remove dripping glue with a gooseneck scraper, inspect with the flashlight and possibly the mirror, and adjust the clamps until the joint is closed nicely along its whole length. When the joint is just as you want it, let it set up overnight; 30 minutes is not enough for a joint held under such light pressure. The next day, early, scrape off the glue with the gooseneck scraper.

Shape the inside surface with a gooseneck scraper and a shaped sandpaper block. Pencil lines drawn across the width, spaced every inch from top to bottom, help keep you aware of where you've removed wood, and keep you from removing too much. I remove glue and rough out the shape with the scraper, then move to a 2-in. by 2-in. by 6-in. sanding block, shaped to the radius of the inside curve. Start with 100-grit paper, sand until tear out and pencil lines are gone. Redraw the pencil lines, move to 150-grit paper and repeat the process. I use an orbital sander with a foam base to work fine sanding grits, say 220 and up for oak.

On the exterior face, plane the joints down with a sharp, finely-set plane to a fair curve, or shape with 100-grit sandpaper on a flat sanding block. As on the inside face, pencil in 1-in. spaced lines across the grain, and move through the grits again, backing the paper with a flat block.

To square-up the panel, place it concave-side-down on a flat surface and mark the high corners. Plane the edges until the panel no longer rocks. To square an end, cut a piece of flexible sheet material (thin plywood, plastic laminate, posterboard) perfectly square. Attach one edge of the sheet flush with the best edge of the panel and wrap the sheet over the surface, as shown above. Scribe the end, bandsaw and plane to the line. Reverse the sheet to do the other end of the panel. If the panel is slightly wider than you'd like, joint the waste off an edge. If it's considerably wider, bandsaw the waste then plane, making sure the panel doesn't rock on a flat surface.

Measuring from the completed panel, you can construct the box or cabinet to suit the actual curve. Sometimes I field the panel and mount it directly; sometimes I enclose a fielded panel in a frame, as for the chest lid. I field a curved panel with a router, a piloted bit and a router sub-base shaped to match the curve of the panel (see figure 2). The sub-base provides a stable bearing surface for routing the edges, as well as the ends. It should be 2 in. wider and 7 in. longer than the router base. Remove most of the waste from the sub-base blank with multiple tablesaw cuts,

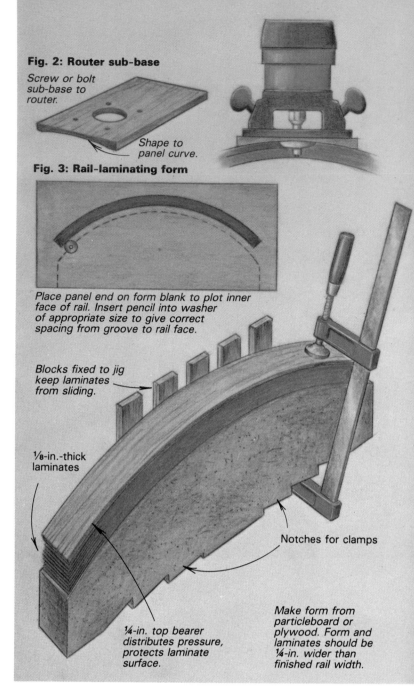

Fig. 2: Router sub-base

Screw or bolt sub-base to router.

Shape to panel curve.

Fig. 3: Rail-laminating form

Place panel end on form blank to plot inner face of rail. Insert pencil into washer of appropriate size to give correct spacing from groove to rail face.

Blocks fixed to jig keep laminates from sliding.

⅛-in.-thick laminates

Notches for clamps

¼-in. top bearer distributes pressure, protects laminate surface.

Make form from particleboard or plywood. Form and laminates should be ¼-in. wider than finished rail width.

scrape and sand to match the panel curve. In use, keep a steady hand and take several shallow cuts rather than one deep one.

In addition to considerations of appearance, framing the panel has definite structural advantages. Like any piece of solid wood, a coopered panel will expand and contract with the seasons. A frame will help keep the radius of the panel's curve from altering with seasonal movement, as well as concealing from view changes in the panel's width due to movement. The straight members, or stiles, are identical to those of a flat frame. The other pieces, the rails, must be curved to match the curve of the panel; I make mine by laminating ⅛-in.-thick strips on a form, like the one shown in figure 3. When making the rail-laminating form, remember to add the length of the tenons and a generous allowance for waste.

I join rails and stiles with a double open mortise and tenon (also called a double bridle joint), and house the panel in a groove, as shown in figure 4. After you square-up the rails and stiles, cut them to length. Figure length just as you would for a flat-panel frame, remembering to allow for panel movement across the grain.

I cut the double bridle joint on the tablesaw with a flat-top,

From *Fine Woodworking* magazine (January 1986) 56:36-39

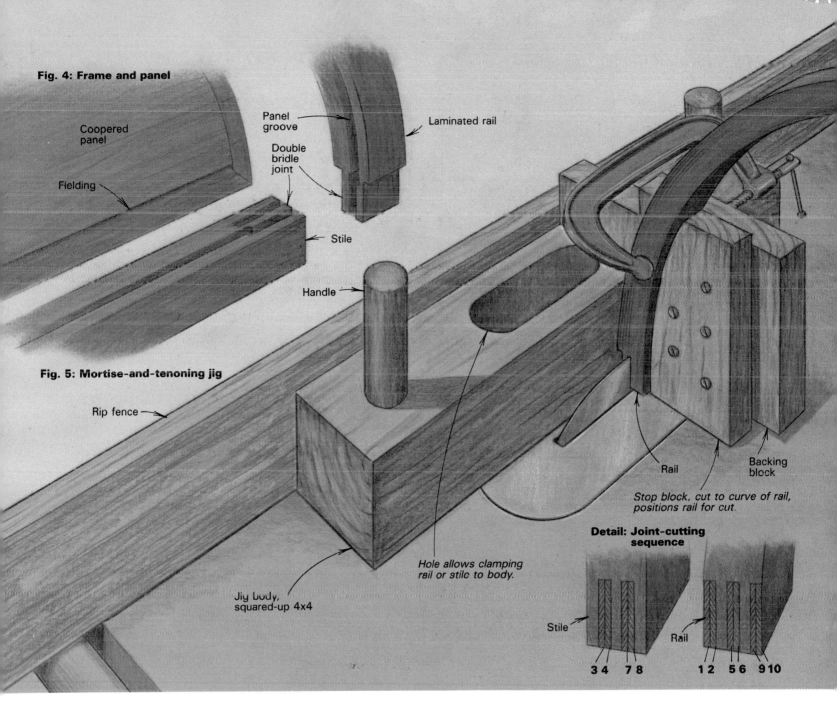

Fig. 4: Frame and panel

Coopered panel

Fielding

Panel groove

Double bridle joint

Laminated rail

Stile

Fig. 5: Mortise-and-tenoning jig

Rip fence

Handle

Hole allows clamping rail or stile to body.

Jig body, squared-up 4x4

Rail

Backing block

Stop block, cut to curve of rail, positions rail for cut.

Detail: Joint-cutting sequence

Stile

Rail

3 4   7 8   1 2   5 6   9 10

chisel-tooth carbide rip blade and a simple jig (figure 5), made of a squared up 4x4, a support for the curved rail and two handles. I make the tenons and mortises of equal thickness, about one-fifth the thickness of the rails and stiles, and cut the tenons on the rails. With a marking gauge, set-out the joint on two pieces of scrap the thickness of the rails and stiles, and use these to set the saw.

The sequence of cuts for making the joints is shown in figure 5. I use the scrap to establish and check the rip fence position before each new cut, then cut all four ends before resetting the fence for the next cut. The first cut is made on the outer faces of the curved rails, the rip fence positioned so the blade just skims, but doesn't cut, the face of the jig. After completing cuts 1 and 2 on the first tenon, move the rip fence away from the blade by the thickness of a saw kerf, to make the first mortise cut on the straight stiles (cut 3). Be sure to check against the scribe marks on the scrap before cutting the stiles. Remember to work from the outside face of the stiles, as well as the outside face of the rails. Continue to alternate from tenons to mortises, as shown, until the joints are finished.

Clear the waste and clean up the shoulders with a chisel if

necessary, assembling the joints to check the fit. Clamp a simple wooden fence, cut to the panel curve, to a router to make the panel grooves. Remember to make the grooves deep enough to allow for panel movement. Plunge the bit into the rails and stiles in the area of the mortise or tenon so that any tear-out at the beginning or end of the stopped cut will be hidden. If you prefer to be able to remove the panel, you can rabbet the frame parts with a piloted bit; the panel is held in place by thin fillets screwed to the frame. Fillets can be glued-up on the rail-making mold as a single, wide ¼-in.-thick piece, then bandsawed to width.

Finish-sanding the rails and stiles, and finishing the panel before gluing up, helps minimize clean-up problems. I glue up the frame first in two L-shaped sections, let them cure, then complete the assembly. Make sure that the panel slides easily in the grooves before the final glue-up. A little candlewax in the grooves near the joints will keep squeezed-out glue from adhering the panel to the frame. When the framed panel is complete, you can make the box to fit its size and curves exactly. □

Skip Sven Hanson, founder of the Albuquerque Woodworkers Association, builds custom furniture in Albuquerque, N. Mex.

Hexagonal Table From Buckled Burl

A new approach to an old pressing problem

by Preston Wakeland

When I was approached by a customer to build a hexagonal table with an elm burl center and walnut trim, I decided on a pattern of triangles whose points would all meet in the center, as shown in the photo below.

Carpathian elm burl veneer is tricky to handle because the sheets are almost always badly buckled and puckered. This makes it impossible to lay out a pattern on the sheets and cut them to exact size. The traditional way of using such veneer is to flatten the slices first, as described in the box on p. 24, then cut the required triangles and tape them all together before veneering. Because burl veneer has grain running in all directions, it is very flaky. The prospect of flattening, cutting and taping 12 matched triangles without losing at least one crucial chip seemed very remote to me.

I decided to try an experiment which, I've since found out, is not entirely my own invention, although it isn't common knowledge either. I laminated the buckled veneer directly onto a ¼-in. fiberboard substrate, then cut the laminated pieces to the necessary shape with a router. I found that the technique makes the traditional flattening step unnecessary, provided that the veneers are not too dried out and brittle and that grain direction is random. Most burl can be laminated down quite well without pre-flattening, but some feather-figure veneer would probably crack up the middle. You can test pieces by trying to flatten them by hand. If they resist too much, dampen and flatten them first.

Once mounted, the backed-up veneers not only resist cracking and chipping, but the router's high-speed action makes cutting a breeze. The process is a little more complicated than conventional methods, but more than one book I have on veneering warns that making several pieces of veneer come together at a point is a difficult task, if not impossible. With this system it's relatively simple.

I began by selecting a grain pattern on the flitch that I thought would look good matched up, then I cut 12 consecutive pieces. It is not important at this stage what shape and size these pieces are, as long as they are big enough to cover the design. Mine, in fact, were rectangular. I arranged the slices as six sets of book-matched pairs and numbered the sheets in the order they came from the flitch.

After selecting the pieces for the face, I cut an equal number for the back of the substrate, using a less attractive area of the same flitch. If both faces of the substrate are not laminated, the work will begin to warp almost instantly when removed from the press. I chose Fibercore (a 48-lb.-density fiberboard made by Plumb Creek, of Columbia Falls, Mont.) for the substrate instead of particleboard or plywood because I couldn't afford any chipping, no matter how small—any chip might take some of the surface veneer away with it. Fibercore has the texture of hardboard, a uniform thickness throughout the sheet and comes flat, not warped.

I use plastic resin glue for veneering, and I bend one cardinal

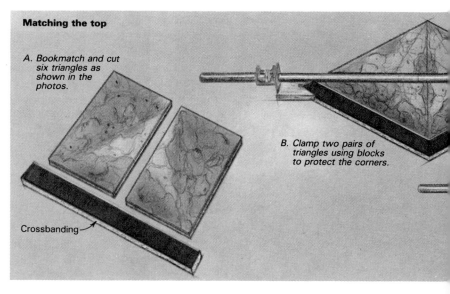

The finished surface of this burl-top table shows no evidence of its multi-layer construction.

Matching the top

A. Bookmatch and cut six triangles as shown in the photos.

B. Clamp two pairs of triangles using blocks to protect the corners.

Crossbanding

From *Fine Woodworking* magazine (November 1985) 55:88-90

At top left, unflattened veneer sheets are laminated onto ¼-in. substrate in a small press made from a solid-core door. Particleboard spacers separate the layers. To rout the first seam, left, clamp the pieces and cut both sides of the seam in one pass, guiding the router against one of the clamp strips. Above, cut the sides of the triangles in two passes, the first with a guide bushing to rough-cut about ⅛ in. from the line, the second by running the flush-trim bit directly along the guide board.

rule because I always apply a very thin coat of glue to the veneer itself, as well as a heavier coat to the substrate. I first apply glue to the substrate with a short-nap roller, then as the roller starts to dry out, I give the veneer a pass—it flattens enough under the pressure to be evenly covered. I take great pains not to get the veneer too wet, because too much moisture would cause it to expand in the press, then shrink and crack after the job was finished. If I don't have enough glue on the roller to get even coverage, I pick up some from the thin layer on the substrate, not from the pan. Using this method I have never had trouble with bubbles or loose edges, and my veneer has never yet cracked from excessive shrinkage.

Instead of my veneer press, which would have been cumbersome to load with so many small pieces at once, I made a press from two halves of a solid-core door and some particleboard spacers. It is imperative that waxed paper be placed between the veneer and the parts of the press, because elm burl is so porous and so full of small checks and cracks that some glue certainly will seep through (the defects are eventually filled with colored wood putty and sanded level). I glued the pieces up in a pair of stacks in the press: first waxed paper, then the bottom veneer with the substrate and the face veneer, then waxed paper and a particleboard spacer. And so on. I then applied pressure with bar clamps and let the whole works sit for 24 hours.

When I removed the pieces, I set them on edge for a day or so

to dry thoroughly. They must not be allowed to lie flat during this time, or moisture will escape faster from one face than the other, causing the pieces to warp.

The first step in bookmatching the tabletop was to make six pairs of matched panels to be cut into equilateral triangles. To cut the first seam, which would end up along the altitude of each triangle, I rough-sawed the joint about ⅛-in. oversize on the tablesaw, then set up to make the final cuts with a new carbide flush-trim router bit. To guide the router, I clamped the two panels as shown above in the lower-left photo. One of the clamp strips is a straight fence located so that the router bit runs down the middle of the seam, cutting about ⅛ in. from each side. With this system, any irregularities are cut into both pieces at once, and the seam closes up with very little pressure during gluing.

When the glue dried, I had six irregularly shaped rectangles with a nifty bookmatched seam up the middle. I used the tablesaw to square the pieces at a right angle to the seam, and glued on my 2-in. walnut crossband trim, which I had laminated to Fibercore in the same manner as the burl.

When these joints were dry, I laid out the other two sides of each triangle so that the baseline would be a tiny bit longer than the sides. This was to ensure that the two halves of the tabletop could be trimmed with the router without removing any of the triangles' points (see step D in the drawing below). I cut the sides of the triangles by laying a straightedge directly on

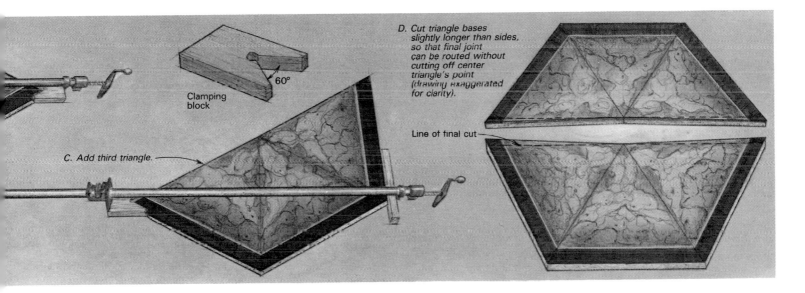

Clamping block

60°

C. Add third triangle.

D. Cut triangle bases slightly longer than sides, so that final joint can be routed without cutting off center triangle's point (drawing exaggerated for clarity).

Line of final cut

Rejuvenating veneers

by Ian Kirby

Spectacular crotch, burl or wild-grain veneers are sometimes so badly buckled, cracked or brittle that they seem practically useless. But such veneers are too beautiful to pass up, especially if you can buy them at bargain prices. Veneer suppliers are often eager to get rid of small parcels of abused-looking veneers and cut-offs from much longer, flatter slices. If you can flatten this stuff, you can create spectacular effects by joining the pieces together end-to-end or with some type of multi-match method.

Veneers become brittle and buckled because of drying out, poor storage conditions and age, but you can rejuvenate them. The usual way is to introduce moisture into the veneer at a very slow rate, in order to increase its flexibility, then to flatten it and allow it to dry under pressure.

You'll need a clean, flat, moisture-resistant work surface—plastic laminate is fine, but you can use a table or floor covered with a plastic sheet. You'll also need a pad of newsprint paper, an inch or so larger than the veneer, and a spray bottle full of clean water. Be sure to use clean newsprint, not your daily newspaper, or you'll get ink all over everything.

Dampen the newsprint and the veneer with a very light spray. Then stack the veneer sheets with two or three sheets of newsprint between each slice. Enclose the entire stack in a plastic sheet, then allow two or three days for the moisture to be absorbed by the veneer.

To test the veneer, lay a piece onto a flat surface and carefully try to flatten it by hand. In some cases, the veneer may resist being pressed or make cracking sounds, it which case it is not yet ready. If necessary, repeat the moisture treatment. Don't try to hurry the process. Raising the moisture content of the material without getting it too wet is a slow process. It's a fine line between sufficient and too much. The result of too much is mildew, which may permanently discolor the veneer.

When the veneer is sufficiently flexible to be pressed, the excess moisture is removed. Stack the veneer with three or four sheets of dry newsprint between each leaf and apply sufficient weight or pressure to flatten the stack. The newsprint will gradually wick the moisture from the veneer. Check the stack's progress after two days, and replace the newsprint with fresh, dry sheets if it seems necessary.

You might have to repeat the treatment a third time, but eventually, the veneer will be dry enough to use.

Now that you have workable sheets of veneer, don't leave them out in the open where they will quickly buckle again. Put a sheet of newsprint between each slice, wrap the whole package in plastic and store it on a flat surface under weight.

An old technique for handling buckled veneer was to size it with a dilute glue solution and glycerine before flattening. This method is messy and has never seemed to me to be worth the trouble.

It has long been the practice with fragile veneers to glue them onto a sturdier backing veneer such as African mahogany or poplar. Even after the pieces of veneer are glued together, store them under pressure on a flat surface.

This whole process isn't as long-winded as it may sound—it's a little work over a long period—and the net result is that you end up with some beautiful and usable material. □

Ian Kirby is a designer, educator and cabinet-maker in Cumming, Ga. He has written a number of articles on veneering for Fine Woodworking *magazine.*

A little water, patience and pressure can transform bumpy veneers (bottom three sheets) into workable material (top sheets).

the marks, then first routing a rough cut using a bushing. To make the final cut to the line, I simply removed the bushing and allowed the bit's shank to bear directly against the straight-edge. After gluing the triangles together using 60° corner blocks as shown in the drawing, I matched the two halves of the top the same way.

The glued top at this stage was about ⁵⁄₁₆ in. thick, and I was prepared to treat it like a pane of glass. Yet when I tested some of the scrap-wood glue joints they turned out to be very strong. I sanded the back so that all surfaces were flush, then laminated the top to a piece of ¾-in. particleboard. The rest of the table was made in a conventional manner using particleboard and walnut veneer fastened with plastic resin glue.

I have used this system several times now, and have come away with the following conclusions: Bumpy veneers require no flattening, thus eliminating the addition of extra moisture into the veneer. Splitting and cracking from cutting are eliminated even when cutting to a sharp point. Differences in veneer thickness can be dealt with by simply putting the faces flush when gluing up the seams. Laminating small pieces first reduces the need for a large veneer press.

I don't pretend that all veneering should be done this way. Certainly, conventional methods are faster and easier most of the time, but for me it provided a very slick way out of what could have been a very sticky situation. □

Preston Wakeland is a full-time cabinetmaker in Lockport, Ill. Photos by the author.

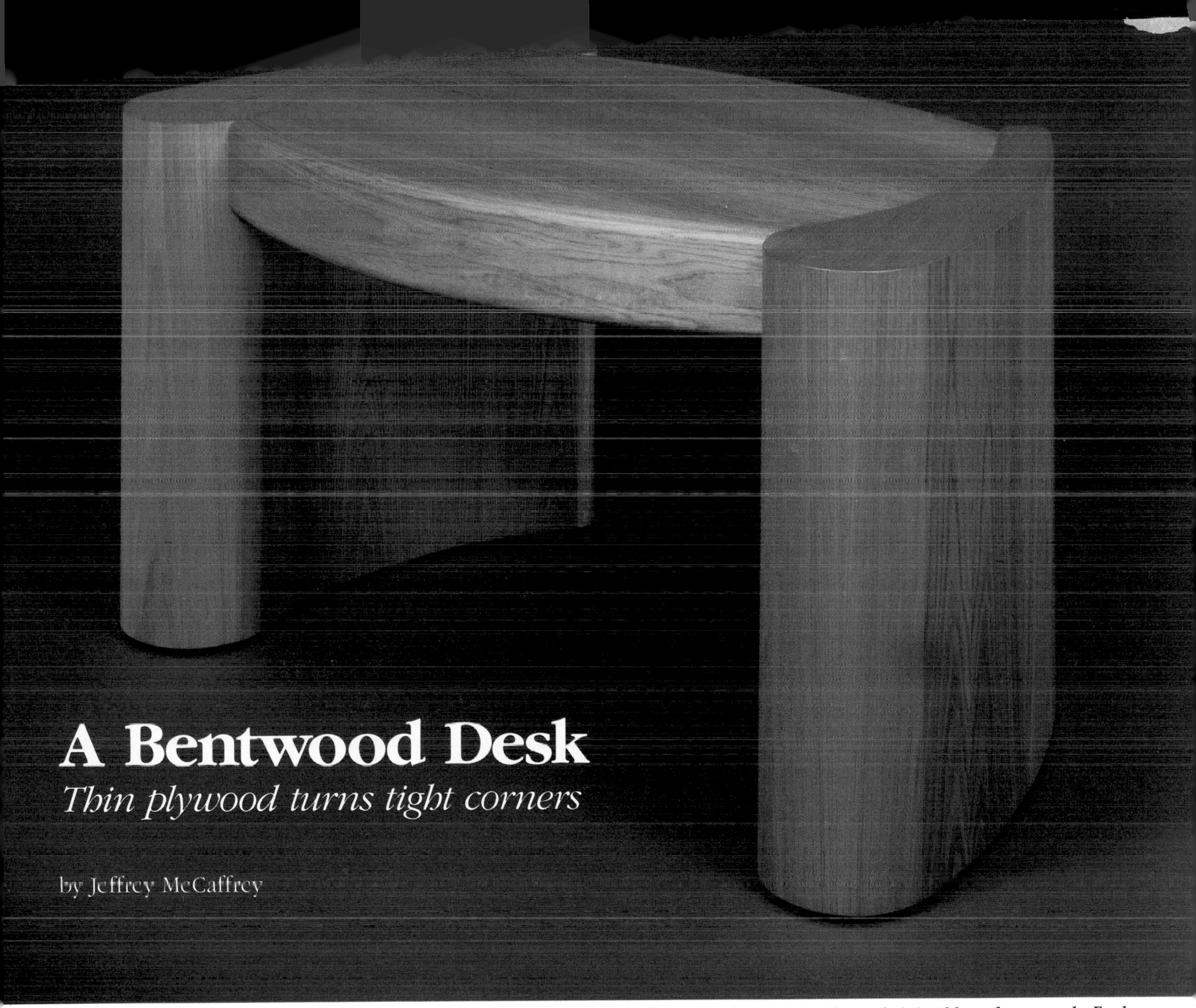

A Bentwood Desk

Thin plywood turns tight corners

by Jeffrey McCaffrey

Author's writing desk suggests solid wood, but it's actually constructed of lightweight, bentwood panels joined by a framework. Each of the desk's two columns consists of three separately bent panels.

I've been working with bentwood since I was a student. For me, it presents an opportunity to create unusual furniture while tackling processes not yet learned—a combination of careful planning and blind ignorance that I find both stimulating and humorous. Like most woodworkers, I learned to bend wood by gluing up thin strips of it around a form. Shaped and joined, these glued-up curves became components of larger structures, perhaps a chair or a curvilinear casepiece.

It was a natural progression for me to widen the strips until it was no longer practical to use solid wood. At this point, I began using ⅛-in.-thick plywoods and my bends became curved planes instead of curved lines. This expanded my design vocabulary to include furniture like the desk shown above. It consists of hollow, monolithic volumes joined together to make a form impossible or impractical to achieve in solid wood. The desk's upright columns are hollow volumes, each made up of several, separately bent panels. They are extraordinarily rigid yet light enough to be easily moved.

In principle, bending plywood panels is a lot like bending solid strips using conventional form lamination. Plywood has some important advantages over solid wood laminae, however. First of all, it's available in sheets at thicknesses suitable for bending so you can skip the tedious, dusty job of resawing thick boards into thin ones. For most applications, plywood will bend to a tighter curve than will an equivalent thickness of solid wood. The columns of my desk, for example, are bent to a radius as small as 4-in. To get away with that in solid wood, the strips would need to be ¹⁄₁₆ in. thick, which is asking a lot of your resawing technique, not to mention requiring twice as many laminae.

Though they aren't sold in a wide variety of species, ⅛-in.-thick plywoods are usually available from local lumberyards or plywood suppliers in oak, ash, walnut and cherry. One supplier here in Portland sells a two-ply ³⁄₁₆-in.-thick lauan plywood capable of bending around a 3-in. radius. Some suppliers sell three-ply bending plywood which consists of a core of soft, bendable basswood faced with another species. Probably the best bargain in bending plywood is the ⅛-in. lauan plywood sold by lumberyards as doorskins for hollow-core doors. If you need a thick bent panel, lay up a core of cheap lauan faced with an outer veneer of nicer wood.

So plywood sheets won't warp, manufacturers generally lay up

Photo: Jim Piper

odd numbers of plies. It's probably good practice to follow this rule where possible, but sometimes an odd number of plywood sheets won't add up to the final panel thickness desired, while an even number will. In this case, I go ahead and use an even number. In laminating multiple sheets, two face plies glued to each other with the grain running in the same direction become, in effect, one ply. Thus, for purposes of stability, two three-ply sheets behave as one five-ply.

Forms for bending panels are more demanding to build than those for bending solid strips. Because they are larger, there's more chance of introducing errors that could produce a twisted panel, so it's important to draw and measure carefully. Your project may require more than one simple curve, in which case you'll have to make a series of bends and then join the parts. Segment the curves wherever it seems logical to do so. I try to divide the curves so the forms and panels will be of manageable size, and so I can clamp with downward pressure only. Lateral clamping makes things too complicated. However divided, you will need a form for each separate curve.

As the photo at right shows, my two-part forms consist of a series of particleboard ribs sawn to the desired curve then mounted on a backing board which keeps them in correct alignment. For accuracy, I make up two templates for each series of ribs—one for one half of the form and the other for the nesting or mating half. I begin with a full-scale drawing of my piece on paper or poster board. I transfer the curves to ¼-in. hardboard, from which I bandsaw out the first template, smoothing lumps or quick turns with a file.

To generate the mating template, set a compass to the desired panel thickness, allowing room for a liner between the form and each side of the bundle of plies. I use a piece of ⅛-in. lauan for a liner. Place the first template on a fresh piece of hardboard and trace the outline for your second template with the compass. Bandsaw, then file the profile fair. For form ribs, I use 1-in. particleboard. It's harder to find than ¾ in., but the extra thickness reduces the number of ribs needed and distributes pressure more evenly. Use the templates to mark out the ribs, then bandsaw close to the line. To finish, screw or tack the template to the rib blank and trim to the line with a flush-trimmer bit in your router or router table.

To assemble the form, place the ribs on a flat surface, curved-side up. Slip a ¾-in. scrapwood spacer between each rib, align the ribs and clamp-up the assembly. Flip the whole thing over and screw a squared piece of particleboard or plywood to the rib backs. This will keep the form from shifting into a parallelogram under clamping pressure.

Now comes the fun part: gluing and clamping. After spending several days planning and building forms, it's thrilling to see if it all works. A dry clamp-up is advisable. This will turn up any problems and you'll find out if you have enough clamps and cauls. For a typical 24-in.-wide panel, you'll need six 4x6 battens the length of the form, three on top and three on the bottom.

If everything checks out, spread glue on the plies (I use plastic resin glue) with a small paint roller. Before laying up the bundle, put a piece of paper between the liners and the bundle so there's no chance of smeared glue sticking them together. As you build the stack, align the long edge of each ply with the edge of the form. This will give you a straight reference edge for ripping the panel to width later. Also, make sure to put the good ply or veneer on the correct side of the bundle. I have an extra panel in my shop because I glued the good face to the wrong side of the bend. Apply clamping pressure first to the center of

Each bent panel requires its own form constructed of 1-in. particleboard ribs spaced ¾ in. apart and fastened together with battens and/or backing boards to keep them aligned. Stout cauls and heavy bar clamps distribute pressure evenly at glue up.

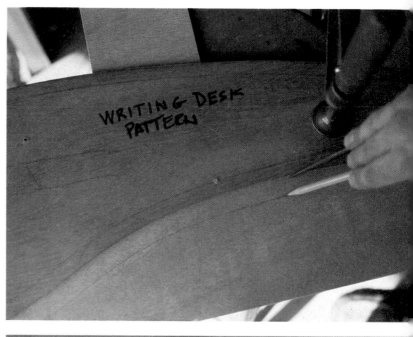

For fair, twist-free panels, ribs must be of consistent size and shape. McCaffrey marks out a template for the mating half of a form (above middle). Tacked to a particleboard blank, the template guides on the pilot bearing of a flush trimming bit, cutting the blank to final size (bottom).

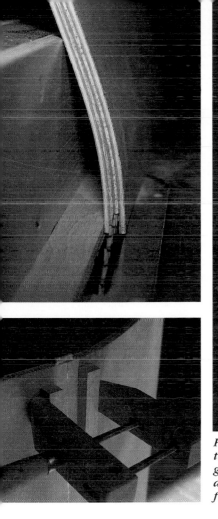

Plywood splines in tablesawn or routed grooves join bent panels together. Blocks temporarily tacked to the panel near the joint with hot-melt glue provide bite for handscrews. Scrap ⅛-in. plywood makes good spline stock. A framework of solid oak joins the desk's two columns, providing support for the top and a hanging surface for a drawer. Bent panels proved too thin for conventional joinery so McCaffrey fitted glue blocks around each frame member—in effect building a mortise around a tenon.

the form, then work outward. Check for inconsistent glue squeeze out, a tell-tale of uneven pressure.

After the glue has cured for 24 hours, I remove and clean up the panels. If one panel edge was held flush to the form, it should be no problem to scrape the glue and hand plane or joint the edge true. With that done, the opposite edge can be table-sawn parallel. Squaring the other edges is trickier. With a T-square, I mark a line along the rough edge then bandsaw to it, supporting the panel so the edge is as square to the table as I can get it. Hand planing checked with a square finishes the job. Actually, it's not as important that these edges be perfectly square as that they be true enough to join cleanly with another panel.

For joining bent panels together, splines seem to work best. If done carefully, a spline accurately aligns the surfaces of two adjacent panels, and it is more than strong enough for most applications. I have three methods to cut grooves for splines. The simplest is to pass the panel edge over the tablesaw, guided freehand against the fence. This is only practical for shallow bends and/or small panels, however. For larger panels, I clamp scraps to both sides of the edge being grooved. This provides a flat surface wide enough for a router and a fence to run against. If the panel is flat enough near the joint, run the router right on it, using a slotting cutter with a pilot bearing. Whichever method you choose to use, make sure that the groove is perpendicular to the edge being joined. Scrap ⅛-in. plywood makes excellent spline stock.

Clamping curved panels is always a challenge and some improvising will be necessary. If the panel assembly is a closed volume, such as the columns of my desk, band clamps might work perfectly. However, clamping blocks temporarily glued to the panels where the joints come together give more control. Cut scrapwood blocks about 1 in. square and 3 in. long. Attach them to both sides of the panels on either side of the joint with

hot-melt glue, as shown in the photo above. Insert the glue-coated spline, then draw the joint together with wooden hand-screws, which can pinch close to the surface without the handles getting in the way. Inspect the joint carefully. If you find any gaps, reposition the clamps to close them up.

Be careful when you remove the clamping blocks once the glue has cured. Hot-melt glue is stubborn stuff—if you try to knock off the blocks with a sharp hammer blow, chunks of the panel may come with them. A safer way is to split the block close to the surface with a chisel, then clean up the remainder with a plane and scraper, being careful not to plane through the show veneer, however.

Assembling bent assemblies into finished furniture calls for unorthodox joinery. The columns of my desk, for instance, are joined by a framework that supports the top and provides a place to hang a drawer. The columns are structurally strong but their walls aren't thick enough for proper mortise and tenons. One solution is to build up the wall thickness in the area of the joint, but I found it more practical (and fun) to mortise through one wall and extend the framework to butt against the opposite wall. It was then a simple matter to glue blocks around the framework, in effect building the mortise around the tenon.

Finishing the desk required some adroit router work. I capped the columns with Baltic birch plywood panels, cut with the aid of a template similar to that used for the form ribs. These caps were then veneered with white oak and another piece of oak-veneered birch plywood was fit between them to serve as the desk top. A shallow pencil drawer fitted beneath the top finished the project. □

Jeffery McCaffrey is head of the wood department at the Oregon School of Arts and Crafts in Portland. Photos, except where noted, by the author.

Bandsawn Veneer

Getting the most out of your precious planks

by Paul Harrell and Monroe Robinson

Colorado woodworkers Brad Walters and Richard Barsky have suggested using a single-point fence for bandsawing thick veneers from a plank. Here's a method we use at the College of the Redwoods. Instead of a single-point fence, we use a long, straight fence and fine blades to saw veneer to the finished thickness right off the saw, without planing or sanding. This gives more usable wood from a plank and it minimizes pattern changes from one veneer to the next.

Where Walters and Barsky recommend a wide, stiff blade, we prefer a narrower one. For sawing narrow veneers (up to 4 in. or 5 in.), we use a ½-in. blade with 6 teeth per inch and very little set. While this blade has limitations and is definitely not for production work, it will give the maximum number of veneers from a plank. For wider planks and resinous woods that may gum the blade, we use a skip-tooth blade with 3 teeth per inch and moderate set. A blade with too much set wastes wood because of the large kerf, and it leaves a ragged surface. With these blades, we get six to eight veneers per inch of plank. We rip wide boards before sawing the veneer. After sawing, the veneers are edge-joined to restore the full width. This produces a better surface with less waste than trying to saw 8-in. or wider planks.

Bandsaw blades almost always have some degree of drift or lead, that is, they won't cut straight if the board is fed at 90° to the front of the table. Drift is constant, so we adjust the rip fence to compensate for it. To find the drift of a particular blade, you will need a bevel gauge and a piece of wood approximately 2 ft. long and thick enough to offer some cutting resistance. Joint one edge of the board, then, with a marking gauge, strike a line on a perpendicular face of the board. With a slow, steady feed, start cutting down the line and try to find the angle of presentation that results in a straight cut. When you are sawing down the line easily without having to make any adjustment, switch off the saw and hold the board in place until the saw stops. The board is now positioned the way the saw wants to cut. Set your bevel gauge to the angle formed by the intersection of the board's jointed edge and the front edge of the table. Don't be surprised if the drift angle is 5° or more off the perpendicular.

Use the bevel gauge to set the fence angle. Position it as far away from the blade as you want your veneer to be thick, then clamp it at both ends. For most surfaces, we use a ³⁄₃₂-in. finished thickness. This is a very general rule, though. Vary the thickness to suit your application. Thick veneers from dense hardwoods, like ebony or rosewood, can exert stress on the core causing warping or cracking, so we cut these ¹⁄₁₆ in. or less. A veneered lid for a jewelry box laid up on a ¼-in. core, for example, will be more stable with ¹⁄₁₆-in. veneers.

We make our fences from Baltic birch plywood faced with plastic laminate to reduce friction and provide a long-wearing surface. It's good to have several fences of different heights. A 6-in. fence for wide boards, and a 3-in. fence for narrower ones will allow the upper blade guides to be brought down close to the work.

When sawing with a properly set fence, you don't have to steer the work at all. Apply steady feeding pressure with your left hand while your right hand pushes the work against the fence just in front of the blade. The smoothness and rate at which you feed is crucial. With a little practice, you can tell from the sound and feel of the saw if you are feeding too fast. The kerf will become erratic and wider if you are forcing the work. Going too slow can cause problems too (burning and wandering) and stopping in the cut almost always results in an uneven veneer. Try to maintain a smooth, steady feed from start to finish. If you're getting uniform veneer, there's no need to surface plane the board between cuts. Minor irregularities can be handplaned before the next cut. A smoothly bandsawn surface is adequate for gluing, and the show side will be handplaned after the veneer is glued to the core.

To edge-glue the veneers before pressing them, we hand-plane the edges on a shooting board, laying the plane on its side as shown in the lower left photo on the facing page. If you are going to make a veneer shooting board, make it with an inclined ramp for the work to rest on. This will allow a fuller width of the plane iron to cut on each pass. To get the best control over pattern matching, we plane one veneer at a time, removing the minimum wood from each. Once matched, we glue up the veneers in the jig shown in figure 1. Ten or fifteen minutes in the jig is long enough for the glue to set, during which time you can shoot the edges of two more veneers.

The process of fine veneer work is time consuming and so should be used when it offers possibilities that justify the extra effort. When deciding whether to use veneer or solid, remember each demands a different style of construction and each gives its own feel to a piece. The clean, refined lines veneer imparts may be ideal for a piece like the cabinet shown here, but on a kitchen table that will get hard use, a solid wood top may better suit both the style and the use of the piece. □

Paul Harrell and Monroe Robinson are graduates of the College of the Redwoods woodworking program taught by James Krenov in Fort Bragg, Calif.

From *Fine Woodworking* magazine (May 1986) 58:44-45

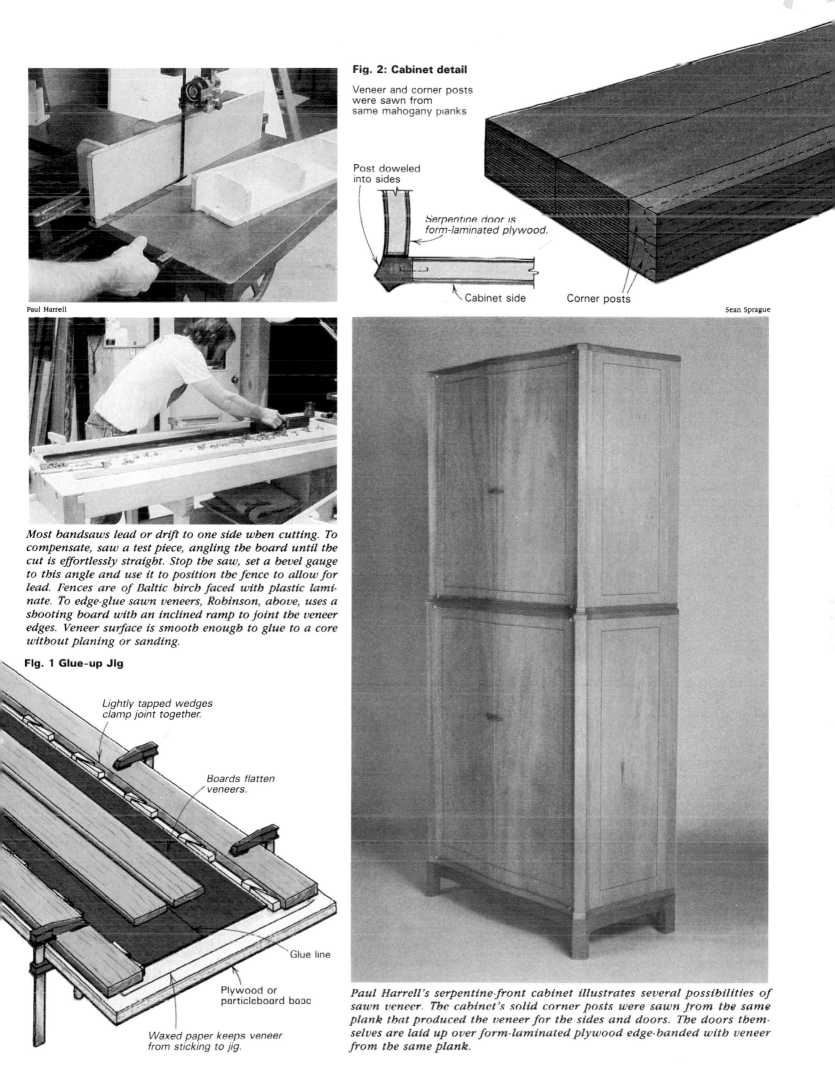

Fig. 2: Cabinet detail

Veneer and corner posts were sawn from same mahogany planks

Post doweled into sides

Serpentine door is form-laminated plywood.

Cabinet side

Corner posts

Paul Harrell

Sean Sprague

Most bandsaws lead or drift to one side when cutting. To compensate, saw a test piece, angling the board until the cut is effortlessly straight. Stop the saw, set a bevel gauge to this angle and use it to position the fence to allow for lead. Fences are of Baltic birch faced with plastic laminate. To edge-glue sawn veneers, Robinson, above, uses a shooting board with an inclined ramp to joint the veneer edges. Veneer surface is smooth enough to glue to a core without planing or sanding.

Fig. 1 Glue-up Jig

Lightly tapped wedges clamp joint together.

Boards flatten veneers.

Glue line

Plywood or particleboard base

Waxed paper keeps veneer from sticking to jig.

Paul Harrell's serpentine-front cabinet illustrates several possibilities of sawn veneer. The cabinet's solid corner posts were sawn from the same plank that produced the veneer for the sides and doors. The doors themselves are laid up over form-laminated plywood edge-banded with veneer from the same plank.

Wrapping the Edges

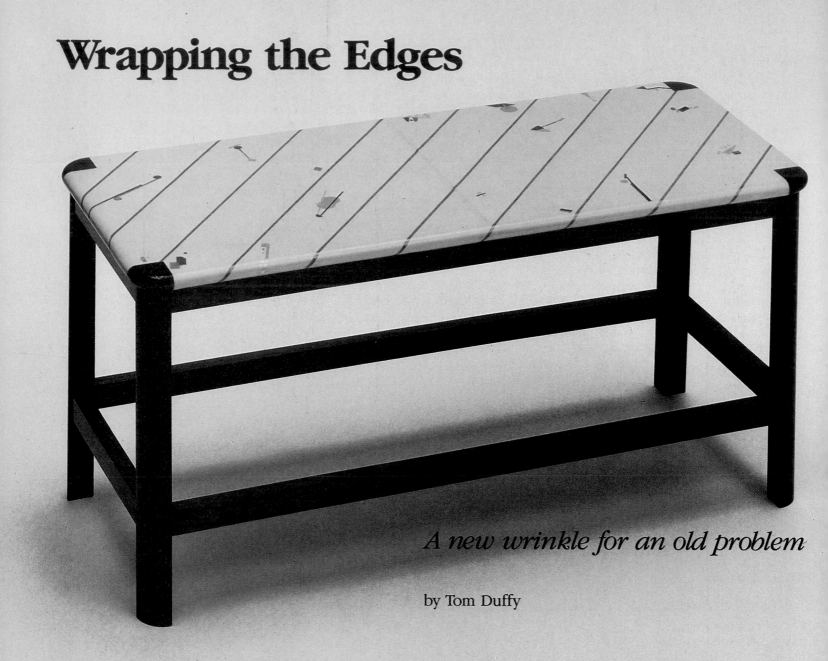

A new wrinkle for an old problem

by Tom Duffy

Tom Duffy's solution to the problem of edge treatment on a veneered panel was to bend the veneer around a bullnosed edge. Positioning the holly veneer strips diagonally allowed him to treat all four edges the same.

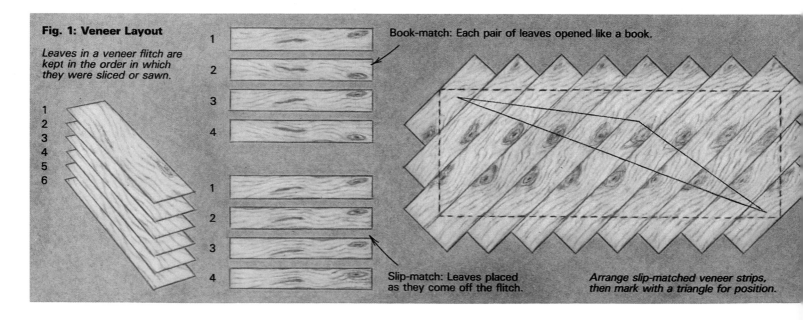

Fig. 1: Veneer Layout

Leaves in a veneer flitch are kept in the order in which they were sliced or sawn.

Book-match: Each pair of leaves opened like a book.

Slip-match: Leaves placed as they come off the flitch.

Arrange slip-matched veneer strips, then mark with a triangle for position.

Photo this page: Courtesy Museum of Fine Arts, Boston; drawings: Lee Hov

My unstudied opinion of veneered work was that it was somehow "cheap." Veneer was covering something and so was participating in some fundamental lie. It wasn't until I was struck by the notion that veneer was *thin* wood that I came to see it in a new light. Removing the idea of veneer as a mask and seeing it as thin wood cleared the way for a deeper understanding of the nature of wood. In its solid form, wood shows itself mainly as structural, a post or beam, for example. Veneer on the other hand is, in fact, a fabric—it can bend and bunch and can be saturated with dye.

Recently, I've been using veneer's fabric-like capacity to bend to solve one of the design problems associated with veneered panels: edge treatment. I don't like the look of solid-wood or veneer strips glued on the edges of the panel substrate; in addition, a glueline might fail or a solid lipping shrink and telegraph through the face veneer. I decided to bend the veneer around the curved edge of a piece to produce a seamless transition from top to bottom. I explored the technique first on a bed design, then used it on the bench shown on the facing page, commissioned by the Museum of Fine Arts in Boston, Mass.

The benchtop is veneered with strips of holly applied diagonally so that each of the four edges is an identical veneered bullnose. Although I chose holly to provide a uniform, light-colored background for the dyed inlays, the wood's shimmering grain also adds life to the surface. I'm keenly interested in this light-reflective quality, called chatoyance, which is a changeable, lustrous, undulating surface appearance. Good examples of chatoyance are seen in figured mahogany, the lightly rippled surface of a stream or the alternating light and dark strips of a newly mowed putting green. Either the eye or the object must move to fully appreciate chatoyance.

The layout of the benchtop involved three related factors: the size of the top, the width of the strips, and their angle across the top. After washing about with these three elements for a time, trying paper strips of different widths across a mock benchtop, they finally assumed their proper place and relationship.

There are a number of ways to match veneer on a panel; two of the most common are book-match and slip-match. To book-match veneer, each successive pair of veneer leaves is opened like a book, producing a pattern symmetrical about a centerline, as shown in figure 1. Slip-matching, the technique I chose, arranges each sheet as it comes off the flitch, creating a pattern of individual, repeating elements. It's critical that the veneer "sisters" are marked for sequence and side-up orientation as they come from the flitch. An inadvertently flipped leaf can reflect light very differently from its right-side-up sisters. With wood as plain as holly this error may not be obvious until the finish is applied.

Slip-matching veneer on a diagonal requires only that you pick a repeating feature—a grain swirl or pin knot, for example—and keep them in line. Once arranged, I marked the sisters with a triangle, as shown in the drawing. Note that each leaf has two lines of the triangle on it. It is quite difficult to flip or get the sisters out of sequence with this method, and it leaves a minimum of pencil marks to be removed later.

For the substrate, I used ¾-in. Baltic birch plywood, cutting a bullnose edge around the entire perimeter with a ⅜-in.-radius router bit worked from both faces of the panel. As this was to be a bench seating two, I decided to suggest this by gluing a very slight fillet to the core. The fillet is triangular in section, with concave faces rising to a peak less than ⅛-in. high.

With the layout arranged and the core prepared, the next step was bending the veneer. I arrived at the bending method by trial and error. I tried hot pipe bending, but couldn't avoid scorching the wood. An elaborate mandrel setup on my lathe proved workable but unnecessarily cumbersome. I found that the best method was a relatively simple combination of moisture and heat. Starting from the middle of the benchtop, I laid a veneer strip in place at the correct angle and put two marks, one at each edge of the strip, where each bullnose started. Then I clamped the veneer on another panel with an edge bullnosed the same as the one for the bench, aligning a pair of marks with the bullnose. Wetting both sides of the veneer in the vicinity of the bend, I waved a 650-watt heat gun across the surface and slowly bent the veneer over the bullnose. (If you don't have a heat gun, pouring boiling water on the veneer should work to bend it.) A block of wood coved to match the bullnose helped ease the bend evenly. Once bent, I removed the strip from the form, held the bend with the coved piece while I thoroughly dried it with the heat gun.

After bending the other end, I glued the strip to the core. For each strip, I made a caul that covered the entire strip up to the bends. A split section of aluminum tubing secured the bends over the bullnose. The veneer past the bend on the underside is also supported with clamped cauls. For the holly strips that crossed the central fillet, I scored the underside of the veneer with a razor

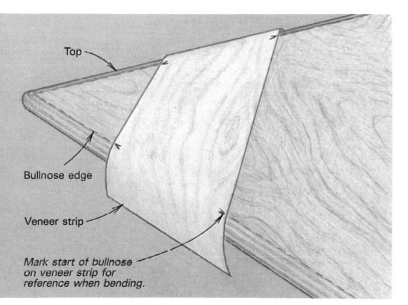

Top —

Bullnose edge

Veneer strip —

Mark start of bullnose
on veneer strip for
reference when bending.

Allen Burns

Duffy bends dampened veneer around a bullnose former. The bend is then fixed with a heat gun.

Veneered columns

by Thomas J. Fannon

I recently completed the altar shown here, commissioned for a 100-year-old chapel at the Catholic University in Washington, D.C. The piece reflects the Romanesque surroundings of the intimate chapel, embellished with touches of the Byzantine, in reference to the nearby National Shrine. Historically, the transition from round column to square beam or arch was handled by a capital of one of the classical orders. The height of the altar wouldn't allow this approach, however, so I drew concentric arches springing from points spaced equally around the tops of the columns. The result was fascinating, reminiscent of the receding arches in the entrances to the classical cathedrals. I flared these arches outward on all sides toward the perimeter of the table. It was a satisfying drawing; building it looked tough.

The mahogany base, or plinth, was straightforward. A router, guided by an air-clamped jig, cut the many archways. A shallow sawkerf housed the tiny boxwood capitals. A shaper and a bit of handwork finished the moldings. If only the ancient temple builders had had it so easy.

Each column consists of five bandsawn discs, attached at equal intervals to eight thin vertical staves. A layer of ⅛-in. bending ply and a layer of ⅛-in. poplar veneer encircles the cage-like framework. Figured mahogany face veneer, with backing veneer, completes the column. I bandsawed the discs then notched them to house the staves. Octagonal plates fixed each end of a stack of discs, bolted together through their centers, made a simple jig for dadoing equally spaced notches on a tablesaw, as shown in the drawing. I notched the ¾-in.

by 1-in. staves to form lap joints with the disc dadoes and assembled the frameworks. Light planing faired the staves to the curve.

The plywood layer was carefully cut to the column circumference, then stapled and glued to the frame. After setting the staples and dressing the surface lightly with a sanding block, the poplar was added. A sheet of stiff (18 gauge or better) galvanized metal serves as a caul, drawn around the drum with web clamps aligned with the internal discs—tightened over the staves,

Column construction

- Plywood disc
- Stave, ¾ x 1
- ⅛-in. plywood
- ⅛-in. poplar veneer
- ¹⁄₂₈-in. backing veneer
- ¹⁄₄₀-in. face veneer

Octagonal plate   Disc

To notch discs for staves, bolt discs together with octagonal plate each end. Dado assembly on the tablesaw, centering a dado on each plate facet.

the pressure would distort or break them. Two ½-in.-square strips along the caul's edges lift the metal bodies of the clamps above the column to avoid damage. I glued the poplar in two halves, and the result is remarkably strong.

After matching and taping the face veneer (four leaves per column), I glued it to a backing veneer using the metal cauls and column as a former, half a column at a time. Removed from the column, these skins are stiff and curved enough to allow exact trimming for perfect lengthwise joints. (I use a hinged printers' knife, 42 in. long, for a veneer trimmer.) Front and back skins were glued to the column one at a time, then the column ends were trimmed flush.

The arch is built up of layers of curved plywood panels, veneered on two forms, one for the front and back, one for the ends. The veneer was an interstellar cloudburst, carefully cut and positioned so the combined layers would create a perfectly flowing pattern. The altar top, like the base, is made of solid mahogany.

I was as pleased with this piece as any I've ever made. But perfection? Maybe never: During the final stages of coloring, I used a felt-tip marker to add accents, then shot the final coats of lacquer and went home for the night. The next morning I was appalled to find that a chemical reaction had turned all the marker accents iridescent green. Yikes! Both columns were completely stripped and refinished in time to keep an appointment with the photographer. □

Thomas Fannon is a woodworker in Alexandria, Va.

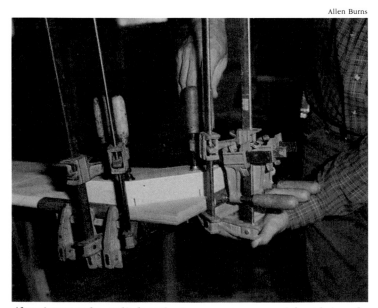

Allen Burns

Aluminum tube, split lengthwise, serves as a caul for gluing the bend. Wooden cauls distribute pressure on the flat surfaces.

knife precisely where it crossed the fillet, and shaped the caul with a chisel to correspond to the fillet's concave shape. After dry-clamping the setup, to make sure everything fit, I applied glue to the core and clamped-up as shown at left. When the glue was dry, I removed the clamps, scraped away the excess glue and repeated the whole process for the next strip. I made no attempt at perfect seams since these would be covered by narrow harewood strips (harewood is most often sycamore or maple dyed silver-gray with ferrous sulphate). I didn't worry about the corners, which would be cut away for purpleheart legs.

Once all the holly was laid, I trimmed the excess on the underside and vacuum-pressed purpleheart veneer onto that surface (run the veneer at the opposite diagonal to the holly for structural balance). No special attention was paid to the joint between the holly and the purpleheart because these edges would be covered by the base skirt rail. (The base is straightforward mortise-and-tenon construction. I turned all the legs at once by gluing four pieces together with paper between the pieces so I could separate them after turning.)

Next, I cut the grooves for the harewood stripes in the top

The columns of Tom Fannon's altar are veneered in figured mahogany wrapped around a plywood-covered frame. Thin marble slabs separate the columns from the solid-mahogany top and plinth.

surface, running a Dremel router against a wooden fence clamped to the benchtop. I cut the stripes to match the groove width with an Ulmia double-knife inlay cutter (available from Lee Valley Tools, P.O. Box 6295, Station J, Ottawa, Ontario K2A 1T4, Canada). Inserting the harewood dry into the groove, I held it in place with cellophane tape, pulling it around the bullnose with the tape for support. (The narrow stripes bent around the curve without wetting or heat.) After scribing along the stripe for the grooves on the curves, I removed the stripe, cleaned out the groove with a narrow chisel and glued the stripe in place. A wooden caul distributed pressure on the top, a short length of split aluminum tube secured the bend.

During the course of making the top I cut inlays that I intended to use and assembled them on double-faced tape. When I position inlay, I think of jazz and of the way strangers assume their separate places on a bus. The backdrop supplied a sublime field for the constellations of inlays and gold leaf. I have never seen black look so black as when it is let into holly.

The actual inlay techniques are rather simple. I scribed around the inlay with an X-Acto knife, lifted the inlay and the excess tape, deepened the scribe line and excavated with a Dremel router or a small gooseneck chisel. After checking the fit, I glued the inlay in place with 5-minute epoxy, covering the whole assembly with clear tape until dry. A sharp scraper quickly leveled and cleaned the inlay.

The completed top required considerable sanding. I used a broad piece of very dense plastic as a block to hold a full sheet of sandpaper to better level the entire surface. Because of the heavy use the bench would receive in the museum, I chose a catalyzed lacquer finish for its durability. It took three days to spray and sand enough coats to build up a good, heavy film, which was given a final rubout with auto-body rubbing compound before applying the gold leaf. Gold leaf contributed a different "frequency" to the chatoyance of the piece—wood grain has a mellifluous chatoyance while the gold "blinks." Ten to fifteen dust coats of lacquer completed the finishing, applied carefully so that no further rubbing was needed, which might have upset the gold. □

Tom Duffy makes architectural woodwork and furniture in Ogdensburg, N.Y.

Vacuum Veneering
Build a bag press

by Greg Elder

Veneering opens up new horizons in design. No longer limited to solid wood, you can cover stable, man-made panels with a choice of veneers in a wide variety of species, widths and grain patterns. Veneering can be done by at least three methods: with a veneer hammer, in a mechanical press, or in a vacuum press. The first requires muscle and skill, the second requires a large, heavy and often expensive piece of equipment, while the third needs only a thin bag and the weight of the air above it. With the air pumped out of the bag, the atmosphere bears on the bag's contents like one huge clamp (2,117 lb. per square foot!), its pressure perfectly distributed. Simple, inexpensive, easy to store, a vacuum press yields consistently excellent results.

My vacuum press consists of a flexible, 16-gauge vinyl bag, a 4-ft. by 8-ft. sheet of particleboard and a second-hand, ⅛-HP vacuum pump. The procedure is simple: After applying the glue, the substrate and veneer, along with a Masonite caul and protective sheet of plastic, are slid into the bag on top of the particleboard press platform. The bag is sealed, the air pumped out and the now-pressed panel is left to cure.

The bag can be any size you wish. Mine takes panels up to 64 in. by 120 in. To get that size, I had to join three pieces of vinyl—two 54 in. wide, one 27 in. wide, all 11 ft. long—to form a tube. The simple, 2-in.-wide lap joints run the full length and are glued with vinyl adhesive. (Vinyl and adhesive can be ordered from Minute-Man, 375 Beacham St., Chelsea, Mass. 02150.)

After applying the adhesive, make the seam, without wrinkles, pressing with a small, firm roller to get a good seal. I found the adhesive joins best when tacky. An extra pair of hands is very useful here, and I suggest wearing a respirator when working with the adhesive. Let the seams set for about 10 minutes, then seal one end of the tube with another 2-in. seam, to form a bag. Wood battens and clamps help seal the end seam while the adhesive sets. Avoid placing the lengthwise seams along the edges of the bag—they would make sealing the end corners difficult.

The press platform is a sheet of particleboard, scored with a 6-in. grid of ⅛-in.-deep sawkerfs to aid the evacuation of the air. A fitting for the pump hose plugs into a ⅜-in. hole bored in the platform edge, aligned with the end of a groove, as shown on the facing page. The hole should be about 1 in. deep and located 18 in. to 24 in. from a corner. A ¼-in. hole, about ¾ in. from the edge, connects the groove and the fitting hole.

The pump-hose fitting is glued to the bag, positioned to align with the fitting hole in the platform. I use a piece of ⅜-in. outside diameter clear vinyl tubing about 10 in. long for the fitting. A flanged, vinyl collar and vinyl reinforcement layer connect the

Brooke Beaird

Elder's vacuum bag veneer press consists of a lightweight, home-made vinyl bag, a particleboard platform and a secondhand vacuum pump. It will handle large, flat panels easily, and can be broken down and stored in a small space.

fitting to the bag. Punch a hole slightly smaller than the tubing through the bag and reinforcement layer. I made a punch by grinding a sharp edge on the end of a length of metal tubing. To make the collar, punch a smaller hole in another piece of vinyl, then cut the flanges with a knife. I glued the collar and reinforcement to the outside of the bag; hand pressure will make the bond.

Vacuum pumps vary in capacity, measured in the number of cubic feet of air they move per minute (CFM) and the vacuum they'll create, measured in inches of mercury. A perfect vacuum will permit the maximum air pressure (14.7 pounds per square inch—PSI—at sea level) to bear on the work. I bought my second-hand pump from a hospital for $50. It moves 2 CFM and attains 22 in. of mercury, which translates to 11 PSI—not perfect, but it's still 1,584 lb. per square foot. Similar pumps are available from scientific catalogs, such as the Sargent-Welch Scientific Co. biology catalog (7300 North Linder Ave., Skokie, Ill. 60077). An air compressor can also be converted by switching the appropriate valves. If the system is well sealed, there should be no problem maintaining a vacuum with a low-volume pump.

From *Fine Woodworking* magazine (January 1986) 56:70-71

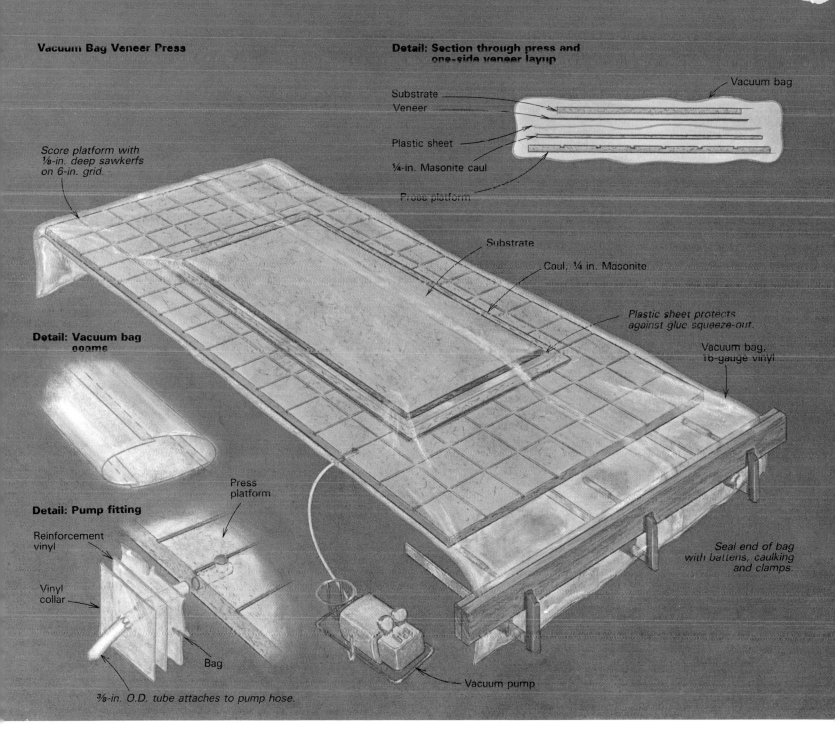

Vacuum Bag Veneer Press

Score platform with ⅛-in. deep sawkerfs on 6-in. grid.

Detail: Section through press and one-side veneer layup

Substrate
Veneer
Vacuum bag
Plastic sheet
¼-in. Masonite caul
Press platform

Substrate

Caul, ¼ in. Masonite

Plastic sheet protects against glue squeeze-out.

Vacuum bag, 16-gauge vinyl

Detail: Vacuum bag seams

Detail: Pump fitting

Reinforcement vinyl

Vinyl collar

Press platform

Bag

Seal end of bag with battens, caulking and clamps.

⅜-in. O.D. tube attaches to pump hose.

Vacuum pump

To use the press, you'll need cauls to cover the veneered surfaces. Mine are ¼-in. Masonite, one 4 ft. by 8 ft., one 3 ft. by 5 ft. A sheet of cheap 2-mil or 3-mil plastic prevents the caul from sticking to the veneer. After preparing the substrate and veneer, I spread a thin, even layer of glue on the substrate—not on the veneer—with a notched trowel, then position the veneer. To keep larger pieces of veneer from shifting during the process, I staple or tape the waste at the midpoint of each end. Lay the plastic sheet on the caul, turn the veneered substrate over onto it, then slide this assembly into the bag. Make sure the caul is smooth and the sheet unwrinkled—bumps on these surfaces can make depressions in the veneer.

Placing the veneer face-down on the caul allows me to press panels in a variety of sizes without making a separate, exact-sized caul for each panel. Under pressure, an oversized caul placed on top of the veneer might bow over the substrate edges, keeping pressure from the veneer near the edges. For large panels that are difficult to turn over, cut the caul exactly the same size as the substrate and slide the assembly into the bag, caul-side up. To

veneer both surfaces of a panel at once, use a caul and plastic sheet top and bottom. Before sliding any assembly into the bag, make sure to ease sharp edges that may damage the bag under pressure. As the vacuum forms, push the bag into the corners formed by the substrate and the caul/platform so that the bag won't bridge these areas and be vulnerable to tears.

I clear the bulk of the air out of the bag with a vacuum cleaner—my low-volume pump would take forever. When the bag is collapsed, remove the nozzle and seal the end of the bag completely with battens and clamps. A sealer strip of Mortite caulking cord (available in most hardware stores) eliminates leaks, which are fairly easy to hear with the pump turned off.

I've found that for a 40 in. by 60-in. panel it takes 8 to 10 minutes from pouring the glue onto the substrate to achieving full pressure. The vacuum cleaner is the key to keeping the time that short. I leave panels glued with Titebond under pressure for an hour, but let the glue cure fully before working the panel. □

Greg Elder makes furniture in Woodstock, Vt.

Leather and Wood
Three clever combinations

by Seth Stem

Leather cemented onto a plywood panel can be an attractive alternative to a solid-wood panel in furniture. After applying contact cement to both leather and plywood, Stem positions the leather carefully and smooths it down onto the plywood.

There are unlimited opportunities to use leather in furniture. Leather's color, texture, and surface character greatly complement the grain pattern and natural warmth of wood. Because its appearance can range from a natural look to slick surfaces or bizarre colors, leather works in almost any context, from utilitarian to purely decorative. I've covered flat surfaces, such as a desk top or panel, with leather, upholstered with it and formed it into three-dimensional shapes that function as containers or ornament on furniture. I'll discuss techniques for doing each of these, but first a little background.

Leather is a durable and strong yet flexible material, made up of fibers interwoven in all directions. Once removed from the animal, the hide is given baths in various chemicals, scraped of its hair and fat then submerged in tanning agents. Tanning keeps leather from putrifying and, depending on the tanning agent, increases its resistance to heat, water and chemicals. Chromium salts and vegetable matter containing tannin—oak bark for example—are the most commonly used tanning agents. (Chrome-tanned leather shows a bluish-gray color in cross section.)

Most retailers sell leather by the square foot in half hides, the hide being divided along the animal's backbone. Half cowhides are usually 20 to 25 sq. ft., and the measurement is stamped on the back side of the hide. It's most economical to buy a half hide, and many retailers won't cut a hide into smaller lots.

Leather is also classified by weight in ounces per square foot, and weight correlates directly to thickness—1 oz. equals 1/64 in. Garment leather is generally 2 oz. to 3 oz./sq. ft., belt leather is 7 oz. to 9 oz./sq. ft., and furniture sling leather is 8 oz. to 14 oz./sq. ft. Quite an amazing range of leather is available—cowhide, deerskin, lizard, pigskin, horsehide, and goatskin are common. Suede is a hide with the skin side removed.

Because there is such a variety of leather available, it's best to visit a leather retailer rather than rely on mail order. If you can't, here is a mail-order source I've used: Berman Leathercraft, 145 South St., Boston, Mass., 02111.

Leather panels in a wood frame are an attractive alternative to all-wood panels. I glue leather to plywood with contact cement, then I fix the panels in the frames using one of the methods shown in figure 1 on the facing page. Use at least 3-oz. leather for panels because surface irregularities in the plywood will telegraph through thinner leather. I also glue leather to both sides of the plywood so there is no chance of the plywood warping, just as it would if you applied wood veneer to only one side. Leather on only one side will probably do if the panel is held firmly in a frame.

The procedure for cementing the leather to the panel is the same for the methods shown in figure 1A, B and C. Cut the plywood panel to size and lay it over an area of leather that is free of defects. Mark and cut the leather about 1/2 in. to 1 in. away from each edge of the panel. I use a razor knife or single-edge razor for cutting and trimming leather. Apply contact cement to both the backside of the leather and to the plywood. Make sure that the gluing surfaces are free from dirt and cement lumps, which will telegraph through the surface. When the contact cement has dried (20 minutes or so), position the leather carefully and, starting from one edge, press it down smoothly on the plywood with the flat of your hand. Trim the excess, then glue and trim the other side.

A panel in a rabbet can be glued or screwed into place (figure 1A) or held by a molding strip (figure 1B). If a screwed or glued panel is to be seen from the inside, I first trim the leather on the inside surface so it overhangs the plywood slightly, then trim it accurately with a razor knife after the panel is in place.

A grooved frame and leather-covered panel can be assembled

From *Fine Woodworking* magazine (July 1985) 53:70-73

permanently, but I prefer to be able to remove a damaged panel. Figure 1C shows a method for the side panel of a desk or cabinet. The panel slides into grooves in the stiles and bottom rail, and is held in place by a two-piece top rail. The outer half of the top rail is mortised to the stiles, the inner half is loose. Chamfer the edges of the panel with a razor knife so they can slide easily into the grooves without peeling the leather off the plywood.

The method shown in figure 1D raises the leather slightly above the frame. I used this method for the top panels on the desk shown at right. The effect of this raised panel is crisp and professional, whereas a flush panel made using the same method will show a crevice between the leather and the frame due to the curvature of the leather as it wraps around the plywood. The depth of the frame rabbet should be half the frame's thickness. Cut a plywood panel to fit snugly in the frame, then rabbet the panel to create a lip that's as thick as the frame rabbet is deep. (The plywood need not be the same thickness as the frame.) I do this on the tablesaw, placing the panel on end, top surface toward the fence for the first cut, then placing it flat on the table, top surface up, for the second. The thickness of plywood varies slightly throughout a single sheet, and this method ensures that the lip will be a uniform thickness.

Next, trim the panel to allow for the thickness of the leather. Place two pieces of leather scrap in the rabbet on each member of the frame, toward the corners, then try the panel in the frame. Saw or plane the edges until the panel fits the opening snugly. It may take several tries, but a good fit here is very important.

Cut the leather for the panel large enough to wrap over the edges of the plywood lip and allow for waste. Contact cement the leather to the face of the panel, then cut small squares out of the overlapping leather at each corner of the panel. The corner of a square should come to within ⅛ in. to ³⁄₁₆ in. of the plywood corner. Cement the overlap to the edges of the lip, stretching the leather over the apex of each corner and smoothing out any puckering. Trim and chamfer the leather all around the panel; no leather should adhere to the underside of the lip. Finally, glue or screw the panel into place. Single-edge razor blades slipped between the leather and the frame work like shoehorns and help slide the panel in. Remember the leather will compress slightly, so a real tight fit is possible.

Simple leather upholstery can be done using the same frame-and-panel system and 1-in. to 2-in. thick foam-rubber padding. The round stool shown on p. 104 has a leather upholstered seat

Stem's desk has raised-leather-panel writing surfaces; the side panels of desk and credenza are flat.

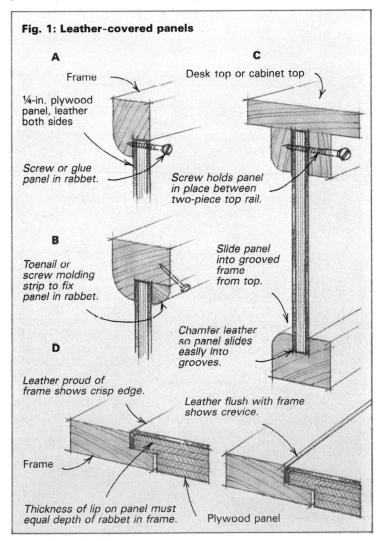

Fig. 1: Leather-covered panels

A

Frame

¼-in. plywood panel, leather both sides

Screw or glue panel in rabbet.

B

Toenail or screw molding strip to fix panel in rabbet.

C

Desk top or cabinet top

Screw holds panel in place between two-piece top rail.

Slide panel into grooved frame from top.

Chamfer leather so panel slides easily into grooves.

D

Leather proud of frame shows crisp edge.

Leather flush with frame shows crevice.

Frame

Thickness of lip on panel must equal depth of rabbet in frame.

Plywood panel

Single-edge razor blades help ease a tight-fitting panel into place in a rabbeted frame.

©Gary Gilbert

By sandwiching foam between the leather and panel, you can adapt the frame-and-panel leatherworking method to upholster a seat, as in this stool made by Matthew Burke.

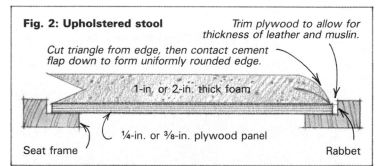

Fig. 2: Upholstered stool

Trim plywood to allow for thickness of leather and muslin.

Cut triangle from edge, then contact cement flap down to form uniformly rounded edge.

1-in. or 2-in. thick foam

¼-in. or ⅜-in. plywood panel

Seat frame

Rabbet

Flat-nosed pliers give added pull when tacking the leather to the seat panel.

fixed in a round frame, but the method will work for seats of any shape. Construct the frame, cut the plywood to fit, then glue the foam to the plywood with contact cement and trim it flush with the edges of the plywood (see figure 2). Left square, the edge of the foam would compress irregularly as the leather was stretched over it. Using a sharp razor blade, I cut a triangular section out of the edge and glue the foam flap down with contact cement so the edge will retain its shape.

Next, stretch muslin over the foam, tack or staple it to the plywood and trim off the excess. First tack the muslin in four places, 90° apart, so it won't gather too much during stretching. The muslin helps make the rounded foam edge uniform, and allows the leather to shift slightly over this surface when the stool is being used, without the leather wearing or pulling directly on the foam. Stretch 3-oz. to 4-oz. leather over the muslin and tack it in the same sequence, using flat-nosed pliers to stretch it if necessary. If the leather puckers or gathers at seat corners or around curves, wet it with a sponge and stretch it smooth. Trim off excess leather with a razor and screw the plywood backing to the seat frame from underneath.

Wet leather can be molded over a form and when dry, it will retain the form's shape. One-layer shells of 8-oz. to 10-oz. vegetable-tanned leather will be extremely stiff and hold their shape well. (Lighter-weight vegetable-tanned leather will also form, but won't be as stiff.) By gluing together two lightweight layers of chrome- or vegetable-tanned leather over a form, you can make a rigid leather shell with finished surfaces inside and out, like the one on the wall-hung basket on the facing page. Leather can be specially tanned to keep stretch at a minimum, so it is best to discuss the intended use of the leather with your retailer.

Single-layer and double-layer shells can be made on the same form. Try slightly rounded or bullnose shapes first, avoiding shapes that cause the leather to bunch or gather. Forms can be lathe-turned or hand-shaped of any material that will hold nails and that won't deteriorate when wet. The final surface must be smooth, as any imperfection will telegraph through the leather. I made the form for the wall basket of fiberboard, with a top layer of plywood to take the nails.

After you've made the form, collect a plastic bucket, regular flat-nosed pliers, a tack hammer and a razor knife or single-edge razor blade. Cut a piece of leather slightly oversize to go over the form. An easy way to measure the piece is to place the form on the leather and roll it to the form's edge, then mark 2 in. or 3 in. from the edge. Roll it to the opposite edge and so on. Soak the leather in a bucket of very hot water for approximately 20 minutes, then tack it along one edge of the form with 1¼-in. brads. Put the smooth side out if you're making a single-layer shell, smooth side in for a double-layer shell. Pull and stretch the leather over the form using flat-nosed pliers, and tack it down. To remove puckering, pull the brads out one at a time and stretch the leather further. Replace the brads with #6 upholstery tacks during the last round of stretching. The leather is dry when it returns to its original color. With a razor knife, remove a one-layer shell from the form now by cutting just inside the tacked area.

For a two-layer shell, stretch the first layer, finished side in, then brush on a very generous layer of yellow glue, such as Titebond, then wet-form a second layer of leather over the first, finish side out. The degree of stiffness can be controlled by the amount of glue applied. For a very hard shell, three or more layers of leather can be glued together.

Formed leather can be attached to a wood frame in a groove,

Leather shells or containers can be made by stretching wet leather over a form. When dry, the leather will retain the shape of the form, and can then be mounted in a wooden frame.

Stretch the wet leather in stages, holding it temporarily in place with brads. Fix it with upholstery tacks during the last round of stretching. Glue two (or more) layers of leather together on a one-piece form for a very stiff shell. Wet, stretch and tuck the first layer to the form. Spread yellow glue on this layer, then stretch and tack the next layer.

Fig. 3: Wall-hung leather basket

Routed keyhole slot

Groove, ⅜ in. deep

9¾

⅜

3¾

1

Laminated frame

5

⅜-in. by ⅜-in. splines

Formed leather

8¾

Alternative fastenings

Glue leather to rabbet in frame.

Glue leather flange to bottom of frame.

Wall bracket

in a rabbet or by a flange, as shown in figure 3. The wall basket is glued into a groove routed in the form-laminated hickory rim; the groove must match the shell's perimeter exactly. The groove is as wide as the thickness of the leather and about ¼ in. to ⅜ in. deep. I usually chamfer the edge of the leather with a razor blade first, to allow for easier entry into the groove.

Leather glued to a rabbet can be stretched slightly to meet the rabbet, then it must be tacked or clamped in place while the glue dries. You'll also need to trim the shell's edge precisely to butt against the rabbet, unless the inside is hidden from view.

If when you cut the leather free of the form you retain the flange (the area of leather tacked to the form), you can glue this to a wood structure. Trim the puckered areas of the flange with a razor knife and pound them flat on the form with a hammer. Then trim the flange ½ in. to ¾ in. wide. If you're gluing the flange down with yellow glue, the frame must allow access for the clamps. If this is impossible, use contact cement. □

Seth Stem teaches at the Rhode Island School of Design and designs and makes furniture in Marblehead, Mass.

Wooden Lamps
Safe wiring for shop-built lighting

by Sandor Nagyszalanczy

Fig. 1: Lamp wiring

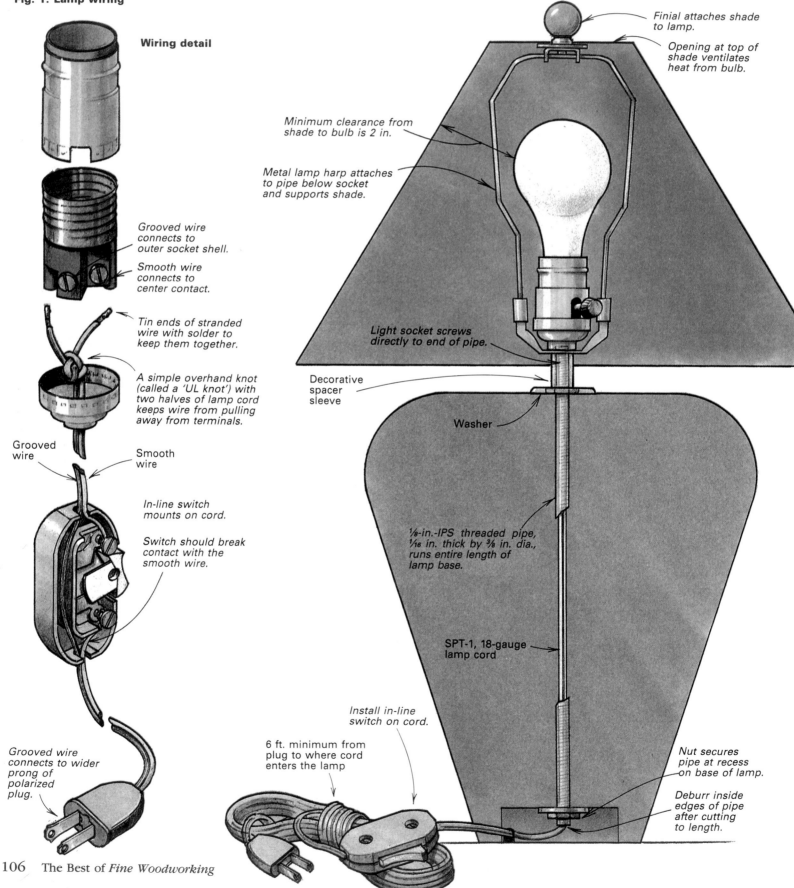

Wiring detail

Grooved wire connects to outer socket shell.

Smooth wire connects to center contact.

Tin ends of stranded wire with solder to keep them together.

A simple overhand knot (called a 'UL knot') with two halves of lamp cord keeps wire from pulling away from terminals.

Grooved wire

Smooth wire

In-line switch mounts on cord.

Switch should break contact with the smooth wire.

Grooved wire connects to wider prong of polarized plug.

6 ft. minimum from plug to where cord enters the lamp

Install in-line switch on cord.

Finial attaches shade to lamp.

Opening at top of shade ventilates heat from bulb.

Minimum clearance from shade to bulb is 2 in.

Metal lamp harp attaches to pipe below socket and supports shade.

Light socket screws directly to end of pipe.

Decorative spacer sleeve

Washer

⅛-in.-IPS threaded pipe, 1/16 in. thick by ⅜ in. dia., runs entire length of lamp base.

SPT-1, 18-gauge lamp cord

Nut secures pipe at recess on base of lamp.

Deburr inside edges of pipe after cutting to length.

A well-designed and skillfully crafted wooden lamp easily rivals the design sophistication and complex construction of even the fanciest furniture: The wooden parts can be turned, carved, stack-laminated, steam-bent, veneered, carcase-built or produced by any combination of woodworking techniques. The lampmaker must be something of a jack-of-all-trades, because fitting lamp hardware involves some metalworking or at least plumbing ability, and making a custom shade may require sewing or glassworking skills. The most important factor, though, is knowing how to wire the lamp safely. An improperly installed cord or a shade too near the bulb can send the lamp, and perhaps the house, up in flames.

Fortunately, you can minimize the fire and electrical hazards by observing some well-established wiring principles. Safety guides for lighting devices, both portable and built-in, are available from the Underwriters Laboratories Inc. (UL), a for-non-profit public safety organization that tests and certifies lamps and other appliances by evaluating the potential fire, electrical and casualty hazards (base stability, sharp edges, etc.). These safety guides are not "how to" books, but they give exact precepts for properly engineering a safe lamp. While UL certification isn't usually required to make or to sell a lamp (check your local electrical building codes), it's foolish to build one without following these nationally recognized safety requirements. Here I'll only deal with the basics of safely wiring a wooden lamp, but for the whole story, order the safety guides listed below.

As you design your lamp, you must consider all the required electrical components. You must decide what wire to use, how to connect it and how to pass the wire through the lamp. Methods for attaching the bulb socket and other lamp parts, such as shades and switches, to the lamp base must be developed. You must provide clearance between the bulb and the shade and a way to vent the bulb's heat. The electrical factors may influence the proportions of your lamp, the size or shape of the shade, or even the way you'll build the wooden body. If you want the wire to pass through the wood base or column, for example, it would be simpler to laminate the column with an open channel in the middle, instead of drilling a long hole through a solid block.

Wire for a lamp must be of the correct gauge and insulation type so the current won't overheat the wires and cause a fire. The most commonly used wire is SPT-1, a two-wire cord often called lampcord or zipcord (because the two individually insulated wires easily peel or "zip" apart). Eighteen-gauge is the recommended size (thickness) wire for lamps with a single bulb smaller than 100 watts. Multiple-bulb lamps may require 16-gauge or larger. Wire is also rated for its insulation qualities as 60C, 75C, 90C and 105C, standing for heat resistance in degrees Celsius. Wire that's 60C is most commonly available from lighting stores, but UL specs for wooden lamps often require 105C-rated wire: The higher-rated insulation will give a wooden lamp more protection from heat and prevent a possible fire. (SPT-1 wire that's 105C-rated is available from local lighting shops or electrical supply houses.) If you're in doubt about which wire to use—or any other specifics about wiring your lamp—consult the proper UL safety guides.

To prevent accidental overloads or short circuits, a lamp should be lined with metal—either pipe, tubing or sheet metal—wherever wires pass through wooden parts. The standard conduit for lamps is a special threaded pipe called ⅛-in.-IPS (the IPS stands for "iron pipe size") available from lamp shops or electrical supply houses. Most standard lamp sockets screw directly onto ⅛-in.-IPS, making it a convenient way to secure a socket to a lamp. The pipe fits through a ⅜-in. hole in a lamp and should be made long enough to extend at least 2 in. past the wood at the socket

end. This keeps any possible shorts that might occur in the socket from igniting the wooden base. Threaded nuts on the ends lock the pipe/socket assembly to the lamp. To prevent jagged edges from slicing into the cord, always deburr inside the pipe's ends with a reamer or sandpaper after the pipe is cut to length with a hacksaw.

Wiring—The socket, plug and switch must be wired for correct polarity (yes, AC current has hot and neutral wires, like DC). First, thread the wire through the lamp, leaving at least 6 ft. of wire for a cord—a UL safe minimum. Notice that the rubber insulation of the SPT-1 cord has a smooth side and a grooved side. At the wallplug end, connect the grooved wire to the wider prong of a polarized 110v plug (I use a Leviton #205). Some plugs have screw terminals, others just clip over the end of the cord. Regardless of the plug type or brand, always use UL-listed lamp plugs and parts for safety. At the lamp-socket end of the cord, pull apart the cord's two halves and tie a "UL knot," as shown in the drawing. This prevents the wires from being pulled off the socket terminals and out of the lamp. If the knot won't fit at the socket, you can provide this "strain relief" by tying a knot anywhere before the cord exits the lamp. A ceiling lamp is sometimes hung entirely from its cord, but this requires a special kind of wire. Consult the UL-57 safety guide on fixtures for details.

To keep the stranded SPT-1 wire from frazzling, apply a little solder to the stripped ends of each wire before screwing them to the socket terminals. The grooved wire goes to the screw feeding the bulb socket's outer shell and the smooth one goes to the center contact. Avoid splicing wires inside the lamp, unless wires from several sockets must be joined together. In that case, use either special UL-rated connectors (I use 3M #557), or solder the wires together and use wire-nut connectors and house the splices in a metal junction box. If there isn't room in the lamp for a metal box, as might happen with a ceiling lamp with several sockets, you can lead the separate wires out of the fixture and then wire these together to the feed wires inside the metal box in the ceiling.

Unless your lamp will be permanently mounted and controlled by a wall switch, you'll need an on/off switch on the lamp or on the cord. You can use a light socket with a built-in rotary switch or pull chain or install an in-line switch right on the cord. In-line dimmer controls are also available so the bulb's brightness can be adjusted. Make sure to use a switch with a current rating higher than the wattage of the bulb or bulbs. When connecting the switch, make sure it breaks contact with the smooth wire of the cord for correct polarity, as shown in the drawing.

Shade design—Lamp shades can be made from just about any material, as long as a few rules are observed. Design the shade so the bulb will stay at least 2 in. from any combustible material, including wood, paper, plastic or fabric. When using a flexible shade material that may sag, make sure the shade frame keeps it from contacting the bulb. The easiest way to attach a shade to a lamp is with a metal lamp harp. The harp's two legs slip in and out of a special clip that fits on the ⅛-in.-IPS, just below the socket. A short, threaded rod secures the shade on top. Harps come in different sizes and heights to work with almost any shade-and-bulb combination. If you decide to support the shade with a wooden frame, make sure the base attachment is secure and the shade can't be easily tipped off the base and onto the bulb. Because incandescent bulbs produce a lot of heat, the lamp shade needs an opening at the top to allow the heat to dissipate. A 6-sq.-in. opening at the top of a shade will be more than enough for a 75-watt bulb, the maximum bulb strength I recommend for a wooden lamp.

The size and type of bulb you use can influence the size and proportions of the lamp base and shade, as well as determine the amount and the quality of light. Bulbs and their corresponding sockets come in a multitude of shapes and sizes to fit the application. For example, a large globe-type bulb is decorative enough and gives off a soft enough light to be used without a shade, while a tubular bulb, the kind often found in aquarium hoods and display cases, may fit a lamp design that has little shade clearance. Although I've limited my talk to incandescents, there are many other light sources appropriate for wooden lamps. A cool-burning fluorescent or neon fixture may be the ticket for a lamp design that doesn't allow much ventilation, while a quartz halogen bulb gives off tremendous amounts of light—great for a floor lamp used to flood a whole room. There are still other light sources

such as LEDs (light emitting diodes) or DC-powered fixtures. While these light sources may fit your lampmaking needs better than garden-variety incandescents, they require different lamp hardware and wiring know-how. If you want to use these, it's best to consult someone from a local lighting shop. □

Sandor Nagyszalanczy is an assistant editor for Fine Woodworking. *Lampmaker Ellis Walentine contributed to this article. Safety guides UL 57 on lighting fixtures, UL 153 on portable lamps, UL 1571 on incandescent lighting fixtures and a free catalog of other lighting publications can be ordered from Underwriters Laboratories Inc., Publication Stock Dept., 1285 Walt Whitman Road, Melville, N.Y. 11747; (516) 271-6200.*

Bright ideas

A well-designed lamp is more than just a good-looking furnishing: It must also provide good light. The definition of good light depends on the lamp's function. A successful floor lamp should give off enough light to flood a room, while a sconce usually only needs to deliver dim, mood lighting. The lampmaker can control the quality of the light a lamp produces by first choosing the appropriate strength and type of bulb. Most bulbs create white light with a more limited color range than sunlight. For example, an incandescent bulb's color will appear warmer than a cool-white fluorescent bulb's color. Secondly, the lampmaker can choose the shade material and control the shape of the shade. A shade made of paper, fabric or thin wood may diffuse and soften the light passing through it and give it a warm color as well. An opaque shade or reflector serves to deflect the harsh light of the bulb and keep it out of our eyes—important for a good reading or desk lamp. The smaller or more open a shade is, the more direct light from the bulb bounces off the walls and ceiling. This not only diffuses the light, but it can create some interesting light patterns as well.

Like a piece of furniture, a wooden lamp can be designed to fit a particular look or style, such as art nouveau, Queen Ann or Post-Modern. Some lamps are designed to harmonize with the furnishings or architectural elements of the room they light. Other lamps are purely sculptural and produce light only as an incidental effect. Consider the lamps pictured in the following pages as illustrations of the many possibilities. The makers range from architects to cabinetmakers to professional lampmakers.   —S.N.

Photo above: Anthony Kamadulski; photo below: Paul Schraub

The 21-in.-high lamp, above, built by Matthew Beardsley of Ennis, Mont., has a shade made from 1/32-in.-thick basswood veneer and reinforced with battens. The tic-tac-toe rosewood base is joined by lap joints, with bridle joints attaching the base to the eight vertical members. The lamp features a copper plate sandwiched into the base and one built into the frame supporting the shade, providing a light-socket platform.

Roy Johnson of Santa Cruz, Calif., is proud that no store-bought hardware shows in any of his lamps. In fact, he makes most of the parts himself, including the glass shades. The stained-glass shade on this table lamp at right has a wood rim supported by four curvacious arms atop a two-piece turned base. All the wood parts are Honduras mahogany, except the ebony pegs in the rim and the carved ebony switch handle out of sight under the shade.

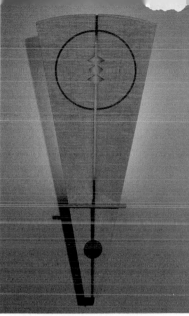

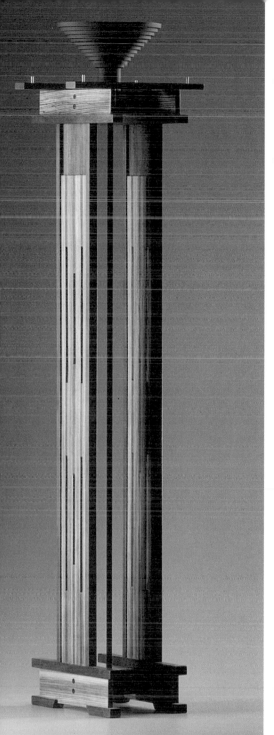

Anthony Beverly of Stephentown, N.Y., built this 76-in.-tall floor lamp, left, with wooden components that bolt together, both to allow the lamp to knock down for shipping and to make finishing easier. The zebrawood and purpleheart lamp is topped by an aluminum shade that's been painted black on the outside with an electrostatic coating process that prevents the heat of the 500-watt quartz halogen bulb from harming the paint. Beverly designed the shade and had it spun to shape by a local metal-spinning shop.

This 18-in.-high wall sconce, right, by Geoffrey Warner, an Exeter, R.I., woodworker, is made from curly maple with padauk line inlay. A turned-padauk knob on the front operates a built-in dimmer switch that adjusts the brightness of the light. Blue European-made glass backs a cutout on the front of the sconce. Warner sandblasted the glass so it would transmit a more diffuse light. A triangular box at the base houses the dimmer and lamp socket. The sconce mounts to the wall by means of a sliding metal bracket normally used to attach bed rails to their posts.

Photo below: Ron Forth; photo above: Paul Ladd

Photo above: Bill Murphy; photo below: Chip Mochel

Tapping into the style and materials commonly found in his ceramic/mixed-media sculpture, Thom Maltbie of Dillsboro, Ind., created these two rice paper and maple Japanese lanterns, above. Maltbie used pinned lap joints for the corners of his lamp frames and let the slats into grooves in the frames for the sides of the narrower lamp at the rear. The latticework is made from split bamboo sticks let into holes in the frame and tied with thin strips of linen. Although Maltbie often uses flourescent fixtures to reduce heat, the bulbs in these two lamps are low-wattage incandescents.

A woodworking school project to design a lamp resulted in Chip Mochel's 'Disclamp.' The spherical lamp, left, is made up of 13 hardwood discs, 1/8 in. thick, with walnut veneer laminated on one side and white plastic laminate on the other. A tubular, incandescent bulb (the kind used for a display case or aquarium hood) mounts vertically in a socket in the crescent-shape arm that holds the discs, and it pierces each of the discs through a 2-in. hole in the center. Mochel lives in Roswell, Ga.

Wood Screws
The basics of the basic fastener

by George Mustoe

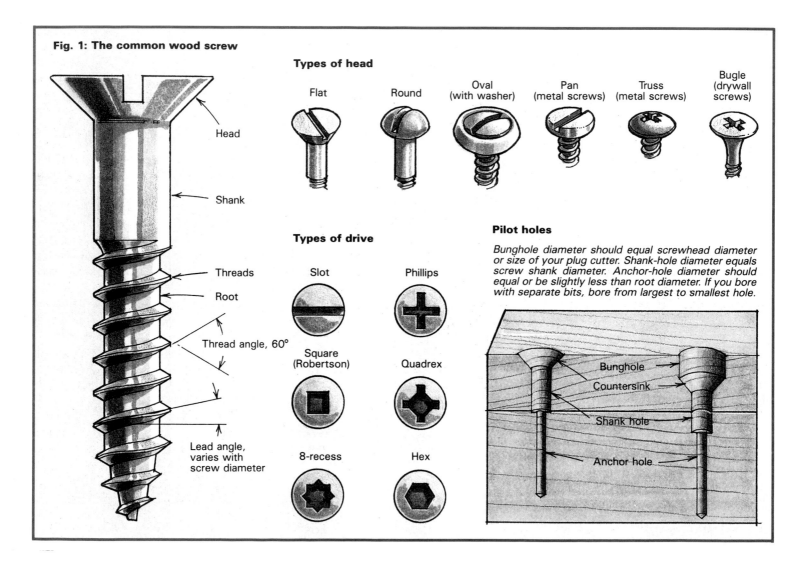

Fig. 1: The common wood screw

Head

Shank

Threads

Root

Thread angle, 60°

Lead angle, varies with screw diameter

Types of head

Flat · Round · Oval (with washer) · Pan (metal screws) · Truss (metal screws) · Bugle (drywall screws)

Types of drive

Slot · Phillips

Square (Robertson) · Quadrex

8-recess · Hex

Pilot holes

Bunghole diameter should equal screwhead diameter or size of your plug cutter. Shank-hole diameter equals screw shank diameter. Anchor-hole diameter should equal or be slightly less than root diameter. If you bore with separate bits, bore from largest to smallest hole.

Bunghole

Countersink

Shank hole

Anchor hole

One day during my late teens I was struck by the desire to build a small sailboat. The fact that I knew nothing about sailing seemed irrelevant, as did my lack of woodworking expertise. After all, I'd built some barn-lumber shelves for my rock collection just the summer before and, as a foolish adolescent, building a boat didn't sound much more difficult. Within a year my 12-foot craft was sunk in a spring storm and I have few memories of sailing it, but, fifteen years later, I still remember the blisters I got driving hundreds of screws to fasten the plywood hull. Since then I've never had a great fondness for wood screws, but I don't share the disdain of purists who believe that metal fasteners are the devil's tool for capturing the souls of cabinetmakers.

Craftsmen who rely on well-cut joints for their finer projects still find screws handy for reinforcing these joints, as well as for attaching hardware, assembling jigs and bending forms, and making the usual run of utility furniture for home and shop (see figure 2, p. 112). Wood screws have gained even greater importance in recent years because of the increased use of particleboard and plywood, materials that are not suited for traditional joinery.

The basic wood screw consists of a head and a shank, roughly two-thirds of which is threaded. Standard wood screws come in lengths from about ¼ in. to 6 in., and a variety of head configurations, as shown in the drawing. In general, flat-head screws are used flush with the surface or hidden beneath a plug.

Round-head screws can be left visible, and, for a fancier touch, you can use oval-head screws seated in nickel-plated finishing washers. Sheet metal and drywall screws are increasingly used in wood (see box, p. 113). Sheet metal screws have flat or pan heads and drywall screws employ bugle heads, which are self-countersinking in sheetrock, most plywood, and softer woods. The drawing also shows some of the variety of drive configurations available. Square-drive screws are common in Canada, where they're called Robertson screws, after their inventor. A square-drive variant, the Quadrex screw, can be driven with either square or Phillips drivers.

Shank diameters are measured in gauge sizes from 0 to 24 (a range from 0.060 in. to about 0.372 in.), the difference between successive gauges being 0.013 in. The solid core of the threaded portion is called the root; its diameter is measured from valley to valley of opposing threads. All screws of the same gauge have the same head, shank and root diameters, regardless of their length. Two angles describe the threads. Single threads viewed in cross section have an included angle of 60°, called the "thread angle." Most wood screws, regardless of other differences, have thread angles of 60°. The "lead angle" is the pitch at which the thread winds around the shank. It varies according to the shank diameter, but is much the same on many common screws—the difference between the lead angle of a #2 screw, with 26 threads per inch (tpi) and a #24 screw, with 7 tpi, is a matter of only a few degrees.

Threads are either cut or rolled on the screw blank. In the first process, metal is cut away on a form of metal lathe. In the second, the blank is squashed between two dies to form the threads. A rolling machine can spit out between 200 and 300 screws per minute, while a thread cutter, which must make half a dozen passes by each blank, can produce only a tenth as many. Chances are, however, that the screws you're using (hardened drywall screws excepted) are cut, not rolled. It seems that third-world countries can produce cut-thread screws cheaper than first-worlders can produce rolled screws. If the outside thread diameter equals the shank diameter, it's probably cut; if the shank diameter is smaller, it's probably rolled. There's no difference in performance, though rolled threads are said to be marginally stronger.

For ordinary wood screws the choice of metal is usually determined by the amount of corrosion resistance that's required, or for appearance. Plain steel screws are not seen much anymore, and most steel screws have a thin plating of nickel, cadmium, or zinc chromate. (Unplated steel screws may stain woods containing tanin, such as oak.) Galvanized screws are better for outdoor uses, but the rough zinc coating makes them hard to drive. Brass and bronze screws are weather resistant and their golden color makes them popular whenever screwheads are visible. Aluminum screws are handy for attaching metal molding and where light weight is important. (Don't use aluminum screws in steel, or vice-versa, as any moisture will cause a galvanic reaction that will rot the hole.) Stainless steel screws offer the ultimate protection against corrosion, but they are relatively expensive.

The mechanical properties of the various types of screws are similar enough and screws appear to be so deceptively simple that workers often give little thought to the engineering considerations that go into a well-planned, screwed joint.

Screwed joints must withstand lateral shearing forces as well as the direct pull of tensile loads. Tensile loads are resisted by the force of the screw threads acting against the head. Lateral loads involve a different type of holding power, namely the friction of the wood surfaces that are being pressed together by the clamping action of the screw. When the surfaces are also glued, the joint's holding power is greatly increased.

The most serious mechanical limitation of wood screws is that they focus stress on a very small area of the joint. This effect is minimized by making sure screws penetrate far enough and are spaced closely enough to distribute their holding power. Several medium-size screws, say #8 or #10, spaced 4 in. to 6 in. apart will be stronger than huge screws placed at 1 ft. intervals. More penetration means more strength. A handy rule of thumb for screw length is that, where possible, the entire threaded portion of the screw should penetrate the piece.

The strength of screwed joints is highly variable according to the size and spacing of the screws, the type of wood, and the grain direction. Withdrawal strength (tensile load), for example, varies according to how deep the screw is inserted and the shear strength of the wood. A #10 wood screw inserted ½ in. into face grain will resist withdrawal up to 678 lb. in maple, but only 346 lb. in yellow poplar. Inserted 1 in., the values rise to 1,400 lb. and 711 lb., respectively. The holding power in any species is about 50% less for endgrain, so screw length should be increased about one and a half times to compensate.

Screws must be kept snug if they are to perform properly. This is a problem particularly with chairs and other solid wood furniture where wood shrinkage, severe overloading or merely the rigors of daily use can cause joints to open up so that the screws are no longer able to maintain pressure between the adjacent wood surfaces. Instead of being distributed evenly over the joint, the loading falls on the shank of the screw. If the screw loosens, it may pull out. More likely, the joint will fail when the wood around the screw tears out or splits.

The strength of the screw metal is not very important in determining the final strength of the joint, for even the softest metals are much stronger than the wood they penetrate. When screws do break during driving, it's almost always because the pilot hole is too small. In effect, you shear off the screw—proof that the lateral strength of a screw is much less than its tensile strength.

Screwed joints don't allow wood movement to take place, so screws cause problems when used to attach solid wood panels to cabinet carcases, or in other situations where humidity changes would cause expansion or contraction along the joint. Several methods of allowing for movement when attaching tabletops or panels with screws are shown in figure 2.

Most screwdriving problems are related to the pilot hole. In fact, the pilot hole consists of several concentric holes, as shown in the drawing on the facing page. The plug or bunghole (or countersink, if a flat-head screw isn't to be hidden) should be at least the diameter of the screwhead or of your plug cutter. The shank clearance hole should be the same diameter as the unthreaded portion of the screw's shank. This allows the shank to slide through the wood without binding so the two pieces are drawn together as the screw is tightened.

The anchor hole is drilled the same diameter or slightly smaller than the screw's root diameter. If the anchor hole is too large in diameter, the holding power is reduced and the screw is likely to strip out of the hole. Too narrow and you're in for some hard driving and the possibility of a broken screw or split lumber. Some wood technologists recommend that anchor holes be 70% of root diameter, larger for denser woods, and

Fig. 2: Screw joints for furniture

Fine furniture

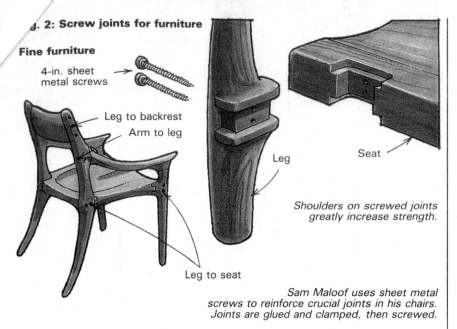

4-in. sheet metal screws

Leg to backrest

Arm to leg

Leg

Seat

Leg to seat

Shoulders on screwed joints greatly increase strength.

Sam Maloof uses sheet metal screws to reinforce crucial joints in his chairs. Joints are glued and clamped, then screwed.

Traditional chairmakers also reinforced joints with screws.

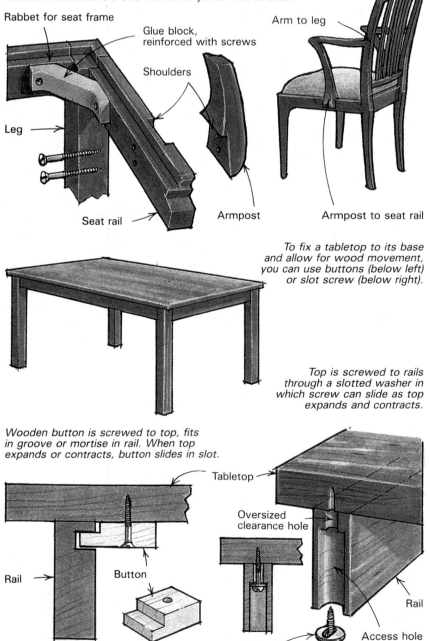

Rabbet for seat frame

Glue block, reinforced with screws

Shoulders

Arm to leg

Leg

Seat rail

Armpost

Armpost to seat rail

To fix a tabletop to its base and allow for wood movement, you can use buttons (below left) or slot screw (below right).

Top is screwed to rails through a slotted washer in which screw can slide as top expands and contracts.

Wooden button is screwed to top, fits in groove or mortise in rail. When top expands or contracts, button slides in slot.

Rail

Button

Tabletop

Oversized clearance hole

Rail

Access hole

File elongated slot in standard washer.

Screws in utility furniture

An Adirondack chair can be assembled entirely with screws.

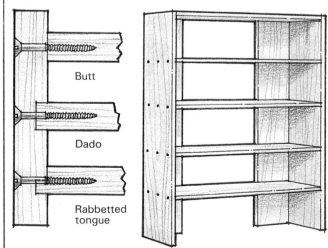

Flat panels for doors, tabletops and carcase sides can be quickly made with screwed battens. Screwing pattern shown here makes no allowance for wood movement, but provides for maximum strength through triangulation.

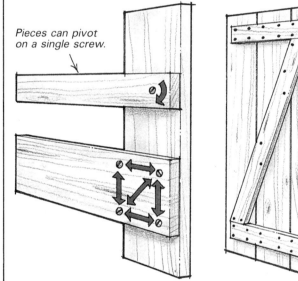

Pieces can pivot on a single screw.

Screws in rectangular pattern resist racking through triangulation of forces between any combination of three screws.

For simple carcases, like this bookcase, screws can provide the primary joint (butt joint), or can reinforce stronger, shouldered joints (dado and tongue).

Butt

Dado

Rabbetted tongue

Wide back battens screwed to carcase top, sides and shelves triangulates the structure and makes it rigid. A full back of thin plywood or Masonite will do the same.

Drywall screws: who needs pilot holes?

by Paul Bertorelli

My hatred of the common wood screw has nothing to do with the purist's view that wood ought not be defiled by metal. Except for dowels, I'll stoop to any method of fastening wood, so long as it gets the job done in a hurry. What I can't stand is rummaging around my drill box for the right pilot bits (usually burned and dull) and my drill's extension cord (upstairs running the fan), only to discover that I've lost the chuck key again.

I had just about resigned myself to common wood screws and their attendant paraphernalia when a friend introduced me to drywall screws six years ago. These case-hardened screws are engineered to penetrate drywall, wood and thin metal without a pilot hole. They were developed during the 1960s when metal framing began displacing wooden studs in commercial buildings. Before long, cabinet and furniture shops discovered how effective they are for woodworking. These days, they are often available in the local hardware store along with low-cost power driving attachments for electric drills.

Drywall screws more closely resemble self-tapping sheet metal screws than regular wood screws. They have a straight shank that terminates in a needle-sharp gimlet point capable of penetrating light metal and wood under power driving. Usually, the shank is threaded right up to the base of the head, but some drywall-type screws have partially unthreaded shanks. Most drywall screws have double lead, which means that two threads wrap their way around the shank rather than just one. The angle at which each of these threads climbs the shank is double that of an equivalent conventional wood screw, so double-lead screws drive faster. Some manufacturers say they have marginally greater withdrawal strength than single

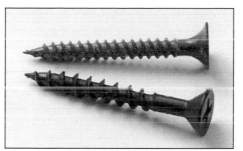

For speed and holding power, drywall screws are hard to beat. Top screw has a double lead, fully threaded shank. Bottom screw has single-lead threads.

leads, but the difference rarely matters in woodworking applications.

The threads themselves are deeper than those of a conventional wood screw, that is, their height represents a greater proportion of the root diameter. Deep threads are why drywall screws work so well without a pilot hole. They bite hard and forcefully pull the screw into the wood, displacing the wood and compressing it rather than actually boring a hole as a pilot bit does. With all that compressed wood crammed into the threads, drywall screws are supposed to be very resistant to stripping, especially in plywood and particleboard where conventional screws don't hold nearly as well. Despite this forceful entry, these screws don't seem to cause much splitting when driven in hardwood, at least in my experience.

Drywall screws aren't available in as many varieties as are conventional screws. The most common sizes are #6 and #8 in lengths from ¾ in. up to 3 in. Some suppliers sell larger and smaller sizes, but I've found that a box each of #8 Phillips head in 1¼-in. and 2-in. lengths covers virtually all of my needs.

Drywall screws have bugle heads, their

undersides gently radiused rather than sharply angled like a regular flat head. In softwood, some hardwoods and plywood, a bugle head will neatly countersink itself. In meaner woods, you may have to help the screw along with a countersink before driving, and a single-diameter pilot hole makes driving easier. But in most applications, you don't need a pilot hole at all.

My weapon of choice for driving drywall screws in wood is a Makita electric screwdriver fitted with a Phillips bit in a magnetic holder. Simply snap on a screw, jab the point into the wood and pull the trigger. You can drive these screws by hand but frankly, I don't see the point of it. One of the reasons they are case-hardened is to stand up to punishing torque of power driving. In six years, I can only remember snapping one.

I pop in a drywall screw anywhere a regular screw might go. For utility shelving out of plywood, for example, I just butt join the parts with four or five screws across a shelf 10 in. wide. Glued carcase joints can be pulled home with a few drywall screws and the screws left in for additional strength. Conventional screws are too wimpy for that kind of barbarism. If I want a neater job I either do a quick countersink or use a brad-point drill fitted with a depth stop to bore a bunghole.

The only thing I don't really understand about drywall screws is why they haven't driven conventional wood screws into complete oblivion. Perhaps it's nostalgia. I've got a couple of dozen boxes of old-style wood screws gathering dust in my shop. I guess I'm saving them for something, but I can't imagine what it might be. □

Paul Bertorelli is editor of Fine Woodworking *magazine.*

most screw manufacturers give away charts listing optimum drill sizes. But it's easy to select the proper drill bits just by holding them up against the screw to compare diameters. It's a wise idea to drill a pilot hole in a piece of scrap lumber to test the anchor hole fit, though. Leave the anchor hole shallow so that the leading two or three threads penetrate solid wood.

A small dab of tallow, soap, beeswax or paraffin makes insertion easier, but lubrication won't be necessary if the proper size pilot hole is used. Try to resist the urge to give that final jerk, which can twist off the screw. If a reluctant screw won't turn quite as far as you'd like, try striking the screwdriver one sharp, downward blow with a mallet. The compression will usually create just enough slack so that the screw can be rotated another one-half turn. You'll also avoid marred screwheads and gouged work by using a driver that fits the screwhead snugly.

To make pilot holes for bunged screws, three different bits are needed: one for the anchor hole, one for the clearance hole and one for the bunghole. This explains why so many impatient workers end up trying to use brute force to make a screw fit into a single hole. If you use more than an occasional screw, it's worth the expense to buy a set of pilot-hole bits, which drill stair-stepped or tapered holes in a single operation, including the countersink or plug hole.

Three styles of pilot-hole bits are commonly available, either

Pilot bits, another view

by Michael Podmaniczky

As George Mustoe has pointed out, the job of properly boring pilot holes for a screw requires three different-size drill bits, one each for anchor, clearance and recess (the bunghole, to a boatbuilder). Boring three separate holes takes time, an important factor to the professional, so various "step" bits were developed. They are indeed faster, but have serious drawbacks. Adjustment is minimal or absent, and waste clearance is ineffective. Tapered bits, for example, cut along their full length, making them prone to overheating, and they are difficult and expensive to sharpen. More often than not, step bits produce burned wood, dull

bits and oversized bungholes from the repeated plunging necessary to clear the waste. If time isn't your main concern, there's a better way to do the job.

Decide on the screw sizes you most commonly use: probably #6, #8, #10 and maybe #12. Trot down to the hardware store and buy four *good* twist bits to match each screw size: two anchors (one each for hard and soft wood), one for shank clearance and one for countersinking and bungholes. This last bit should allow for the smallest-size bung possible, and should be ground to match the shape of the underside of the screw head. To en-

sure a very tight bung fit, I've also had the diameters of the bung bits professionally ground a few thousandths undersize. If you're feeling flush, buy brad-point bits as well for countersinking round-head screws—they produce a flat bedding surface for the screw head.

Mount all of these bits in a nicely finished block of wood, stand it on the shelf over your workbench and you are ready for anything. □

Michael Podmaniczky of Williamstown, Mass., is a contributing editor to Fine Woodworking.

Pilot bits range in sophistication from the one-piece, non-adjustable bit at bottom right to the three-piece tapered twist drill with countersink/bunghole and depth collar at top right. Between is a two-piece rig consisting of a common twist bit and a countersink/bunghole cutter. From left are a brad point twist bit, two plug cutters and a Vix pilot bit, which centers a twist bit in hardware holes—hinges, locks, strike plates and so on.

as individual bits or in sets that cover the most common screw sizes (examples are shown in the photo at left). The least expensive kinds are single-piece flat or half-round steel bits. Their limitation is complete lack of adjustability—a #12 bit, for example, might work great for a 2-in.-long screw, but poorly for longer or shorter sizes. For only a little more money, you can buy pilot bits having an adjustable cutting sleeve. With these, the shank hole depth remains constant, but you can vary the depth of the anchor hole. Some of these adjustable bits have flat cutters, but the best ones use a twist drill for the anchor hole. A set of four costs about $7. Tapered twist bits cut both anchor and shank holes at the same time with exceptional accuracy, and they stay sharp longer than the other two types. Each screw size requires a bit, a matching countersink/bung borer, and a collar depth stop. A set of seven can cost from $50 to $70. They're worth the cost if you use a lot of screws, especially when working with very hard wood. □

George Mustoe, a geologist and woodworker, lives in Bellingham, Wash.

Sources of supply

A wide variety of screws, pilot bits and screwdrivers are generally available at hardware stores. Here are some other sources:

Screws—Reed and Prince, one of the largest screw manufacturers in the country, doesn't sell small quantities direct; to find the distributor nearest you, write to Judy Hogan, Reed and Prince, 1 Duncan Avenue, Worcester, MA 01603, or phone (800) 225-7260. Trend-Lines (375 Beacham St., Chelsea, MA 02150) carries a good selection of wood and drywall screws. Parker-Kalon (395 Roberts Road, Campbellsville, KY 42718) makes a drill-point drywall screw for use in heavier metals, and Woodshop Machines (70 Regional Drive, Concord, NH 03301) sells Quadrex screws. Write for information.

Tools—Pilot bits, brad-point bits, power-drive bits, plug cutters, and a variety of hand and power drivers are carried by Garrett Wade Co. (161 Avenue of the Americas, New York, NY 10013), Woodcraft (41 Atlantic Ave., P.O. Box 4000, Woburn, MA 01888), and Trend-Lines (see above).

Hanging a Cabinet Door
Swinging with brass butt hinges

by Roger Holmes

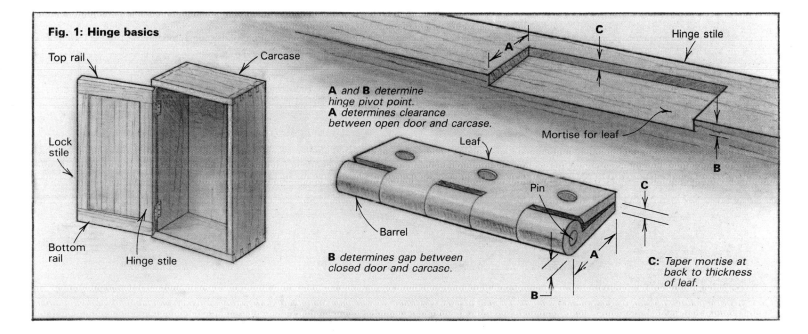

Fig. 1: Hinge basics

Top rail

Carcase

Lock stile

Bottom rail

Hinge stile

A and *B* determine hinge pivot point.
A determines clearance between open door and carcase.

Leaf

Barrel

Pin

B determines gap between closed door and carcase.

Mortise for leaf

A

C

Hinge stile

B

C

C: *Taper mortise at back to thickness of leaf.*

B

A

B

Hanging a cabinet door well is as important as making it well—unsightly gaps, a sloppy fit or a sticky door can ruin the effect of the loveliest wood and most meticulous joinery. You can hang a door with anything from interlocking clenched nails to space-age plastic inserts. Solid, extruded (or drawn) brass butt hinges have a nice look and feel, and I prefer them for most quality work. Accurate layout and a careful, step-by-step approach are essential to making butt hinges work properly, as well as look nice. Although I will describe how to hang a flush door (one hung inside the carcase, flush with the carcase edges), the steps are much the same for butt-hinging other types of doors, too.

You may have a little trouble finding extruded hinges. Most hardware store brass hinges are stamped or pressed from a single sheet, and the hinge barrels are bent around the pins. Although these hinges are cheaper than the extruded ones, their leaves are thin and often rattle around the pin. Extruded hinges, made by forcing hot brass through dies shaped to the desired cross-section, are generally heavier, tighter and sturdier than pressed hinges. (Extruded brass hinges in a variety of sizes are available from Garrett Wade, 161 Avenue of the Americas, New York, N.Y. 10013.)

Hinges are commonly described by their height and open width, in that order. A 2-in. by 1½-in. hinge, therefore, has leaves ¾-in. wide, measured to the center of the barrel. The width of the hinge needed for each door depends on the thickness of the

door stile and width of the hinging surface on the carcase. You can figure widths on a full-scale drawing or by trying various hinges against the door itself. If you want a rough general rule, double the thickness of the stile (or carcase surface if it's narrower) to get the hinge width. A ¾-in. door, for example, can accommodate a 1½-in.-wide hinge. The barrel protrudes beyond door and carcase, allowing the door to swing open and making room for a stopped mortise, which hides the edge of the hinge from view on the door's inside face. Long hinges give more support, for obvious reasons, but balance length against looks—I seldom use hinges longer than 2 in. on all but the largest cabinets.

The leaves of extruded hinges can be rectangular in section or tapered. A tapered hinge is lighter for the same strength, but the difference is insignificant for cabinet-sized hinges; there are only minor differences in installation. Most cabinet butts I've found have been tapered. I recommend fixed-pin hinges for cabinet doors; the convenience of loose-pin hinges, which can be disassembled during installation, is outweighed by the sloppy fit of pin to leaves.

I use two butt hinges for most cabinet doors, adding a third in the middle of doors over 30 in. high. The position of the top and bottom hinges is mostly a matter of taste. I usually try to line them up in some way with the top and bottom rails of frame-and-panel doors. The middle hinge isn't necessary for strength as much as to keep the center of the hinge stile from moving slight-

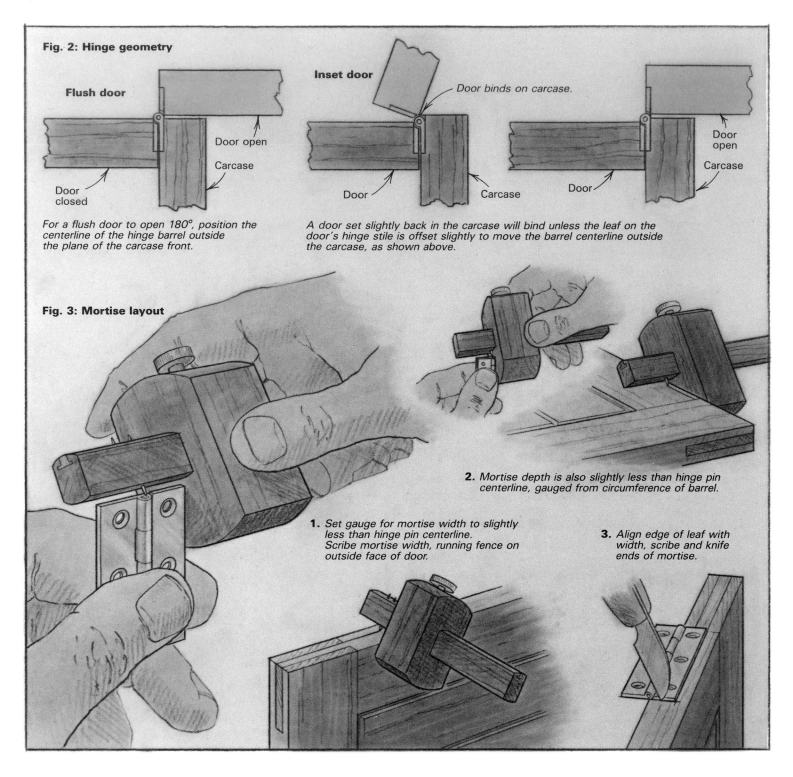

Fig. 2: Hinge geometry

Flush door

Door open

Carcase

Door closed

For a flush door to open 180°, position the centerline of the hinge barrel outside the plane of the carcase front.

Inset door

Door binds on carcase.

Door

Carcase

Door open

Carcase

Door

A door set slightly back in the carcase will bind unless the leaf on the door's hinge stile is offset slightly to move the barrel centerline outside the carcase, as shown above.

Fig. 3: Mortise layout

1. Set gauge for mortise width to slightly less than hinge pin centerline. Scribe mortise width, running fence on outside face of door.

2. Mortise depth is also slightly less than hinge pin centerline, gauged from circumference of barrel.

3. Align edge of leaf with width, scribe and knife ends of mortise.

ly and binding the door. A center hinge can help to pull a slight bow out of a door, too. The position of the centerline of the pin, which is the pivot point of the hinge, determines how far the door will open, as shown in figure 2. A full-scale section drawing through door, hinge and carcase will help determine hinge position—rotate the hinge on a push-pin pivot to see how far the door will open.

I think a well-fitted door should show a uniform gap between it and the surrounding carcase. It should open smoothly, without binding or sticking. For doors that won't expand or contract much with changes in ambient humidity, such as frame-and-panel or veneered doors, I shoot for gaps of 1/32 in. all around; more if I'm hanging the door during the dry season. The larger the door, the greater the gap should be. You can vary the size of the gap between hinge stile and carcase by varying the depth of the mortises

for the leaves. Making the mortises half the diameter of the barrel (the centerline of the pin) will bring the stile flush to the carcase. Shallower mortises give greater clearance. The barrel diameter of most cabinet-size brass butts is greater than the combined thicknesses of the two tapered leaves. A closed hinge will, therefore, taper. To make a neat job, I taper the mortises from front to back so that the back edge of the hinge will be flush with the surface.

When you build the carcase, make it as square as possible, especially at the door opening. Sight over the carcase or frame around the opening, as you would over winding sticks, to check for twist, and plane off high spots. Make the door slightly larger (at least 1/16 in. overall) than the opening. Then, regardless of the type of door—frame and panel, veneered, board and batten—make sure it's flat. It's virtually impossible to correct all but the slightest of twists during hanging. Check for twist by rocking the door on a flat surface or by sighting over winding sticks. A slight twist can be planed out, but if you find yourself thinning the door down appreciably to remove a twist, make another door.

Next, fit the door to the opening. First plane the edge of the door's hinge stile flat and square to the door's face. Try the door to the opening, pressing the hinge stile against the carcase side and the bottom rail against the carcase bottom. Plane off the wood necessary to make the bottom rail conform to the carcase. Try the door to the opening again, then plane the top rail to fit; repeat for the final stile. The order isn't important, as long as the result is a door that slips into the opening with very little play up or down. You can plane the door to create the clearance now and hang the door using shims—small pieces of card or veneer as thick as the desired gap—inserted between door and carcase. I prefer to hang the door first, then plane for clearance.

After determining the position of the hinges, I mortise the door first. (I'll describe fitting a door flush with the carcase, a fine gap all around. Alter the marking gauge settings to suit your taste.) Put the door hinge-stile-up in the vise, set a marking gauge from the edge of the leaf to just shy of the pin centerline. This locates the pivot point outside the carcase and allows the door to open 180° (figure 2). Mark the edge of the hinge stile at the hinge locations, running the fence against the outside face of the door (figure 3). Set another gauge for the mortise depth; again, just shy of the pin centerline. The amount by which the setting is shy of dead center equals half the finished gap between door and carcase. (Two gauges are useful for hanging a flush door, as the settings are the same for laying out the mortises on the carcase.) Scribe this setting on the face of the door at the hinge locations. Position the hinge on the door, its long edge aligned with the first gauge mark and knife against its ends. This ensures a snug fit in the mortise—the ends of few hinges are exactly square to the edges.

Now chisel out the waste. I carefully score the gauged and knifed lines with a sharp chisel, then make a series of chops, as shown in figure 4, along the length of the mortise, about $\frac{1}{32}$ in. from the scored outlines and as near the final depth as possible. The chops break the wood fibers and make it easy to clean to the bottom of the mortise by paring with a wide chisel. Finally, slice down to establish the outline and try the hinge in place.

I fix the hinge through only one hole at this time, in case it needs adjusting later. Centering screws in hinge holes can be terribly frustrating, particularly in open-grained woods. I position the hole with a carefully placed awl and a steady hand. Deepen the hole with the awl when the position is right, to keep the pilot-hole bit from wandering. I place the screw just off-center toward the back of the mortise, so it will pull the hinge tight. It is prudent to use steel screws during fitting. Brass screws have an infuriating tendency to twist off; steel screws prepare the way for the final installation with brass screws, thereby avoiding much gnashing of teeth.

Next, fold the hinges shut and slip the door into the carcase; the lock stile won't go in all the way because of the hinges. Knife the positions of the hinges on the carcase side (figure 5). If you've already planed for clearance, place the shims before knifing. Remove the door and gauge the mortise width and depth on the carcase. Align the hinge with the knifed position marks and knife the mortise ends, as for the door. It's most convenient to chop and pare the mortises with the carcase side supported on the workbench.

Now screw the door to the carcase, one screw to a leaf. I plane

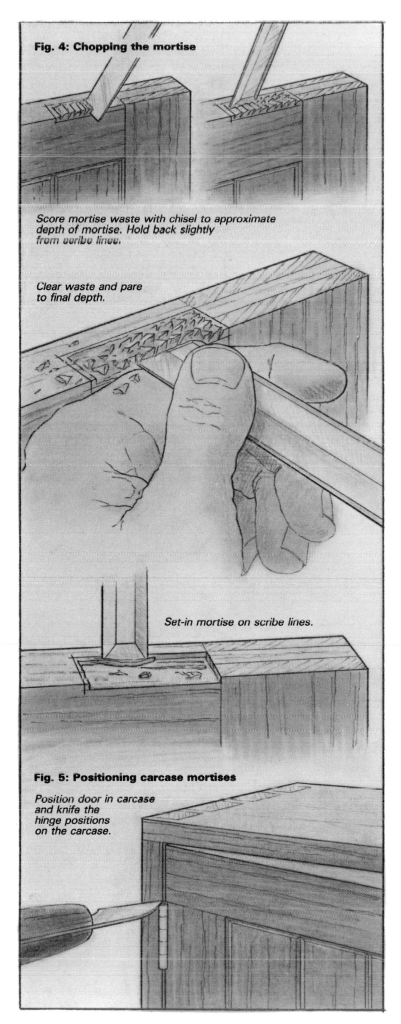

Fig. 4: Chopping the mortise

Score mortise waste with chisel to approximate depth of mortise. Hold back slightly from scribe lines.

Clear waste and pare to final depth.

Set-in mortise on scribe lines.

Fig. 5: Positioning carcase mortises

Position door in carcase and knife the hinge positions on the carcase.

clearance on the lock stile first, beveling the edge back from the front to allow for the radius of the swing. Then plane top and bottom rails. You'll probably have the doors on and off two or three times to do this, so remember to use the steel screws. Uniform gaps make a single door look good and a row of doors look even better, so it's worth a little extra trouble.

Though attractive, simple and durable, butt hinges aren't built for adjustment. Vertical movement is impossible without plugging screw holes and extending mortises. You can adjust the gaps by packing out one or more hinge mortises with paper, card

or veneer shims. You make a slight twist in a door less noticeable by adjusting the width of a mortise. If, for example, the bottom of the lock stile is set farther back from the carcase edge than the top is, widen the top carcase hinge mortise. This will pull the top of the hinge stile in and push the bottom of the lock stile out. This is just a balancing technique, evening the twist out around the door; it can't be relied upon to take the twist out of the door. □

Roger Holmes is an associate editor of Fine Woodworking.

Router mortising Soss hinges   by C.B. Oliver

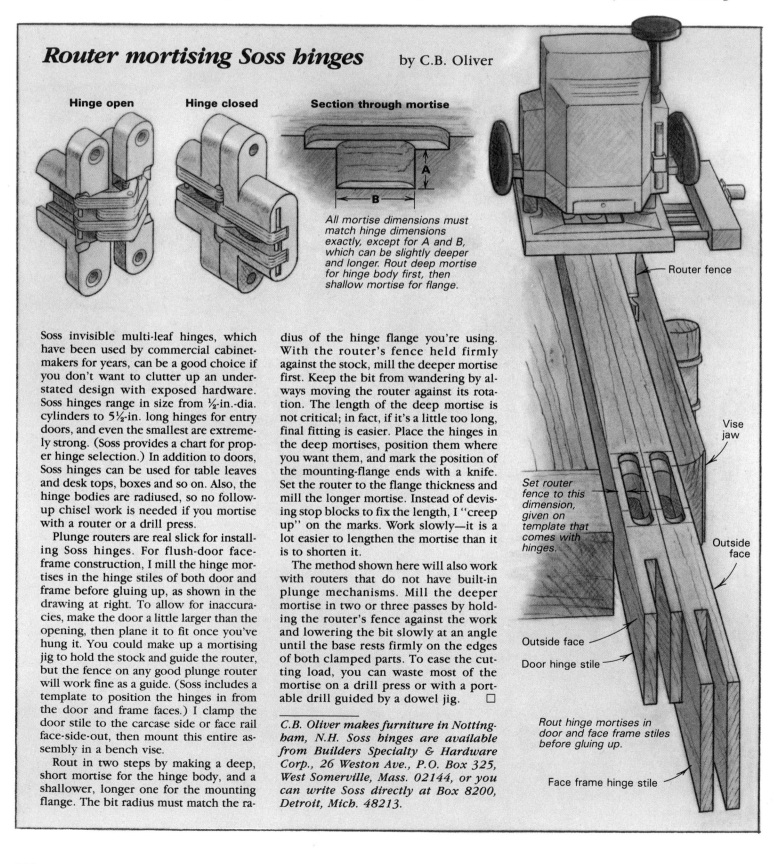

Hinge open

Hinge closed

Section through mortise

All mortise dimensions must match hinge dimensions exactly, except for A and B, which can be slightly deeper and longer. Rout deep mortise for hinge body first, then shallow mortise for flange.

Router fence

Vise jaw

Set router fence to this dimension, given on template that comes with hinges.

Outside face

Outside face

Door hinge stile

Rout hinge mortises in door and face frame stiles before gluing up.

Face frame hinge stile

Soss invisible multi-leaf hinges, which have been used by commercial cabinetmakers for years, can be a good choice if you don't want to clutter up an understated design with exposed hardware. Soss hinges range in size from ½-in.-dia. cylinders to 5½-in. long hinges for entry doors, and even the smallest are extremely strong. (Soss provides a chart for proper hinge selection.) In addition to doors, Soss hinges can be used for table leaves and desk tops, boxes and so on. Also, the hinge bodies are radiused, so no follow-up chisel work is needed if you mortise with a router or a drill press.

Plunge routers are real slick for installing Soss hinges. For flush-door face-frame construction, I mill the hinge mortises in the hinge stiles of both door and frame before gluing up, as shown in the drawing at right. To allow for inaccuracies, make the door a little larger than the opening, then plane it to fit once you've hung it. You could make up a mortising jig to hold the stock and guide the router, but the fence on any good plunge router will work fine as a guide. (Soss includes a template to position the hinges in from the door and frame faces.) I clamp the door stile to the carcase side or face rail face-side-out, then mount this entire assembly in a bench vise.

Rout in two steps by making a deep, short mortise for the hinge body, and a shallower, longer one for the mounting flange. The bit radius must match the ra-

dius of the hinge flange you're using. With the router's fence held firmly against the stock, mill the deeper mortise first. Keep the bit from wandering by always moving the router against its rotation. The length of the deep mortise is not critical; in fact, if it's a little too long, final fitting is easier. Place the hinges in the deep mortises, position them where you want them, and mark the position of the mounting-flange ends with a knife. Set the router to the flange thickness and mill the longer mortise. Instead of devising stop blocks to fix the length, I "creep up" on the marks. Work slowly—it is a lot easier to lengthen the mortise than it is to shorten it.

The method shown here will also work with routers that do not have built-in plunge mechanisms. Mill the deeper mortise in two or three passes by holding the router's fence against the work and lowering the bit slowly at an angle until the base rests firmly on the edges of both clamped parts. To ease the cutting load, you can waste most of the mortise on a drill press or with a portable drill guided by a dowel jig. □

C.B. Oliver makes furniture in Nottingham, N.H. Soss hinges are available from Builders Specialty & Hardware Corp., 26 Weston Ave., P.O. Box 325, West Somerville, Mass. 02144, or you can write Soss directly at Box 8200, Detroit, Mich. 48213.

Wooden Hardware
Giving your furniture the right pull

by Jay McDougall

One challenging design problem for many furniture-makers is developing pulls and handles that enhance their designs. It's rare to find that elusive "perfect pull" in a catalog or at a local hardware store. You can't have too many options in this area, so here are three ideas to stuff into your burgeoning bag of tricks.

The coved pull shown below has been a real workhorse for me, since it can be modified for many different applications. It's made with a tablesaw and hand tools, then simply glued to the edge of a drawer front or door. A second option is to employ the same design on a smaller pull, which can be shaped with a router. The final example is an undercut crescent pull, ideal for contemporary "Deco revival-style" furniture. When painted black or some other accent color, the pulls, shown on p. 121, exude a classic look, much like shirt studs on a tuxedo.

The size of the pull always depends on the dimensions of the door or drawer on which it will be mounted. A typical blank for tablesawn coved pulls, like the ones shown in the photo series on p. 120, is 2 in. wide and ¾ in. thick and long enough to span the door or drawer. For side-by-side drawers, you may want to cut the stock longer so you can have uninterrupted grain patterns in abutting drawers. This is a must if you have continuous grain in the drawer fronts themselves. Allow yourself extra length for waste,

experimentation and (don't kid yourself) mistakes.

To begin, I form the coves with a 6-in. dado head, set for a ¼-in.-wide cut (see photos, top of next page). The fence is set at an 18° angle to the blade. Next, I rip the coved pieces. Note that each piece is ripped twice—first with the blade set at 45° to remove the front corner of the pull, then with the blade set at 90° to remove the waste at the back of the pull. This step establishes a ridge that aligns the pull on the drawer or door edge. For a continuous pull, all that remains is to glue on the pieces and fair everything with spokeshave, chisel or scraper/sandpaper. For a contoured pull, make a template of the curve, trace it on the cove side and saw it out with a coping saw or bandsaw. Fine sandpaper makes a good non-slip template for small pieces.

The procedure for making smaller coved pulls is the same, except the coves are cut with a router fitted with a fence attachment and a core-box bit. Again, the size of the pull is determined by the dimensions of the door or drawer; I most often use 4-in. pulls cut from ¾ in. thick stock. To prevent the stock from flexing, and to provide an adequate bearing surface for the router, I usually rout the pulls in stock that's at least 3 in. wide, then rip off strips of pulls.

Routing is pretty straightforward. Make a template defining the profile of the pull and the length of the coves. The profile is marked only on the face of the stock, but the cove length must be transferred with a square to the back side of the board. Depending on your taste, you can cut through coves or stopped coves on each side of the pull. Set the router's fence (or guide strip) so the cove will be centered in the pull's width, ⅜ in. from the front edge. The depth of the cove cut is a matter of taste. Just a hair (about ¹⁄₆₄ in.) over ¼ in. works well for this size pull. Cut the coves between your layout lines with a ⁷⁄₁₆-in. core-box bit. Flip the board over and cut the corresponding cove marked on the flip side. (Here's where a plunge router pays for itself.)

You can save yourself untold aggravation by sanding the coves and rounding off the front edges with a spokeshave and/or sander before you cut out the individual pulls with a bandsaw or coping saw. Coarse 80-grit paper rounds off the hard edges on the coves and produces a nice-feeling pull. When ripping the two ¾-in. strips of pulls, keep the ¾-in. strip on the side of the blade away from the rip fence to avoid kickback. Bandsawing the pulls apart and fairing all the surfaces completes the process.

To make a crescent pull like the ones shown on p. 121, cut out a wooden circle, undercut or chamfer its back edge, then cut off two sections, or arcs, to form crescents. For 4-in. diameter or larger pulls, I use ¾-in.-thick stock; ⅝-in. or ½-in. stock is fine for smaller pulls. If the pulls will be painted, they should be cut from a dense, close-grained wood such as maple, birch or beech. You

Handshaped hardwood pull adds a distinctive touch to drawers. The pulls are coved on a tablesaw, then shaped on a bandsaw.

From *Fine Woodworking* magazine (May 1987) 64:78-80

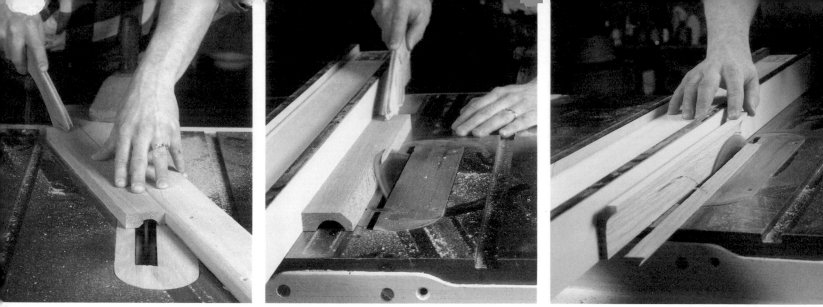

After ripping out 2-in.-wide blanks, author McDougall coves the pulls on a tablesaw with a dado head set for a ¼-in. cut, above left. The narrower the dado setting, the smaller the flat spot on the top of the cove. The fence angle is 18°. Several passes are needed to make a ⅜-in.-deep cove, with its edge about ¼ in. from the front of the blank. The cove blanks are then ripped twice with a sharp, preferably carbide-tipped, blade. McDougall sets the blade at 45° to rip off the front corner of the blank, above center. The fence setting is 2⅛₆ in. Next, he sets the blade at 90° with a 1-in. depth of cut and rips the waste from the back of the blade, above right. The fence is set slightly under ⅜ in. from the blade, creating a small ridge that serves as a guide when gluing the pull to a door or drawer edge. The pull will be about ¼ in. proud at the back and must be planed or scraped.

The pulls are glued and clamped to the drawer fronts in pairs, back-to-back, left. For a contoured pull, McDougall traces a template onto the cove, above, then band-saws the curve before finishing with spokeshave, chisel and sandpaper.

Small hardwood door pulls like the ones above are shaped with a router and a core-box bit. The 3-in.-wide stock resists flexing and provides a stable surface for the router and its fence attachment, right. Then, the strips of pulls are ripped apart.

The contemporary-looking crescent pulls above are two halves of a bandsawn disc, which is cut apart after being chamfered.

could also use the same wood as you used for the furniture, or some nicely contrasting species.

To speed up the process, make the jig shown at top right to bandsaw rough-cut squares into discs. Cut a sawkerf to the middle of a piece of plywood that can be clamped to the saw table. Then, install a pin and a pivoting arm to carry each disc into the blade as the discs are rotated and cut round, as shown. The same jig also holds the discs when you chamfer and sand them. To lay out the discs, cut several round Plexiglas or hardboard templates. Drill a center hole in each template, then a second hole 1 in. from the center for a stabilizer pin to lock the blanks when you don't want them to spin. I make the pins from ⁵⁄₃₂-in.-diameter brazing rods. Use a template to mark the two holes on the blanks, aligning the holes with the grain, and drill the ¹¹⁄₆₄-in. center and stabilizer holes.

Next, mount the jig on the support table of a stationary bench sander set in its vertical position. Position the jig's long edge ⅛ in. from the belt, as shown at right, and mark a new center pin hole so that ¹⁄₁₆ in. to ³⁄₃₂ in. will be sanded off the discs when they are rotated against the belt. While you have the jig on the sander, you should also true and sand the template/shim discs, which will be needed in the next step. Once you've sanded true circles, you can rout around the blanks to chamfer their back edges to form the pulls' finger grips. Use the Plexiglas template to mark a ⅛-in. hole near the center pin so you can use the stablizer pin to secure the disc. Shim the discs with the templates to raise them away from the jig (allowing clearance for the chamfer bit's bearing guide), and insert the center and stabilizer pins. With the shims and pull blank in place, back side up (see photo, far right), rout the chamfers. The chamfers are sanded much the same way as the edges were, except the sander table must be tilted 45°. I also mount the discs on the jig when I hand sand to soften the edges.

The final step is to cut the crescents. Use the template to mark the center and stabilizer holes about 2½ in. from the long edge of a 9-in. by 12-in. piece of plywood. Bore the holes parallel to the saw's line of cut. Mount the discs face down for a larger bearing surface. Set the tablesaw fence, as shown at right, to rip the size crescent you want from the disc, mounted on the plywood. Make the initial cut with the crescent on the side of the blade opposite the fence, then rotate the remaining piece 180° before mounting it on the pins for the second cut. If you dislike holding the pull this close to the blade, install a lever-action clamp on the jig.

After sanding, I attach the pulls with screws from the inside of the door or drawer front. The screws help position the pulls properly, but you could get away with just using glue. The end product will be a versatile pull that feels as great as it looks. ☐

Jay McDougall is a furniture designer and builder in Fergus Falls, Minn. Photos by the author.

Discs are cut from 3¾-in. squares on a jig mounted to a bandsaw table. A hole is bored in the center of each square, so it can be mounted on a swinging arm, which carries the blank into the blade as it's rotated through the cut. The pin on the arm is located so that the distance between it and the blade equals the radius of the disc and is tangential to the blade's line of cut. A stop pin secures the arm in cutting position.

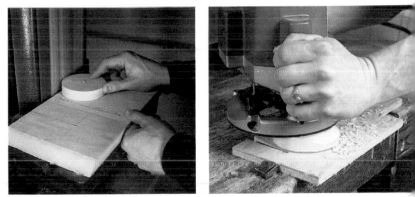

Each disc is rotated on a pin and trued against a sanding belt, above left. Two pins secure the disc when its back edges are routed, above right. Plexiglas shims under the disc provide clearance for the chamfer bit's bearing guide.

A piece of plywood serves as a carrier for ripping crescents from the shaped discs. The discs are fastened to the plywood with two ¼-in. brazing rod pins. Set the fence as shown, above, to cut the desired crescent size. After ripping off one crescent, rotate the remaining piece 180° and rip off the second.

Buying and Drying
How to find and season your own lumber

by Todd Scholl

Fig. 1: Log yield

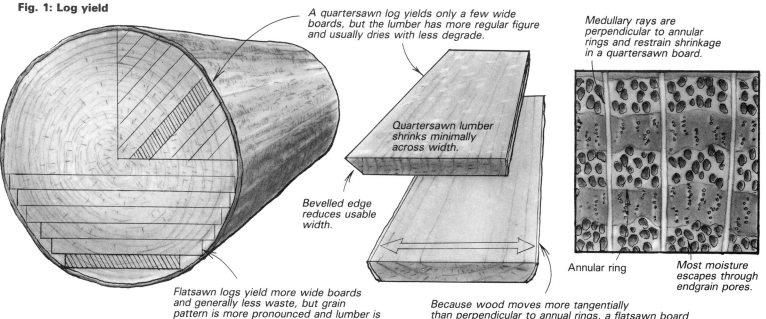

A quartersawn log yields only a few wide boards, but the lumber has more regular figure and usually dries with less degrade.

Medullary rays are perpendicular to annular rings and restrain shrinkage in a quartersawn board.

Quartersawn lumber shrinks minimally across width.

Bevelled edge reduces usable width.

Annular ring

Most moisture escapes through endgrain pores.

Flatsawn logs yield more wide boards and generally less waste, but grain pattern is more pronounced and lumber is more susceptible to warp.

Because wood moves more tangentially than perpendicular to annual rings, a flatsawn board shrinks and swells considerably in width.

Getting lumber from the sawmill to the tablesaw yourself can be a long and difficult process, but it is a worthwhile one. Professionals and amateurs alike can realize hefty savings by buying lumber right at the mill and drying it themselves. You can save 50% or more by dealing directly with a sawmill instead of with a lumber retailer.

Economics aside, there are other less-tangible benefits. Having operated my own small sawmill at one time, I enjoy talking to sawyers and rummaging around sawmills. I've developed a greater understanding of wood and have learned that handling it carefully early on produces better material and ultimately benefits the furniture I build. I find great satisfaction in buying green lumber, drying it and turning it into a fine piece of woodwork.

Before you set out to hunt lumber at the source, you need to decide what species, size and quality wood you want. If you're building furniture, you'll probably be most interested in hardwoods, but you'll need to get straight on the thickness (4/4, 6/4, 8/4, and so on); the width (typically most mills saw boards in random widths up to 16 in.); and the lengths (which are also most often random). For the best furniture work, the highest hardwood grade, firsts and seconds (FAS), is appropriate. But good bargains can be had in the lesser grades that most sawmills are likely to deal in. For more on grading, consult the reading list at the end of this article.

The entire business of grading is a tricky matter. Often sawyers' interpretations of grading will vary so greatly from the official rules that it renders the issue moot. In fact, "run-of-the-mill" is the most common grade I've found used by backwoods sawyers. Any board that comes off the mill is given this general designation, good or bad. Some mills are only slightly more sophisticated, separating lumber into vague categories like "good" or "bad." Good is anything that's No. 2 common or better; bad is anything worse. This is further confused by regional terminology: In central Kentucky, where I ran my mill, what a lot of sawyers called "barn lumber" would be called utility, pallet or secondary lumber in other parts of the country. Disregard this hazy grading and learn the official rules. That way, you'll be less likely to be duped by a fast-talking sawyer and better able to compare prices quoted by various mills.

The output of small sawmills varies widely. At my mill, we sawed lumber for a variety of purposes, including furniture, but many of the neighboring mills sawed only for barn wood or pallets—a grade that's of little use to woodworkers because it has too many defects and is often too thin after drying to produce a board usable for furniture work. If possible, you should locate a mill that saws for grade rather than for yield. Grade sawmills treat logs more carefully and they're equipped and willing to saw logs that will produce furniture-grade lumber. Those that saw for

From *Fine Woodworking* magazine (January 1988) 68:58-61

yield are more interested in large volumes of lower-quality lumber. I know many sawyers who don't know (or care) about sawing for grade and are more interested in production; the more board feet the better. Having been in the business, I can sympathize. Frankly, it often doesn't pay for a sawyer to sort out and market the few furniture-grade boards a marginal log yields. Often high-quality logs never make it to the sawyer anyway, having been skimmed off and sent directly to a veneer plant.

Finding a mill—One of the best ways to find a sawmill is by talking with other woodworkers. If you can find a woodworker who deals directly with a mill, you've eliminated 80% of your worries. First off, you'll be talking with another woodworker—someone who speaks your language. You'll also be dealing with a mill that has worked with a woodworker and thus should have a better idea of what you'll need.

There are other ways to find green lumber. Try the Yellow Pages for sawmills or lumber dealers. Local lumberyard workers may have knowledge of local mills, or you can consider contacting the local forest or agricultural extension agent, because many mills get their logs from government land. If all this fails, a drive in the hills might turn up a shed or barn built of freshly sawn lumber. You might stop and ask where the lumber was purchased and go from there.

I have lived in many parts of the country and have always found a suitable mill within 50 miles of my home. Once I have a lead on a mill, I usually call (if there's a phone) to find out what wood species the mill saws, what they charge per board foot, green, and whether their lumber is graded. I also ask if the lumber is stacked and stickered, if it's covered, and if I can pick through the pile. If the answers sound promising, I'll check out the mill in person.

It's useful to walk around the mill before you buy to see what kinds of logs are being sawn, how they're sawed and what kind of job the mill is doing. If you don't know what you're looking for, you're in a less-desirable bargaining position and missing a good opportunity to learn more about lumber buying. Check to see if the lumber is sawn heavy, which means it is ⅛ in. oversize in thickness. If you're buying green 4/4 lumber, it should be at least a full inch thick and, ideally, ⅛ in. thicker. If it's not the full 4/4, you'll be lucky to get a ¾-in.-thick finished board when it shrinks and dries. Consistency is the measure of a well-run mill, too. A worn-out head rig, sloppily operated, might saw a 4/4 board that's a full inch thick at one end, but 1½ in. thick at the other end. Such boards are trouble. When you feed the thin end into the planer, it jams when the feed rollers encounter the greater thickness.

Ideally, the lumber stacks should be level, stickered properly, covered against the weather and sorted by grade and species. Steer clear of lumber from crooked stacks sitting in a muddy yard or bleaching in the sun, no matter how inexpensive the lumber is. Such stacks are likely to contain lots of warped, bowed and crowned lumber, which only causes grief later. If the mill checks out, ask the sawyer specifically what he charges. As in any purchase, quality costs money and you'll probably pay more at a well-run mill where the sawyer takes time to stack his wood. At our mill, we charged 25 cents per bd. ft. for run-of-the-mill oak—stacked, but not graded—and 30 cents for No. 2 or better. Some mills won't dicker with you on price, some will. We were always willing to discount the price if the buyer helped out by stacking lumber. But be clear on what you are getting into before you offer to trade labor for lumber. Find out too if the sawyer

Dick Pawloski, a sawmill operator in Bethel, Conn., hefts a flat-sawn FAS 4/4 oak plank fresh from the mill. The board has been edged, trimmed to length and graded, and is ready for drying.

Sawyers can get so busy that they often don't have time to properly stack the lumber they've sawn. The back stack is good, but steer clear of lumber piled like that in the foreground. Lumber from such piles often contains a high percentage of cracked, cupped, bowed and twisted boards.

will let you pick through the stacks if you promise to restack and resticker it. We found, however, that most people didn't know how or didn't care to restack our lumber. Assure the sawyer you'll be different from the rest.

Custom sawing—An interesting way to work with sawyers is to bring your log to the mill and have it sawn to your specifications. You'll need a basic knowledge of sawing and a good rapport with the sawyer before you try this. My experience with custom sawing has been good and I've enjoyed sawing other people's logs for them. If you have your logs sawn, make sure they are clean and free of rocks, nails, and especially barbed wire. If we hit wire, nails or any foreign object, it was our policy to charge the customer for a new set of sawteeth. Before having your log sawn, find out what the sawyer will charge for a damaged blade. It can cost anywhere from $200 to sharpen teeth to $1,000 or more to replace a blade. A sawyer will want to know whether a tree came from the forest or from someone's yard where it could have acquired any number of metal objects, such as fence wire, pocket knives, nails or screws. Forest trees will likely be cleaner, but avoid trees along boundary lines. Look for deformities on the bark that indicate metal lurking within.

If it's your log being sawn or the sawing is being done to your

Rhode Island woodworker Geoff Warner's drying shed has a large overhang to protect lumber against rain. Although not critical, lumber sheds should be oriented to be open to the north, with the southern exposure covered to prevent losses from rapid drying.

specifications, consider having the lumber quartersawn. Left to their own, most mills don't like to quartersaw because it's slow and somewhat wasteful. As is shown in figure 1, a quartersawn log produces more narrow boards, many of which will have beveled edges that reduce their usable width. But in exchange for narrower boards, quartersawing in species like oak and ash yields delightful grain patterns. In addition, quartersawn lumber is more stable than plainsawn, because its annual rings are perpendicular to the face of each board rather than tangential; as a result, most shrinkage occurs in the board's thickness rather than its width. Even a log that is plainsawn, however, will produce a few quartersawn boards at its center.

Drying your find—Once you've bought a load of lumber, you need to dry it. This process begins with air drying, progresses to indoor drying, or to custom drying done at a commercial kiln. The lowest moisture content you can air dry wood to in most climates, except for the desert, is about 12%, but ranges from 15% to 20% are more likely. Kiln drying will further reduce moisture content to the 6% to 8% suitable for furniture.

Air drying lumber is not particularly difficult, but because you're at the mercy of the weather, it's not a controlled procedure like kiln drying, so some precautions are necessary. Long before I consider stacking the lumber, I take steps to reduce rapid moisture loss, which will cause end checking. Immediately after bucking logs to length, or taking possession of them, I coat their ends with glue, polyurethane varnish or paraffin to reduce moisture loss through endgrain. I see to it that the logs are sawed into boards as soon as possible and then preferably stacked immediately after sawing, because this is when the most rapid drying takes place. If I've bought already-sawn lumber, I end coat the boards as soon as I pick them up at the mill or immediately after stacking. This is critical during the summer: A board left in the hot summer sun for an hour could split disastrously, and end coating helps to reduce radical moisture loss.

Some sawmills dry lumber in the open without cover, some stack it vertically on racks, and some just dead stack it (without stickers between the layers). I strongly recommend against all these methods, because they are likely to produce a high degree of degrade lumber, ranging from cupped or bowed boards to fungi stains that form when damp boards lie together. I have been most successful in drying lumber in a well-ventilated shed built for that purpose or in a drafty barn. Such a structure protects wood from too-rapid drying from direct sunlight, while shielding

it from rain and snow. A reasonable size for a drying shed is about 20 ft. long, perhaps 10 ft. wide, with an open-facing long wall on one side and a louvered, or burlap-draped wall on the other. Its siding boards should have no more than 2 in. and no less than ½ in. between them to allow for air circulation. Variations on this design are endless, but the point remains: The lumber needs to be protected from rain without being sealed off from breezes that will carry away the moisture.

I stack the thinnest boards at the bottom so wood stacked on top will weigh them down against bowing. Where possible, wider boards should go inside the pile rather than near the edges where too-fast drying might cause them to split. Boards that are very long should be stacked on the bottom of the pile as well—an unsupported end from a long board sticking out from the center of a stack may sag as it dries, crooking the board. To separate each layer from the next, place ¾-in.-square stickers about 24 in. apart along the length of the pile. As you build the stack, keep the stickers vertically aligned to keep uneven weight distribution from kinking your boards. For stability, the stacks should be neatly piled and level. This could require that you keep a few extra stickers on hand that are a little thinner or thicker than ¾ in. to make up for inconsistencies in the thickness of the lumber. Leave a foot or two between each stack to ensure adequate air movement. If your shed has a dirt floor or you are just drying wood outside with a sheet of plywood over it, support the stack at least a foot off the ground. A foundation of timbers supported on concrete blocks spaced about 16 in. on center, front of the stack to back, works well.

The old-timer's rule of a year of air drying per inch of thickness is, at best, a speculative way to determine when your lumber is dry enough. The only sure-fire way to track all of the variables at work in air drying is to use a moisture meter to periodically test a sample board. You can buy a moisture meter for about $100 or make your own (see the reading list). In any case, select a board from *inside* the stack for testing and measure the moisture every few weeks until it gets down to 20% or lower. This could take anywhere from a few months to a year or more, depending on the species, its thickness, the location of the stack and the climate where you live. Far and away, temperature and humidity most affect how fast wood dries. Generally, the best drying period runs from July to September, but the farther north you go, the shorter the season. Thus, a stack of 4/4 oak that dries in a single season in Alabama might require two years or more to dry in northern Minnesota.

If you intend to make a habit of air drying, keep records of how long it takes to dry the various species you are working with. Also, date each stack of lumber; it's easy to loose track of how long a stack has been drying, especially when you have several going at once.

Finish drying—Once your wood has dried to the 20% range, you're ready to finish dry it. If you've paid 30 cents per foot for 100 bd. ft. of FAS oak, you now have an investment of $30 plus your time. You must now decide whether you want to hold your costs to the bare minimum by drying the wood in a heated room, or spring for the additional cost of drying in a commerical kiln. Commercial drying is affordable, provided you have enough lumber to make it worth transporting to the kiln. Typically, expect to pay 15 cents to 20 cents per bd. ft. for kiln drying.

In the East and Midwest, hardwood kilns are quite numerous; the sawyer you buy from is likely to know where one is located or you can check the phone book for leads. If the kiln does custom drying, the operator will want to know what species and how much lumber you have, its thickness and length, the current moisture content and what you want the finished moisture content to be. In most cases, this will be 6% to 10%. Plan as far ahead as you can. Every species requires a different drying schedule, and where one kiln might mix species in a drying run, another will not.

Final inspection—Kiln operators don't generally guarantee results, so inspect your lumber carefully before and after it comes from the kiln. The boards should emerge bright, free of stains, cracks and cup, and they should machine normally. Lumber that's been pushed too fast through the drying schedule might become casehardened. This occurs because the board's outside shell dries too fast, causing it to shrink around the wet core. This puts the shell in tension and causes it to set oversize. When the core eventually shrinks, the shell is pulled into compression. (Or, the wood itself may give during improper drying, which can cause deep surface checking or internal failures such as collapse and honeycombing.) Kilns usually try to ensure against casehardening by conditioning the wood, slowly raising the humidity at the end of the drying cycle. Figure 2, right, shows how to test for casehardening and reverse casehardening, which occurs when the conditioning is carried too far, causing the core to be in compression and the shell in tension. For more information on kiln degrade, I suggest reading the *Dry Kiln Operator's Manual* (see reading list). The good news is that if you find the lumber has been casehardened, you can take it back to the kiln and ask the operator to condition the lumber again. If the lumber is reverse casehardened, however, it's ruined.

If you plan to dry several hundred board feet yearly, heated-room drying is the most economical way to go. Of course, you can't do thousands of feet of lumber (unless you have a very large house), but it is feasible to dry up to 800 bd. ft. a year. And, I find it satisfying to see wood that will later become furniture drying in my living room. You can also use your attic, but be careful here: During the summer, an attic will get too hot, accelerating drying and causing horrible checking. Be sure the attic is well ventilated, preferably with a fan, so the moisture released from the wood can escape.

Before bringing it indoors, inspect your lumber for pests such as spiders, ants and more-destructive boring critters like powderpost beetles or termites. If you find suspicious-looking holes in the wood or tiny frass hills, leave it outside. Strip off any bark or decayed areas on the boards that might conceal insects. And though you may be tempted to hasten the drying process, leave adequate space between a stack and radiators, electric baseboard heaters or hot-air ducts. Similarly, stacking wood near a wood stove or fireplace is inviting splits and cracks, not to mention the danger of fire. Stack the lumber as you would outside, with evenly spaced stickers.

With your moisture meter, continue to monitor your lumber. As soon as its moisture content nears 10% or less, remove the stickers and dead stack the lumber. Leaving the stickers in place will encourage air flow between the boards and they'll actually begin to pick up moisture rather than lose more. Store your lumber in a rack or blocked up off the floor in the shop or the place where you intend to use it. That way, the wood will arrive at an equilibrium moisture content with the environment, reducing the chances of unexpected twists, warps and bows. Once machined, it's important to stack boards on a flat surface and weigh them down to reduce bowing or cupping. By the way, the same holds true for glued-up panels—they only look stable, and if left on their own, they can bow or cup. Wood will always move, so cover

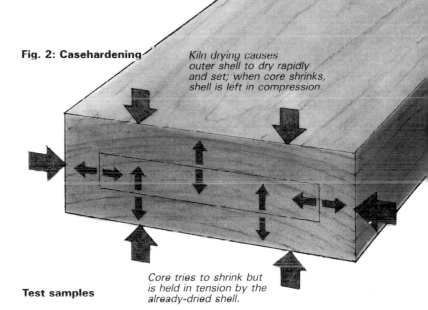

Fig. 2: Casehardening

Kiln drying causes outer shell to dry rapidly and set; when core shrinks, shell is left in compression.

Core tries to shrink but is held in tension by the already-dried shell.

Test samples

Saw core from sample piece

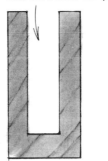

In correctly conditioned sample, prongs remain parallel.

Prongs turn inward if the board is casehardened.

A reverse casehardened sample shows results of overconditioning. Core is in compression and shell in tension, turning prongs outward.

the panels to prevent marring and then weigh them down.

How much can you save by drying your own wood? I can buy run-of-the-mill green walnut at 80 cents per bd. ft. From a lumber dealer, kiln dried FAS walnut would cost $3 or more per bd. ft. Even after driving to the sawmill, picking through the stack, stacking, air drying and moving it indoors, I will not have significantly added to my cost. If I decide to pay an extra 20 cents to have 1,000 ft. kiln dried, I'd still save about $2,000 that I can invest in more machinery or, better yet, more wood. □

Todd Scholl is a woodworker and teacher. He lives in Wray, Colo. Barbara Rowley, a freelance editor, contributed to this article. She lives in Florissant, Colo.

Further reading

Rules for the Measurement and Inspection of Hardwood and Cypress, $5.00 ppd.; *Introduction to the Grading and Measurement of Hardwood and Cypress*, $1.25 ppd. National Hardwood Lumber Association, P.O. Box 34518, Memphis, TN 38184-0518. *Drying Eastern Hardwood Lumber*, $5.50 ppd.; *Dry Kiln Operator's Manual*, $7.00 ppd.; *Air Drying of Lumber, A Guide to Industry Practices*, $4.75 ppd. Superintendent of Documents, U.S. Government Printing Office, Washington, DC 20402-9325. *Understanding Wood, A craftsman's guide to wood technology* by R. Bruce Hoadley, 1980, $17.95; *FWW On Wood and How to Dry It*, $7.95; containing articles on wood species, how to air dry wood, how to build a kiln, how to build a moisture meter and related topics such as sawmills and basic woodlot management, 1986. The Taunton Press, Box 355, Newtown, CT 06470.

Index

If you enjoyed this book, you're going to love our magazine.

A year's subscription to *Fine Woodworking* brings you the kind of practical, hands-on information you found in this book and much more. In issue after issue, you'll find projects that teach new skills, demonstrations of tools and techniques, new design ideas, old-world traditions, shop tests, coverage of current woodworking events, and breathtaking examples of the woodworker's art for inspiration.

To try an issue, just fill out one of the attached subscription cards, or call us toll-free at 1-800-888-8286. As always, we guarantee your satisfaction.

Subscribe Today!
6 issues for just $25

TAUNTON MAGAZINES
...by fellow enthusiasts

The Taunton Press
63 South Main Street,
Box 5506
Newtown, CT 06470-5506